WHAT ~~WOULD~~ *Did* JESUS DO?

And What His Followers Are To Do

KEVIN ANTHONY KEATING

WESTBOW
PRESS®
A DIVISION OF THOMAS NELSON
& ZONDERVAN

WestBow Press books may be ordered through booksellers or by contacting:

WestBow Press
A Division of Thomas Nelson & Zondervan
1663 Liberty Drive
Bloomington, IN 47403
www.westbowpress.com
844-714-3454

Scripture quotations are from The ESV® Bible (The Holy Bible, English Standard Version®), copyright © 2001 by Crossway, a publishing ministry of Good News Publishers. Used by permission. All rights reserved.

ISBN: 978-1-6642-4966-0 (sc)
ISBN: 978-1-6642-4965-3 (e)

Print information available on the last page.

WestBow Press rev. date: 11/29/2021

Other Books by the Author

MUSTARD SEED: A Story of Jesus' Little Sister

THE HANDS OF JESUS: A Scriptural and Pictorial Meditation and Devotion

MODELING THE HEAVENLY FATHER TO EARTHLY CHILDREN:
A Thoroughly-Incomplete Guide for Christian Dads

Dedication

To
Suzette Mary, Dennis Joseph, Nanette Gabrielle,
Christopher Edward, and Michael B –
followers of the Lord

Royalties

All royalties from this book are donated to Mercy Ships,
a trusted Christian charitable organization
that serves the needs of the world's forgotten poor and impaired
in the name of Jesus.

CONTENTS

PART ONE

Introductory Ideas

INTRODUCTION

Remember those wristbands that were popular a few years ago which said, "What Would Jesus Do?" They were an attempt to encourage people to consider the person of Jesus and make application of His life and teachings to modern day situations. Thinking of buying a house? *What kind of residence would Jesus select?* Making career plans? *Which job would Jesus get?* Evaluating a relationship? *What sort of person would Jesus choose to be with?* Thinking of changing churches? *Where would Jesus attend services?* Election coming up? *Who would Jesus vote for?* Intending to get married and raise a family in the future? Well, that's a tough one since Jesus did neither of these. (More on that later.) Choices from the significant to the trivial, from the sublime to the mundane, anything really could be considered through the hoped-for clarifying lens of Jesus' life.

While I understand this desire by Christians to do what is in accord with the will of the Lord, I believe that another, less speculative question can also be asked regarding our life situations, namely, not *"What WOULD Jesus do?"* but *"What DID Jesus do?"* What actions did He take? What decisions did He make in his life? What did He do with His time here on earth? How did He choose to live? That is the focus of this book then: looking at His activities and deeds so that we who seek to follow Jesus can see clear examples of righteous behavior which He modeled for our benefit and which can be incorporated into our lives. In doing this, we will be more able to pursue Christlikeness in very practical ways.

Now, certainly many of the specific situations we face today were not something that Jesus had to deal with. For example, Jesus never had to decide what kind of car he should drive or how much screen time He should spend on His cell phone. However, it is my hope that by looking at what Jesus did in His life, we can relate the principles by which He lived to some of the day-to-day challenges we face in the 21st century.

To do this, I am focusing on specific events in Jesus' life, though certainly not all, as viewed from my far-from-perfect understanding of a general chronological sequencing of the canonical gospel stories about Him. In this book, I don't reference the teachings of Jesus very much (nor do I but rarely quote from the rest of the New Testament), and I don't emphasize His spiritual accomplishments, such as our redemption, justification, and atonement, as significant as they are; rather, I concentrate on Jesus' activities – what He physically did, His actions, and it is from these that I hope to draw application to our lives as we followers of Jesus seek to become more godly, selfless, and virtuous in how we lead our own lives.

Having said that, let me candidly say that I am neither theologian nor biblical scholar; I'm just someone who has great interest in and some familiarity with the sacred scripture and who has committed his life to Christ. So, it is with utmost humility that I embark on this journey, praying for the guidance and inspiration (lower-case i) of the Holy Spirit of God, without whom we cannot hope to accomplish anything of true value.

GOAL

In a remarkable scene from the life of Jesus, on the night before He would die, while eating His final meal with all his disciples, Jesus washed each of their feet, including those of the men who would soon desert Him, those of the man who would soon deny knowing Him, and those of the man who would soon betray Him. Jesus' purpose was to give His followers an object lesson in humility and service, and in a greater sense to teach them what it means to be His disciple. As He explained:

"You call me Teacher and Lord, and you are right, for so I am. If I then, your Lord and Teacher, have washed your feet, you also ought to wash one another's feet. For I have given you an example, that you also should do just as I have done to you. Truly, truly, I say to you, a servant is not greater than his master, nor is a messenger greater than the one who sent him. If you know these things, blessed are you if you do them." (Jn. 13:13-17)

For Jesus – the Lord, Master, and Teacher – a goal in following Him was to become like Him and to do what He did. Not just know about His life, but to follow His lead actively and seek to emulate Him purposefully in behavior and deeds. We Christians – His students (for that is what "disciple" means), His servants – are to become like Him; in Jesus' words: *"It is enough for the disciple to be like his teacher, and the servant like his master" (Mt. 10:25a).*

We need to be aware, however, that becoming Christlike in our actions is not a one-time, momentary event. It is a lifelong process. It is the day-by-day dedication and discipline to submit to our Father God and allow Him to work in us to become more like His Son Jesus. We must be committed to Christ, willing to say "no" to what we want for ourselves and "yes" to what He wants for us. As Jesus declared: *"If anyone would come after me, let him deny himself and take up his cross daily and follow me" (Lk. 9:23).* The Lord calls us to every day surrender our own selfish desires to Him; to every day devote our hearts and hands, our energy and resources, to Him and His mission; to every day yield all that we are and all that we have to Him; to every day live in obedience to His way.

Yet, while becoming like the Lord is our aim, it is an ideal that none of us will ever perfectly realize, for inevitably we will fall short in emulating Jesus' example in all things. However, thankfully, when we do fail to follow His lead, we are encouraged and instructed to acknowledge our waywardness, to turn back to Him, and then to continue on our spiritual journey.

We pray for the Lord's support and strength to accomplish the goal of becoming more like Him.

OBJECTIONS

Focusing on the actions of Jesus rather than on His specific teachings might raise the objection that we cannot separate the Lord's words from his deeds, that they are integrally linked together. In fact, I don't disagree with this idea. What Jesus said and what He taught cannot really be disconnected from what He did.

Yet, though I strongly uphold the sacred importance of Jesus' verbal directives and explanations about life, both physical and spiritual, it is my intention in this book to concentrate on the specific acts of Jesus – what He did in certain situations, how He reacted to actual conditions, how He behaved in particular circumstances. These provide us with examples that we, Jesus' disciples, can strive to emulate today so that we can become more Christlike in our own lives.

Does that mean that because Jesus wore a cloak, His followers must also? Or, since Jesus ate some fish, do we have to include that in our diet? (Well, actually, yes, fish is good for you!) But I am focusing not so much on merely copying explicit customs from 1st century Israel; I am more interested in dealing with the universal deeds which transcend culture and historical era that we might glean from the life of Christ and incorporate into our own behavior – actions such as reaching out to those in need, knowing the Scripture, communing in prayer with the Heavenly Father, or denying ourselves for the benefit of others.

Another possible protest might be that Christlikeness is primarily an internal growth generated by the active working of the Lord's Holy Spirit in the life of the believer which then manifests itself externally in our attitudes and behaviors. Again, I absolutely agree with this point. It is yielding ourselves to the inner promptings of God, hearing and obeying His voice that will result in outward words and deeds that reflect Jesus. By living intentionally in the presence of the Lord and developing the mind of Christ in us (i.e., His way of thinking), we will steadily move toward genuine Christlikeness. I stress the word "genuine," for true Christlikeness is not merely robotically or phonily mimicking Jesus' behavior without real conviction or perhaps just to be seen by others as some kind of "super-Christian." Instead, it is devoting our lives to Him and honestly giving our hearts to the Lord so that He can mold us to become more like Him.

And as I stated earlier, becoming more like Christ does not happen instantaneously. It is rather a lifelong process of understanding the Lord's life and seeking every day, moment by moment, to follow his lead. And that is the express purpose of this book: to focus on what Jesus did in His short time on earth so that we can learn better what to do with our own few years of mortal life. Let us walk in Jesus' footsteps in order to lead more Christlike lives.

ACTIONS BEYOND OUR CAPABILITIES

Jesus exercised divine power. He performed miraculous healings, such as giving sight to the blind and causing the lame to walk. He defied the laws of nature, like walking on water and calming a raging storm. He exerted His dominion over the spiritual forces of darkness as He cast demons out of those who were satanically possessed. He manifested His heavenly authority by pardoning the sinful. And ultimately, He even conquered death through His resurrection.

But what does this mean for a disciple's pursuit of Christlikeness? Are we expected to mirror the Lord's supernatural abilities by restoring hearing to the deaf or multiplying loaves or raising the dead? After all, Jesus did state that *"whoever believes in me will also do the works that I do; and greater works than these will he do ..." (Jn. 14:12).*

While I personally have never witnessed an actual authentic contravention of natural laws like those mentioned above, I do think that we believers can allow ourselves to be used of Christ to be involved in the miraculous, all in His name: We can contribute our abilities and our finances to the medical health and nutritional wellbeing of those in our community and beyond; we can work in conjunction with the Creator of all things to protect the environment and to provide relief for those who have been ravaged by devastating tempests and natural calamities; we can offer comfort to those suffering from the inner turmoil of depression, mental illness, and spiritual angst; we can reach out and embrace those marginalized and ostracized by our society – the dispossessed, the indigent, the struggling immigrant; and we can bring the message of the forgiveness and new life in Christ to those who desperately seek release from the burden of sin and the shackles of spiritual oppression and death. These are the miracles that we can engage in by letting God's supernatural power and lovingkindness work in and through us to touch the lives of others.

WHAT JESUS DIDN'T DO

We can learn a good deal from the canonical gospel accounts about certain specific aspects of Jesus' life: He prayed; He spent time fasting; He knew and quoted Scripture; He trained people to be His disciples; He had a close and personal relationship with God.

The gospels also show us much about the general tenor of Jesus' life, which can be looked at from both a positive and negative viewpoint (i.e., what He did and didn't do). For instance, He didn't appear to worry and didn't rely on Himself but always trusted His Heavenly Father; He didn't expect others to serve Him but rather dedicated His life to serving God and other people; He didn't focus on material, temporal, or earthly things but instead concentrated on the spiritual, eternal and heavenly; He didn't seek self-fulfillment but came to give abundant life to those who would believe in Him; He didn't pursue fortune, fame, or settled family life with a home, wife, and kids, but instead devoted Himself to His God-appointed mission of preaching, teaching, and healing, and to laying down His life as a sacrifice for our sinful world. Additionally, there are particular instances in which Jesus actively rejected or refused to do something, such as His withdrawal from an attempt to make Him king by force after feeding the five thousand or His refusal to rebuke His disciples for their vociferous praise as He triumphantly entered Jerusalem.

So, though in this book we are focusing on the things that Jesus did during His earthly lifetime, we might also ask whether it is valuable to think about what He *didn't* do. For example, as stated above, Jesus never seemed to have gotten married or had children. Also, He apparently did not own much in the way of worldly possessions. Are these behaviors that we as His disciples are to follow if we are to be more Christlike? A simple response is that many situations are personal matters between the disciple and God, and they call for study of the Scripture, time spent in fervent prayer and meditation, and listening to the voice of the Lord, the Good Shepherd, who said, *"My sheep hear my voice, and I know them, and they follow me"* *(Jn. 10:27).*

I must also offer a caveat here: Where the scriptural record is silent, we ought not to formulate beliefs and practices based on speculation or educated guesses. Surely, discussion and research are needed to deepen our understanding of the life of Jesus, but as we seek to become more like Him, let's stick to what is clearly shown in the Gospels. To echo Jesus' words, *"It is enough ..."* *(Mt. 10:25a).*

CHRONOLOGY

It is in no way a simple task to try to harmonize chronologically the gospel accounts of Jesus' life, and I confess that my attempts to do so have often resulted in some frustration. Seeing how John's gospel fits with the synoptics is especially challenging. While there is certainly a general flow of events that is readily evident in the life of Christ, the exact timing of specific incidents or occasions and of particular teaching passages is sometimes difficult to ascertain with assurance.

Thus, what is presented in this book is not, by any means, to be seen as a strict chronology of events. I list many, though definitely not all, of the actions taken by Jesus during His life as described by the gospel writers, and sometimes these actions appear in this book to follow a precise timeline, but at other times they do not. As a result, occasionally, some incidents may seem to be out of time-sequential order. While I have consulted the storylines presented in gospel harmonization resources such as Tatian's *Diatessaron,* Johnston Cheney and Stanley Ellisen's *The Greatest Story,* John Macarthur's *One Perfect Life,* Jerry Peyton's online *NET Bible Synthetic Harmony of the Gospels,* and Marshall Thomas' *The Gospel of Jesus,* the aim of this book is not to offer a strict chronology of the life of Christ; it is rather to show what He did in His life and how we, His followers, are to emulate the attitudes and actions of our Lord.

SOME KEY TERMS

Let me explain my usage of some terms that appear frequently in this book. They are based on my understanding of their meaning as spoken by Jesus.

▷ *Repent*: To have a change of heart and mind regarding our past wrongdoings and to turn away from an old, sinful and selfish life to a new life of righteousness, altruism, and obedience to God.

▷ *The gospel*: This is the good news that Jesus brought of the welcoming and forgiving love of a merciful and gracious Heavenly Father to those who have faith in Christ, turn to God in repentance, and trust His promise of a restored relationship and eternal life with Him. On another level, the evangel was (and still is) the proclamation of a new kingdom in which the sick and disabled would be healed, the weak would be empowered, wrongs would be righted, the victims of unfairness would receive justice, the broken would be mended, the oppressed would be freed, the hungry would be filled, those thirsting for righteousness would be satisfied, the poor would be made rich, the needy would be provided for, the sorrowful would be comforted, the marginalized would be received, and the shunned and excluded would be embraced.

▷ *The Kingdom*: Initially, the imminent appearance of God's supernatural intervention to bring about His reign of heaven on earth through Christ, the Son of Man who is spoken of in *Daniel 7*; currently, submission to the inner, immanent reign of God the King in the hearts and lives of people and obedience to His rule: Wherever God reigns, wherever persons submit to His Kingship, there is the Kingdom of God; eventually, the coming, final manifest supremacy of God's reign on earth through Christ.

▷ *Ministry*: Not just the work of ordained clergy, but the mission of every Christian to minister to (i.e., care for) the spiritual, physical, and emotional needs of others. Thus, all those who follow Jesus have a specific ministry of service in the place where God has put them.

A NOTE ON CAPITALIZATION
AND ABBREVIATIONS

While the version of Scripture that I am using for quotes in this book, the English Standard Version, does not capitalize pronouns referring to Jesus, I personally have always done so and thus follow that habit throughout. Also, relating to Scripture, *(v.)* stands for "verse;" *(vv.)* stands for "verses;" *(ff)* stands for "and following verses;" *(Chs.)* stands for "Chapters." Citations of Scripture with verse numbers followed by lower case letters, such as *32a* or *15b*, refer to the first and second parts of the verses, respectively. And when writing particular years, I use the commonly-accepted abbreviations CE, which stands for Common Era (meaning AD – *Anno Domini*), and BCE, which stands for Before the Common Era (or BC – Before Christ).

ABOUT THE ARTWORK

The works are 19th-century engravings by Julius Schnorr von Carolsfeld. These religious pieces are stylized, dramatic, devotional, often symbolic and not exact representations of the Biblical narrative, at times anachronistic, but always reverential.

PART TWO

What Jesus Did & What His Followers Are To Do

AND THE WORD BECAME FLESH

In the beginning was the Word, and the Word was with God, and the Word was God ... And the Word became flesh and dwelt among us ... (Jn. 1:1, 14)

<u>WHAT JESUS DID:</u>

John's Gospel opens with the description of the heavenly Word, the *logos* of God, taking on a body of flesh in the person of Jesus and living with us humans. Jesus was the corporeal presence of God on earth. God's mind, God's will, God's intention, God's very nature, all were expressed and made manifest in Jesus. Jesus was God's speech in action.

Almighty God resided uniquely in Jesus, as shown in His miraculous powers and His life-giving words of truth. And yet, Jesus willingly and sacrificially humbled and gave Himself for our wellbeing throughout His life, even to the point of His death. Jesus saw our need for reconciliation with God and salvation from sin, and so He did what was necessary to meet that need by living and dying for us. The Lord's entire life was one of complete altruism: He considered our needs greater than His desires. His actions displayed genuine, dynamic love in that He was aware of our condition, separated by unrighteousness as we were from God and walking a path that led only to death, and then took the measures required to restore our relationship with the Father and secure the promise of eternal life.

<u>WHAT HIS FOLLOWERS ARE TO DO:</u>

Without probing the mysterious, theological depths of Christ's incarnation, we can see this descent by the *logos* from the ethereal to the tangible, from the spiritual world to that of the physical, as a prime example which the Lord gave for us to follow. We can emulate Christ by giving flesh to words, turning immaterial wishes and plans into substantial care and material provision. Rather than merely talking about a problem or offering lip-service solutions, we can display God's love and kindness by taking real, practical, active steps to help others in whatever way we can. Just as Jesus did everything in His power to redeem and enrich our lives, we His followers should use whatever God has given us for the wellbeing of others.

If we hope to accomplish any of the above, it is vital for followers of Jesus to embrace His humble attitude and spirit in our daily lives. As He said: **"Take my yoke upon you, and learn from me, for I am gentle and lowly of heart"** *(Mt. 11:29a)*. Let's not think of ourselves as better than others; instead, let's put the needs of those in our lives as more important than our own. We should not feel that we are special and therefore should receive advantages above the people around us. Let us serve rather than be served. We must be willing to give up our privileges so that others might benefit and be lifted.

As we seek to show God's lovingkindness in very real ways to those in need, giving ourselves sacrificially for others' welfare and behaving humbly, we will be emulating the Lord and displaying true Christlikeness.

JESUS, THE CHILD, GROWS IN BODY, MIND, AND SPIRIT

And the child grew and became strong, filled with wisdom.
And the favor of God was upon him. (Lk. 2:40)

WHAT JESUS DID:

While little is revealed in the canonical gospel accounts of Jesus' childhood, three characteristics are mentioned here regarding Jesus the child: growth, strength, and wisdom.

We can likely assume that Jesus' parents provided for both His physical and spiritual nourishment that enabled Him to grow and develop. It is probable that Jesus helped His father as a builder, a carpenter – hard, manual labor which gave Him muscular strength – and that He learned the Hebrew scriptures, which offered Him religious knowledge and divine wisdom. And from His earliest years, Jesus was blessed with God's grace.

WHAT HIS FOLLOWERS ARE TO DO:

We Christians, regardless of age, can seek to emulate Jesus even in His childhood by staying physically healthy and by filling our hearts and minds with knowledge of God and insight into His character and what He deems to be right, just, and good.

This first means that we adhere to simple health guidelines, like eating and drinking nutritious foods and liquids in moderation and getting adequate physical exercise to offset our increasingly sedentary lifestyle. It also requires that we not engage in unhealthy practices like smoking or over-indulgence in sweets or fats. Additionally, we should not be averse to hard work, whether physical or otherwise, and never allow ourselves to become indolent.

More significantly, following Jesus demands that we devote time to the study of and meditation on the Holy Scriptures, so that we can make practical application of what we learn, which is in essence exercising wisdom. As we commit ourselves to the discipline of knowing God and of obeying His revealed Word, we will grow and become strong in spirit as Christ was. And the result? We will enjoy the favor, the grace, and the blessing of the Almighty.

JESUS AS A BOY IN THE TEMPLE

Now [Jesus'] parents went to Jerusalem every year at the Feast of the Passover. And when he was twelve years old, they went up according to custom. (Lk. 2:41-42)

WHAT JESUS DID:

Even at an early age, Jesus engaged actively in a deep spiritual life. So, when His parents made their annual trip to Jerusalem, the boy Jesus ended up in the Temple sitting with the learned men, asking them questions and listening to their answers *(v. 46)*. He was always about the things of God. Thus, as He said, He needed to be in the temple, His Father's house *(v. 49)*, participating in discussion with religious teachers. Jesus had probably displayed to these teachers knowledge of the *Torah*, and from their reaction, one of amazement at His understanding and wisdom *(v. 47)*, it was clear that this young man, though still in His adolescence, had a special relationship with the LORD.

And yet, despite his precocious sagacity, Jesus humbly submitted Himself to His parents *(v. 51)*, living with them in obedience to their God-given authority.

WHAT HIS FOLLOWERS ARE TO DO:

We disciples of Jesus, in pursuit of Christlikeness, should also give priority to life in the spirit. We too should dedicate ourselves to developing a close relationship with God, Whom Jesus taught us to call "Father." As we seek to live our days in the presence of the LORD, wherever we are, we can truly and confidently say that we are in our Father's house.

Our connection with God can most certainly be strengthened by the study of Scripture and by thinking about how its words can be applied practically to our lives. That is, after all, a definition of wisdom – the practical application of knowledge. Our goal in delving into the Holy Writ is not to impress others with our biblical expertise; rather, it is to be able to utilize what we learn in our everyday activities so that we can lead godly lives. And it's not only for ourselves that we study the Bible. Instead, God can use His word to speak to others through us. Just as Jesus discussed with others about the LORD, we also can share what we have learned as needs arise.

It also occurs to me that Jesus was not satisfied with His knowledge but sought out teachers and listened to them and asked them questions. Were all His questions rhetorical, merely asked as a kind of Socratic method of leading people to truth? While that might be partially true, I see in this temple incident an active mind that is eager to learn and hear the views of others. Let us follow His example and never feel as if we've arrived at the pinnacle of knowledge and need to go no further, especially when it comes to our comprehension of things divine. We should consider what other people have to say regarding their spiritual understanding and experience as we keep exploring the infinite depths of the person of God.

Finally, Jesus exhibited once again His incomparable humility as the placed Himself under parental authority at the appropriate time. He was neither proud nor selfish in His behavior, and we, His followers, can also determine not to be demanding of others. There are occasions when it is correct and proper to submit ourselves to certain authority, and when those times arrive, we ought not haughtily resist or refuse. Let us instead live deferentially and respectfully as Jesus did.

JESUS' BAPTISM

Then Jesus came from Galilee to the Jordan to John, to be baptized by him. (Mt. 3:13)

WHAT JESUS DID:

We are told that Jesus began His ministry at about age 30 *(Lk. 3:23)*, and one of His first acts was to be baptized by John. However, John was reluctant to baptize Jesus *(Mt. 3:14)*: John's baptism was one of repentance, but he knew Jesus was without sin. John eventually acquiesced to Jesus' request and performed His baptism. As Jesus came out of the water, the synoptic gospels describe the presence of God's Spirit and the vocal affirmation by the delighted Heavenly Father of His Son Jesus *(Mt. 3:16-17; Mk. 1:9-11; Lk. 3:21-22)*.

There are many ideas about why Jesus desired to be baptized. Perhaps in this initial step of His ministry, Jesus was identifying with a sinful humanity whom He came to redeem, and was in a sense binding Himself to them and committing Himself to their deliverance. But Jesus explains the reason humbly and plainly: to *"fulfill all righteousness"* (Mt. 3:15) He always did the right and godly thing, and being baptized at that time and that place was right, as witnessed by the divine response.

WHAT HIS FOLLOWERS ARE TO DO:

Does the baptism of Jesus imply that His disciples are to emulate Him by being baptized? Of course, there is much debate about the topic of baptism, and while there are legitimate points that support the opinions of those with various views, my simple, non-dogmatic answer to the question would be, Yes. Whatever one believes about the significance of baptism, Jesus did it, and we should follow His lead and encourage others who are devoted to Him to do so as well. I'm not suggesting a blind, rote, robotic response to Jesus' action; there must be knowledge and understanding of baptism's meaning and purpose, and that demands study and prayer before a step is taken into the water.

Additionally, from the example of Jesus' lining up with the other people to be baptized, we should strive to look beyond our own lives and learn to identify with those in need – both physical and spiritual. If we are indifferent to the plight of others, we will never be used by God to touch their lives. Let's be willing to join others who are genuinely seeking God, to devote ourselves to their wellbeing, to enter into their world and their experience, and to see in what practical ways we can actively assist them.

There is also a basic lesson in Jesus' baptism from which we can glean a significant rule to follow in our own lives: do what is right in God's eyes. Jesus was ever concerned with righteousness – i.e., with godliness, justice, morality, honesty and rectitude. For our Lord, it was always vital to do what was good and ethical and fair. Integrity was His hallmark. For us who follow Him, that means that we are to be judicious in our behavior, to choose good over bad, morality over immorality, honesty over dishonesty, equity over prejudice, right over wrong. We are faced daily with options about how we spend our time, our abilities, and our money. How do we direct the energy that God gives us every hour of every day? How can we use our skills and talents to help and benefit others? In what ways can we make the lives of those in need better by using the resources with which the LORD has blessed us? We should commit ourselves to yielding to Jesus' guidance as we seek to answer those questions. Let's always do what is right.

JESUS IS TEMPTED IN THE WILDERNESS

*Then Jesus was led up by the Spirit into the wilderness
to be tempted by the devil. (Mt. 4:1)*

WHAT JESUS DID:

The first thing which stands out is that Jesus followed the leading of God's Spirit. We are not told how this guidance was manifested, but Jesus was certainly conscious of the movement of the Spirit, and He allowed God to direct His way.

It is also stated that Jesus engaged in fasting – here, for forty days *(v. 2)*. Later in His ministry, in the Sermon on the Mount, the Lord would give some specific instructions to His disciples about fasting *(Mt. 6:16-18)*, so we can assume it was likely a practice of His – going without food as a means of focusing on spiritual nourishment.

During His time of fasting, Jesus was confronted by Satan, the evil tempter, who sought to seduce Jesus through physical needs (by changing stones to bread), through questioning His trust in God (by throwing Himself from the top of the temple and expecting God to catch Him unharmed), and through the lure of power (by bowing to Satan in exchange for worldly dominion). Of note is the way Jesus responded to each temptation: He quoted Scripture, thus showing His reliance on God and not on Himself. *(Mt. 4:3-10)*

WHAT HIS FOLLOWERS ARE TO DO:

Let us, as Jesus was, be led by the Holy Spirit. Through prayer and meditation on the Scripture, by fostering a closeness with God and continually living in His presence, we will develop an awareness of the Spirit and sensitivity to His guidance. And as the Spirit directs us with the words of Scripture and a divine, inner voice that speaks to our hearts, minds, and souls, let's be willing to follow.

If Jesus fasted, should we do likewise? In His directives on fasting in the Sermon on the Mount, Jesus said, *"When you fast"* *(Mt. 6:16)*, not "If you fast," which indicated that it is something expected of us. What kind of fast, how often, and what allowances and restrictions are not outlined; rather, I believe those considerations are up to individual disciples as we seek God's leading. The simple guideline Jesus offers on fasting is to avoid making a show of it in order to be seen as pious by others; it is between the disciple and the

Heavenly Father. Fasting is instructed by Jesus, so let's obey Him in practice and concomitant behavior.

We can also view Jesus' resistance to the temptations as instructive for our own lives:

▷ Jesus refused physical gratification (turning stones into bread) and kept His spiritual focus. Though we have physical needs, we should not indulge those desires which interfere with our drawing near to God and our pursuit of leading righteous lives.

▷ He refused to test God (throwing Himself from the pinnacle of the Temple and expecting God to save Him) and maintained His firm trust in God's constant care. Let's not be foolish or reckless and put ourselves in dangerous situations just to prove our faith that God will come to the rescue.

▷ He refused to worship anything other than God, even with the reward of worldly power presented before Him (all the kingdoms of the earth and their glory) and held fast to obeying God. We must always direct our lives toward serving God, not to accumulating wealth or fame.

One other significant lesson we can learn from this event in Jesus' life is a couple of ways to defend against the inevitable temptations of the Devil, namely, relying on God's empowerment and citing Scriptural truth. When we are being enticed to disobey God, to do what we know is wrong, to depend on ourselves rather than on the LORD, to prioritize materialistic comfort over spiritual development, let us turn from the sinful impulse and allow the Holy Spirit to give us the strength to resist. Also, we must speak the Word of God boldly to repel the attacks of Satan and to remain firmly submitted to the will of the Father. If we employ these methods, we can perhaps hope for the same result as in Jesus' case: ***Then the devil left him, and behold, angels came and were ministering to him*** *(Mt. 4:11).*

JESUS MEETS HIS FIRST FOLLOWERS

[Two disciples of John the Baptist] followed Jesus. Jesus turned and saw them following and said ... (Jn. 1:37-38)

WHAT JESUS DID:

In Jesus' meeting His first followers in Judea and then in Galilee, two specific actions by the Lord stand out: He looked and saw them and then spoke to them personally. He repeated this with Peter, Philip, and Nathaniel *(vv. 39-47)*. It might seem like an obvious progression – you need to see people in order to talk to them. But Jesus met people right where they were, *really* looked at them, *really* saw who these individuals were. Jesus looked past the outside of persons and addressed their true inner selves. Thus, upon meeting Simon, Jesus gave him a new name, Cephas (in Aramaic) or Peter (in Greek) meaning "Rock" *(v. 42)*. In this renaming, Jesus recognized Simon's potential and directed his development of character. And when Jesus met Nathaniel, who had spoken honestly of His disdain for anyone from Nazareth *(v. 46)*, Jesus identified and acknowledged Nathaniel's candor as a positive trait, for he spoke without any deceit *(v. 47)*.

WHAT HIS FOLLOWERS ARE TO DO:

We too can make a point to really see people for who they are. This means initially to make eye contact with the people with whom we interact, acknowledging their presence by the simple action of seeing them. That behavior should be extended to all people, rich or poor, charismatic or reserved, friends or strangers, well-known celebrities or commonfolk. Each individual is a unique creation of Almighty God, and we should see everyone as the inestimable work of the Father's hands.

Then, let's strive to look beyond people's exteriors and try to know who they are on the inside. We ought not settle for cursory chit-chat that barely scratches the superficial identity of someone. Without making it feel like an interrogation, we can ask authentic questions about a person's life, showing that we genuinely care, and then listen intently and respond to the answers. Our speech should reflect an awareness of others and concern for their needs, whether physical, emotional, or spiritual.

And as we converse with one another, let's speak words of encouragement and positivity. No doubt, Jesus' calling Simon "Rock" would help him to become a person of strong character that others could depend on, and Jesus' praise of Nathaniel's honesty would exhort him to always speak the truth. So, just as Jesus did, let's see people and acknowledge their areas of potential and laud their prominent, constructive character traits to urge growth and development.

JESUS TURNS WATER INTO WINE

Jesus said to the servants, "Fill the jars with water." And they filled them up to the brim. And he said to them, "Now draw some out and take it to the master of the feast." (Jn. 2:7-8)

WHAT JESUS DID:

Jesus had returned from Judea to Galilee. His first miraculous sign which pointed to His true, glorious identity was at a marriage feast in Cana where the supply of wine had run out. Jesus' mother told Him the situation *(v. 3)*, and by turning six 20- to 30-gallon stone jars of water into wine, Jesus not only spared the bridegroom some embarrassment but also gave His followers ample reason to believe in Him.

Jesus was made aware of the need, He understood the possible negative consequences if the need was not met, and He took action to solve the problem. But notice that He also engaged others in the process: He could have just produced the wine directly into the jars, but instead He told the servants to fill them with water first. Why? I believe because He wanted them to be active participants in this extraordinary event so that they might understand their role in helping others and also so that their faith in Him might grow and be strengthened.

We are to join Jesus in performing wonderous acts of love and kindness. As we go about our daily lives, we should be ever mindful of the myriad needs of those around us: a friend in need of encouragement and a sympathetic ear; a family struggling to get by in need of material or financial assistance; a lonely acquaintance in need of social embrace. We can all do our part to offer our hearts and our hands, our time and our resources, to the Lord and to allow Him to use us to touch people's lives.

Through our loving words and kind actions, we can help bring about transformation. Like turning water to wine, we can give reassurance to change anxiety into comfort; we can bring understanding to change bitterness into gratitude; we can offer material assistance and change want into supply; and we can mediate peace to change anger and separation into calm and reconciliation. The result of Jesus' transforming power was to create something that was good, something that brought relief, joy and appreciation, and that should be our goal as well: to follow Jesus, to yield ourselves to Him, and to actively participate as He transforms lives for the better.

JESUS CLEARS OUT THE TEMPLE

In the temple he found those who were selling oxen and sheep and pigeons, and the money-changers sitting there. (Jn. 2:14)

WHAT JESUS DID:

Being an observant Jew, Jesus traveled to Jerusalem for the Feast of Passover *(v. 13)*. He had been to the Temple in Jerusalem for Passover before *(Lk. 2:41-42ff)*, so He knew what would be happening there – the sale of sacrificial animals and the exchange of currency. Though the sacrificial system had been detailed in the *Pentateuch*, it seems that the purpose of worshipping God had been subverted and turned into a business operation, with the animal sellers and money changers making an inordinate profit off of dutiful pilgrims, many of whom did not have the required unblemished animals or who came from far away and could not bring their own animals or who carried unacceptable foreign, non-Temple-approved currency. Thus, Jesus, filled with fervor for His Father's house of worship *(Jn. 2:17)*, reacted to this crass, materialistic venture and the profanation of this sacred place with righteous anger by forcefully herding the animals out with a kind of whip He had made from some rope and by knocking over the tables of money *(v. 15)*. It was a direct and pointed challenge to the prevailing corrupt system and to those that governed the practices in the Temple.

(Note: The synoptics similarly describe this event, though set during the week of Jesus' death, and some commentators believe these are two separate occasions.)

WHAT HIS FOLLOWERS ARE TO DO:

Is nothing sacred anymore? Increasingly, the answer appears to be an emphatic "No!" But Jesus gave us an example to follow here in His actions at the Temple: uphold that which is holy, and oppose that which is immoral. When we who follow Jesus become aware of attempts to undermine godly values of goodness, probity, and justice and to supplant them with clearly unethical attitudes and unrighteous behavior, we must not sit quietly by and allow things to proceed; we must take a strong and principled stand against them. Like Jesus, we need to be ardent in our dedication to the things of the LORD and moved to take action.

JESUS' DISCERNMENT REGARDING TRUST

Now when he was in Jerusalem at the Passover Feast, many believed in his name when they saw the signs that he was doing. But Jesus on his part did not entrust himself to them, because he knew all people. (Jn. 2:23-24)

WHAT JESUS DID:

Jesus evidently performed some miracles, called *"signs"* in John's gospel, during His stay in Jerusalem *(Jn. 21:25* states that Jesus did many more things than are recorded in his gospel.), and as a result, numerous people became convinced that He was the One sent from God. However, Jesus did not trust their commitment to Him because, apparently, it was superficially based on seeing the miraculous: They had merely been swayed by the spectacular. But Jesus knew people and could discern their hearts. He understood that human nature is fickle and changeable. Consequently, He did not invest His time and energy with these people, seeming to know that they would not fully embrace His call to discipleship.

WHAT HIS FOLLOWERS ARE TO DO:

As Christ followers, we have been called to make disciples *(Mt. 28:19)*. This means we need to spend time sharing and teaching God's word, developing their spiritual habits and experiencing Christian life together, and working closely with those who are truly committed to becoming obedient to the Lord and to His word. So, as Jesus did, we too should exercise discernment with those around us who confess Christ to determine whether their dedication is genuine or momentary. Jesus spoke of people who receive His message joyfully and even may grow for a while but then wilt when troubles occur or when they get distracted by a pursuit of worldly riches *(Mt. 13:20-22)*. At some point, we need to recognize if our time and energy is being well-spent with the individuals we are mentoring, and if not, to direct our efforts elsewhere.

JESUS SPEAKS WITH NICODEMUS

Now there was a man of the Pharisees named Nicodemus, a ruler of the Jews. This man came to Jesus by night ... (Jn. 3:1-2a)

WHAT JESUS DID:

Jesus and His small group of disciples had come to Jerusalem for Passover. In John's gospel, it was at this time that Jesus went into the Temple and drove out those selling animals for sacrifice and the money changers. He made bold claims about His authority to do such an action and also performed signs which caused many to believe in Him. *(Jn. 2:13-25)*

Nicodemus, whose name in Greek means "victory of the people," is described as a Pharisee and a Jewish leader, perhaps suggesting that he was a member or even a head of the Sanhedrin. His meeting with Jesus is presented only in John's gospel. Much speculation has been made as to why Nicodemus met with Jesus at night. Was this a secret meeting? Was he afraid to be seen by his fellow Pharisees or other Sanhedrin members with this upstart preacher and miracle worker from Galilee and thus needed to talk with Jesus under the cover of darkness? Or, maybe Nicodemus was just a busy man during the day and only had free time at night. Whatever the reason, Jesus (who was also busy!) met and talked at some length with him.

Nicodemus' initial statement that Jesus' miraculous signs show that God was indeed with Him might have been an attempt to soften Jesus with flattery but may also have been just a genuine declaration of belief. At any rate, Jesus immediately cut to His crucial teaching about the need to be born again to see God's kingdom. Nicodemus had more questions, and Jesus answered patiently and forcefully. We are not told Nicodemus' immediate reaction to Jesus' words, but he appears to have been deeply touched as he later appears two more times in John's account: first, when he spoke out to a group of Pharisees against unlawfully arresting Jesus *(Jn. 7:50-51)*; and then again as one who brought expensive ointments to prepare Jesus' body for burial *(Jn. 19:39)*.

WHAT HIS FOLLOWERS ARE TO DO:

When God brings people into our lives who are truly wanting to know Him and to understand His ways, let's do what we can to accommodate them so that we can have a chance to share the gospel with them. This may mean changing our schedules so that we can meet at times which are more convenient to them. And if those seekers desire to talk with us privately, we should try to appreciate where they're coming from and agree to meet when it is most opportune and comfortable for them Like Jesus, we need to be flexible so that we can answer their honest questions and point them to the One who said, *"For God so loved the world, that he gave his only Son, that whoever believes in him should not perish but have eternal life"* *(Jn. 3:16)*.

JESUS' MINISTRY OF BAPTISM

After this Jesus and his disciples went into the Judean countryside, and he remained there with them and was baptizing. (Jn. 3:22)

WHAT JESUS DID:

Jesus incorporated baptism into His early ministry in Judea, in a place where water was plentiful, and many responded *(v. 23)*. We are told later that Jesus Himself didn't perform the actual baptizing; rather it was His disciples *(Jn. 4:2)*. Like John the Baptist, Jesus was preaching a call to repentance, but so great was the response to Jesus that John's disciples were concerned that everyone was going to Him instead of John, to which John, understanding that his role of preparing people for the coming Messiah was nearing its end, replied that it was time for his work to decrease and for Jesus' ministry to grow *(Jn. 3:30)*. At the end of Jesus' time on earth, He instructed His followers to make disciples, and this included teaching and baptizing them *(Mt. 28:19-20)*.

<u>WHAT HIS FOLLOWERS ARE TO DO:</u>

In obedience to the directive of Jesus, as we share His message of repentance and the promise of God's grace and forgiveness of sins, we are to encourage new disciples to consider the need to be baptized once they have been adequately taught and sufficiently understand its significance. This ritual of submersion into and emersion out of water is to be an outward symbol of inward change of heart and mind, a public testimony of a turning away from an old life devoted to self and towards a new life dedicated to the Lord. If there is a real commitment on the part of believers in Christ to follow Him, let them take this important step of faith.

Baptism was part of Jesus' ministry, and He told us to baptize others who commit themselves to Him, so let's follow His lead and fulfill His command.

JESUS AND THE SAMARITAN WOMAN

Jesus, wearied as he was from his journey, was sitting beside [Jacob's] well. ... A woman from Samaria came to draw water. Jesus said to her, "Give me a drink." (Jn. 4:6a, 7)

<u>WHAT JESUS DID:</u>

Jesus and His disciples had spent some time in Judea baptizing new followers. But when word came that John had been arrested by Herod *(Mt. 4:12)* and that the religious leaders were aware of Jesus' activities and His growing number of disciples, He judiciously headed back to Galilee, passing on His way through Samaria *(Jn. 4:1-4)*.

Recorded only in John's gospel, Jesus conversed with a woman while sitting near a famous, ancient well (perhaps in an area purchased by Jacob in *Gen. 33:18-19*). In speaking to a woman, and to a Samaritan woman, Jesus was breaking a couple of cultural taboos of the time: a man speaking to a woman when no one else was present (the passage in John tells us that Jesus' disciples had gone into town to get food [v. 8]) and a Jew speaking to a Samaritan, with whom the Jews had an antagonistic relationship (v. 9).

But Jesus was not bound by artificial social restraints. He was under the authority of His Father in heaven and abided by His holy law. Jesus had a message of good news that He wanted to share with all that He met. For Him, every encounter with someone was a God-ordained-opportunity to offer the life-changing words of the gospel, and He would not let manmade rules prevent Him from doing that.

As a result of this initial meeting with the woman and her testimony about Jesus, many in the village believed in Him, so Jesus stayed there two more days sharing His message and teaching, and even more people came to faith in Him. (Jn. 4:39-42)

WHAT HIS FOLLOWERS ARE TO DO:

We all grow up in a certain social milieu in which we learn the values and morals of our families and friends and the customs and traditions of our culture. We are taught what is right and what is wrong, what is acceptable behavior and what is not. And the question we followers of Jesus must continuously ask ourselves is whether we adhere to the ever-shifting principles of the world or to the divine, eternal precepts of God.

Does our family, society, or culture dictate with whom we can interact or have a relationship? Do these external forces define how we are to engage with certain individuals? Specifically, are we discouraged or even prohibited from having any significant affiliation with people of some other races or countries or religions or sexuality? If so, perhaps it is secular forces which are seeking to mold us into their image.

We who call Jesus Lord can see how He stepped beyond the boundaries of cultural and social prohibition and should let Him guide us to do so as well. We can be used by God, just as Jesus was, to touch the lives of all those with whom His Holy Spirit brings us into contact, regardless of race, ethnicity, skin color, country of origin, divergent lifestyle or religious belief. God seeks to reach out through us to share His redeeming message of hope and love to everyone.

There is also here in this meeting between Jesus and the woman at the well a clear illustration of how the gospel can spread. One person hears the words of Jesus and receives Him and His promises of God's forgiveness and grace, and that person tells others who in turn accept the message. It is a people-driven way of expanding the rule of the Kingdom of Heaven on earth, and our responsibility is to keep spreading the good news.

JESUS HEALS AN OFFICIAL'S SON

And at Capernaum there was an official whose son was ill. When this man heard that Jesus had come from Judea to Galilee, he went to him and asked him to come down and heal his son. (Jn. 4:46b-47a)

WHAT JESUS DID:

Jesus had returned to Galilee and was well-received there because of what He had done in Jerusalem at the Passover (v. 45), possibly a reference to His actions at the Temple and perhaps also to some unrecorded miracles He had performed. Jesus came to the village of Cana, where He had changed the water into wine, and it was there that He was met by this royal or governmental official (v. 46). The official had made the more than 16-mile trip from Capernaum southwest to Cana to beseech Jesus' help for his sick son. Jesus responded initially that people needed to see miracles before they believed in him, but then assured the man that his son would live (vv.48-50a). The account in John's gospel continues that the official believed (v. 50b) and that his son became well at the very moment that Jesus spoke His words of healing (v. 53), described as the second miracle that Jesus performed in Galilee (v. 54).

What is of note to me here is Jesus' initial, somewhat harsh reaction – that He at first chided the distraught official for His lack of faith – but that He then without further comment pronounced the son healed. Jesus was displeased with and criticized the official's well-founded concern for the physical health of his son because of the man's lack of spiritual perspective; however, ultimately, He understood and sympathized with the official's anxiety and pain for his loved one and responded to His need.

WHAT HIS FOLLOWERS ARE TO DO:

There are certainly times when we, Jesus' disciples, are called to minister to others whose motives and sincerity we question. They may express real, earthly concerns or hardships, but we are quick to dismiss them by disparaging their absence of spiritual outlook or heavenly viewpoint. However, let's take a cue from the Lord in such a case: Though they may not be believers in Christ or even interested in His message of salvation, and though we may question or even want to indict their attitudes and behavior, we should still do that which is within our power to help and to offer solutions to people's genuine difficulties.

Most assuredly, the official's faith in Jesus was bolstered by the healing of his son, and we can also hope that our reaching out to provide for those in need in the name of the Lord will instill in them a greater openness towards Christ's words and even a longing for a closer relationship with God.

JESUS READS SCRIPTURE IN THE NAZARETH SYNAGOGUE

And as was his custom, [Jesus] went to the synagogue on the Sabbath day, and he stood up to read. (Lk. 4:16b)

WHAT JESUS DID:

Jesus had returned to His home region of Galilee empowered by God's Spirit, and news about Him spread throughout the province as He taught in the synagogues to the acclaim of those who heard Him. *(Lk. 4:14-15)*

Following the *Torah* and Hebrew tradition, Jesus was in the habit of going to the synagogue on the last day of each week to join with other Jews to hear a reading or recitation of the Scripture. On this occasion in His hometown of Nazareth, Jesus stood in reverence to read a passage from the scroll of the prophet Isaiah which speaks of the LORD's anointed one *(Isa. 61:1)*, the Messiah, and applied the verses directly to His own life and person, saying, **"Today this Scripture has been fulfilled in your hearing"** *(Lk. 4:21)*.

WHAT HIS FOLLOWERS ARE TO DO:

We are reminded here, first, that our spiritual strength and energy come from God, not from ourselves. As we yield our wills and desires to Him and allow God's Spirit to fill us and move in us, He will give us the guidance and power to engage in fruitful ministry.

Also, though I am not advocating for strict adherence to seventh-day religious laws, I do believe it is important for disciples of Jesus to set aside a time out of the mundane, busy work week to regularly assemble together for the purposes of spiritual edification and corporate prayer and worship. I consider all time to be sacred as we live in God's constant, immanent presence; however, meeting with those of like faith to be instructed in the way of the Lord on a specific day and time offers the benefits of building each other up and creating a strong sense of community. Whether in a church or home, led by clergy or lay people, structured or free-flowing, a local body of believers should meet to listen to, talk about, and meditate on the teaching of Holy Writ. We need to treat the word of God with devotion and respect, as Jesus did. And let's diligently seek to understand its depth of meaning and its relation and application to our lives and relationships.

JESUS IS REJECTED BY HIS HOMETOWN

When they heard [what Jesus had said about Himself], all in the [Nazareth] synagogue were filled with wrath. (Lk. 4:28)

WHAT JESUS DID:

The people in Jesus' hometown of Nazareth rejected His teachings and His claims to be anointed by the LORD. So incensed were they that they forced Him out of town to a nearby cliff where they intended to throw Him off *(v. 29)*. However, remarkably, He merely walked through the angry crowd and left for another city, Capernaum, and when He spoke in the synagogue there, people were amazed at His powerful and authoritative teaching *(vv. 30-32)*.

Let's note that Jesus didn't lose His temper in this situation, that He didn't engage the mob in heated argument, that He didn't attempt to convince them of the error of their ways, that neither He nor His disciples fought against those even seeking His death. Instead, He just departed for a place that was more receptive to His words. Jesus did not give up despite this rebuff in Nazareth. He pressed on to another town to continue His God-ordained ministry.

WHAT HIS FOLLOWERS ARE TO DO:

Of course, not everyone will readily embrace the message of Jesus; there may even be outright hostility toward it and its messengers, i.e., His followers. How are we to react to overt and perhaps even irate refusal of the gospel?

Following Jesus' example, we are not to return the anger of those who openly and vocally oppose Christ with an indignant response, nor are we to intensely contend with them. Rather, we are to present His clear message, understanding that some will accept it while others will not. And when there is angry opposition and refusal, the best thing to do is just lovingly walk away and take the message elsewhere to places where there are more receptive and amenable minds and hearts. Let's follow Jesus' example of persistence when we experience setbacks, disappointments, or failures: Don't give up, trust in the Heavenly Father, and carry on with the mission of spreading Jesus' good news.

JESUS THE GALILEAN FULFILLS PROPHECY

And leaving Nazareth [Jesus] went and lived in Capernaum by the sea ... (Mt. 4:13a)

WHAT JESUS DID:

Jesus, rejected by His hometown of Nazareth, traveled some 20 miles to the northeast to live in Capernaum, a fishing town on the northern shores of the Sea of Galilee. This would become His home base, as it were, for the bulk of His ministry. Several of Jesus' disciples who were eventually chosen as apostles came from Capernaum, including the pairs of fishermen-brothers Peter and Andrew and James and John, and the tax-collector Matthew. The rest of His apostles and closest followers also came primarily from the region of Galilee.

The writers of the Christian New Testament saw the life, death, and resurrection of Jesus as a fulfillment of specific passages from the *Tanakh* (Hebrew Scripture), as their frequent citations indicate. Matthew's Gospel, for example, described Jesus' luminous presence in Galilee as a prophetic fulfillment of *Isaiah 9:1-2*, written perhaps in the 8th century BCE. Jesus was moved and guided in His life by the same Spirit of God that had inspired the pronouncements of the ancient prophets of Judah and Israel, and thus, His words and actions became a completion of their proclamations made centuries before.

WHAT HIS FOLLOWERS ARE TO DO:

In a sense, we Christians of today are called to fulfill the truth of the Bible as well, not as Jesus did in fulfilling specific prophecies made about His coming, but as living out the clear teaching of Christ and following His example. For instance, as we share the good news of God's grace and mercy in Christ and instruct others to follow Him, we are fulling His commission to *"make disciples"* (Mt. 28:19). Or, as we lead lives of goodness and righteousness, we fulfill Jesus' description of us as *"the light of the world"* (Mt. 5:14). As we engage in acts of lovingkindness and compassion, such as feeding the hungry, we will fulfill the words He spoke to His disciples when faced with huge crowds: *"You give them something to eat"* (Mk. 6:37a). Or, as we seek to be led by Jesus and exhibit real gentleness and genuine humility, we will fulfill His words to *"take my yoke upon you, and learn from me"* (Mt. 11:29). As we are generous with all we have and give priority to spiritual riches rather than material wealth, we will fulfill Jesus' teaching that *"life does not consist in the abundance of [one's] possessions"* (Lk. 12:15). And as we demonstrate active and sacrificial love for one another, we fulfill the promise that *"by this, all people will know that you are my disciples"* (Jn. 13:35).

Yes, we can fulfill the words of Scripture through a faithful walk with Christ.

JESUS BEGINS TO PREACH

From that time Jesus began to preach, saying, "Repent, for the kingdom of heaven is at hand." (Mt. 4:17)

WHAT JESUS DID:

John the Baptist had been arrested, and Jesus had left Judea to return to His home region of Galilee. There, He began a more public ministry. One crucial aspect of Jesus' mission was to preach, i.e., to proclaim His message to the world. As stated here in Matthew's gospel account, His theme was quite simple: a command to turn from doing evil because God's reign was near. Jesus mandated a change of mind, a change of heart, a change of life direction away from selfish enmity with God and toward a life dedicated to righteousness and submission to the will of the Father in heaven.

And what is "the kingdom of heaven" or "the kingdom of God" that Jesus referred to? There was certainly a physical, eschatological significance to the term, as would have been understood by a 1st century audience. God would intervene supernaturally and dramatically into history through His Messiah, the Son of Man depicted in *Daniel 7*, to overthrow the ruling empires of the world – including and especially Rome – to reign as supreme king over a holy realm. People needed to prepare for that soon-to-arrive day by turning from their sinful ways. (There continues to be an eschatological sense to the expression "kingdom of God" or "kingdom of Heaven" as the eventual, final manifest supremacy of God's reign on earth through Christ.)

There is also a definite spiritual, perhaps mystical, meaning: The kingdom of God is the any place where God is sovereign, where God's rule is supreme, and its constant proximity makes it readily accessible to all those who cede the throne of their lives to Him. It is the yielding of our own desires and plans to God, and making Him our LORD, just as Jesus taught us to pray, *"Your kingdom come, your will be done, on earth as it is in heaven"* (Mt. 6:10). As stated earlier in the Introductory Ideas section, the kingdom of God is submission to the inner, immanent reign of God the King in the hearts and lives of people and obedience to His rule. Wherever God reigns, wherever persons submit to His Kingship, there is the kingdom of God.

<u>WHAT HIS FOLLOWERS ARE TO DO:</u>

Jesus brought a message to all those who heard and continue to hear His voice. And His followers today are to communicate that same message to the people with whom we come in contact. Our Lord's straightforward demand to redirect ourselves away from wrongdoing and towards a life under the rule of the Heavenly King should be our message to others as well. Additionally, we are to proclaim the constant presence and availability of God's kingdom here on earth as we give up the control of our lives and place ourselves under His dominion in an attitude of loving obedience and trust.

Jesus came with a clear and uncomplicated message; we, His servants, are to share the words of the Master to a world that desperately needs to hear them.

JESUS CALLS HIS FIRST DISCIPLES

While walking by the Sea of Galilee, [Jesus] saw two brothers, Simon (who is called Peter) and Andrew his brother, casting a net into the sea, for they were fishermen. And he said to them, "Follow me." (Mt. 4:18-19a)

<u>WHAT JESUS DID:</u>

It will be recalled that in John's gospel, Jesus first met Andrew and his brother Simon in Judea. They had been disciples of John the Baptist, but he had told them to follow Jesus. It was at that time that Jesus gave Simon the new name Peter, which is Greek for "Rock." *(Jn. 1:35-42)*

When John the Baptist was arrested, Jesus made His way back to Galilee *(Mt. 4:12)*, where He again encountered Simon Peter and Andrew, who apparently had returned to their fishing business on the Sea of Galilee. Jesus issued a more definite call this time to the brothers, telling them that their new occupation would be **"fishers of men."** *(Mt. 4:19b)*, and they responded by leaving everything and following Him. Jesus then also called two more brothers, James and John, later to be nicknamed by Jesus **"the sons of thunder"** *(Mk. 3:17)*, and they too left their work and family to become disciples of the Lord *(Mt. 4:22)*.

WHAT HIS FOLLOWERS ARE TO DO:

Let us also, as Jesus did, call people to truly follow Him, not to just verbally affirm allegiance to Him, though that is important, but to also leave their old lives behind and become dedicated disciples of Christ. Following Jesus means to accept His direction and guidance in our lives, to yield our wills to His leading. We need to encourage those who seek a relationship with God to have a change of heart and mind about the life they are living and to turn to actively abiding by the way of Jesus.

Of course, it is often difficult and even wrenching to leave the familiar and the comfortable and to embark on a new way of life. The pull to go back to the old way of being can be extraordinarily strong. So, we should continually remind those striving to follow Him (including ourselves) that all of us, in a sense, have been given a new name by Jesus, a new identity which we can grow into as Christ-followers. We also have a new reason for living, a new focus that can help define who we are and what we do. The former self which was separated from God has been born anew as a child of the Heavenly Father. Old preoccupations and priorities can be dropped and left behind as we move to follow Jesus and to become more like Him.

His call to newness of life was made two millennia ago, and it continues today.

JESUS COMMANDS AN UNCLEAN SPIRIT

And they went into Capernaum, and immediately on the Sabbath [Jesus] entered the synagogue and was teaching ... And immediately there was in their synagogue a man with an unclean spirit. (Mk. 1:21, 23)

WHAT JESUS DID:

Jesus was confronted in the Capernaum synagogue by a man who was under the control of a demonic presence that held complete sway over his words and actions. The diabolical fiend recognized Jesus as the *"Holy One of God"* and feared that He had come to destroy them *(v. 24 – The plural "us" is used here).* Jesus responded swiftly and decisively, commanding the spirit to be silent and to leave the man, and the spirit obeyed, however reluctantly, the authoritative word of the Lord, convulsing the man as it came out. The reaction of the crowd predictably was one of amazement, and news of Jesus' power spread quickly around the entire region *(v. 28).*

WHAT HIS FOLLOWERS ARE TO DO:

Today, there continues to be a very real demonic presence in our world. We often come across people who are controlled by a variety of unclean, selfish spirits that manifest in behaviors such as anger, greed, lust, indolence, gluttony, envy, and pride. (You may recognize these as the "Seven Deadly Sins.") Additionally, many individuals in our world are dominated by evil spirits of lying and dishonesty, prejudice and bigotry, callousness and indifference, and downright wickedness. How are followers of Jesus to respond to this?

I believe we can first pray and speak authoritatively in the name of Christ against any and all demonic powers to limit, remove, and prevent their influence on the spiritually unprotected. Also, through our acts of love and kindness, we can help others to overcome hatred and mean-spiritedness; through our attitude of empathy and understanding, we can bring about a change of heart in those bound by bitterness and intolerance; and undoubtedly through our courage in the strength of God, we can and must confront wrongdoing and malevolence and stand against those who would do harm to others, especially to the innocent.

But in order to confidently command ungodly spirits, we as Christians must maintain godly lifestyles that reflect well on our Lord, not overindulging in food or drink, not given to avarice and the unbalanced desire for material accumulation, not obsessed with physical gratification, not exhibiting laziness or succumbing to jealousy. Instead, as we lead lives of righteousness, moderation, industry, and contentment, we will have the right to call out the evil we see in others and in our society.

So, when we hear dishonesty, we must call it out. When we see injustice, we must call it out. When wrongdoing occurs, we must call it out. And we must not just call these evils out, but we must also be willing to take specific, pragmatic action against them, realizing that a sacrificial price might have to be paid in doing so. Thus, I'm not advocating for a milquetoast, Pollyanna type of response to the powerful demons that are still at large and infecting people these days. We have to be spiritually and morally strong and absolutely dedicated to God to be able to fight against them. Jesus, the holy one, allowed no sin or wickedness or uncleanliness of spirit to dictate any aspect of his life. As we strive in the power of the Holy Spirit to do the same, we will be emulating our Lord.

JESUS CURES SIMON'S MOTHER-IN-LAW

[Jesus] left the synagogue and entered the house of Simon and Andrew, with James and John. Now Simon's mother-in-law lay ill with a fever, and immediately they told him about her. (Mk. 1:29-30)

WHAT JESUS DID:

The disciples of Jesus here made Him aware of the illness afflicting Simon's mother-in-law. Jesus' compassionate response was predictable: go to her, be near her, touch her, lift her up, and heal her *(v. 31a)*. In Luke's account of this incident, the fever is described as *"high,"* indicating its seriousness, and Jesus ordered the fever to leave her *(Lk. 4:38-39)*. Because of Jesus' curative power, the woman was returned to health and able to serve and minister to them *(Mk. 1:31b)*.

WHAT HIS FOLLOWERS ARE TO DO:

As we become aware of particular problems facing those around us, whether they be physical, emotional, or spiritual, our reaction should be one of kindness and empathy, with a mind and heart toward helping to solve those difficulties. Even if it means giving up something ourselves, we must be willing to approach others in need, to draw close to them, to stand with them, to touch their lives, to raise them up out of their troubles, and to offer whatever we can to bring about resolution, healing, and restoration. Once renewed in strength, they can then devote their energies to serving others. That is how Jesus reacted, and that should be our response as well.

JESUS HEALS MANY BUT DOES NOT ALLOW DEMONS TO TESTIFY

And [Jesus] healed many who were sick with various diseases, and cast out many demons. And he would not permit the demons to speak, because they knew him. (Mk. 1:34)

WHAT JESUS DID:

News of Jesus' power to heal spread quickly throughout Capernaum, and by sundown people were crowding around Simon Peter's home *(v. 32)*. They brought with them the sick and demon-possessed, and Jesus cured and restored them *(v. 33)*. And as we saw earlier, Jesus would not allow the evil spirits that He had exorcised to testify to who He was.

WHAT HIS FOLLOWERS ARE TO DO:

We who follow Jesus must be open about our faith and lead lives of righteousness and compassion. By doing so, we will be known in our communities as devoted people who truly care for others, and the LORD will bring to us those who need physical and spiritual help. And if we respond with lovingkindness and do whatever we can to assist and provide for their needs, our ministry of healing and spiritual cleansing will grow and flourish for the glory of God.

It is also interesting to me that Jesus did not permit demonic spirits to testify to His identity, and I believe there is a lesson here for us: Don't seek the testimony of those who practice evil and lead ungodly lives. We often love to hear popular celebrities, successful businesspeople, champion athletes, and powerful politicians talk about their relationship with Jesus, even though their attitudes and actions are in direct contradistinction to His ways and words. These people may express gushingly about their love for God, but out of the other side of their mouth come lies, cursing, boasting, and insults.

They may put on airs of humility for the cameras but in real life are prideful, vindictive, envious, and selfish. They talk about their wonderful savior but are guided not by His life and teaching but solely by their unrighteous desire for luxury, material excess, self-gratification, and worldly prosperity. These are not the kind of people that we want as spokespeople for Christ. Jesus would not let evil ones talk about Him, and we should discourage that as well.

JESUS SPENDS TIME ALONE IN PRAYER

And rising very early in the morning, while it was still dark, he departed and went out to a desolate place, and there he prayed. (Mk. 1:35)

WHAT JESUS DID:

Before the sun rose, before the day of work and ministry and the challenges He faced, Jesus retired from others and privately spent time in prayer with His Heavenly Father. Jesus understood that He could do nothing unless it was decreed by the Lord God *(Jn. 5:19)*. He realized that His words and deeds, His power and authority, all came from His unique relationship with the Almighty. Knowing this, He set aside part of His day in intimate communication with His Father in heaven. Jesus and His disciples then went throughout the region of Galilee, in synagogues and elsewhere, preaching and exorcising demons, for that was the mission He had been sent to accomplish *(Mk. 1:38-39)*.

WHAT HIS FOLLOWERS ARE TO DO:

Quite simply, we who follow Jesus need to pray as well. Jesus felt the necessity to be in continual communication with God through prayer, and so should we. And the way Jesus went about this time of prayer should be instructive to us: He prayed early in the morning before the demands of the day pressed in on Him; He prayed at a time when others would still be sleeping and when the distracting sights and sounds of the dawn would be limited; He prayed in in a deserted area where no one would interrupt Him or divert His attention. (For us today, that would mean not even an intruding cell phone.) Let's embrace Jesus' habits to better our own spiritual prayer life.

Through prayer, we can praise and worship the LORD, we can confess our sins and seek forgiveness, we can give thanks for all the blessings we see in our lives, and we can beseech God to provide for specific needs. Prayer is a way of maintaining an awareness of God's presence, a way of not only speaking to Him but listening to His voice, a way of yielding to His will, a way of recharging our energy to be of greater service to Him as we are sent, like Jesus, to engage in ministry.

Prayer was a crucial part of Jesus' life; it is of vital importance for us, His followers, also.

JESUS' MINISTRY

And [Jesus] went throughout all Galilee, teaching in their synagogues and proclaiming the gospel of the kingdom and healing every disease and every affliction among the people. (Mt. 4: 23)

WHAT JESUS DID:

Jesus ministered in many ways: teaching, preaching, healing, and exorcising demons. Thus, His ministry had intellectual, emotional, physical, and spiritual aspects. As a result of the power of His words and deeds, news of Him spread so that He quickly became famous, and large numbers of people from all over the entire region and beyond began to follow Him wherever He went *(vv. 24-25)*.

WHAT HIS FOLLOWERS ARE TO DO:

Our ministry can be multi-faceted as well. We can teach the word of God found in the Holy Scripture, bringing people to a better understanding of the true nature of our Heavenly Father. We can call individuals to a change of heart, a change of mind, and a change in the way of living, and share with them the good news of God's promises of grace and forgiveness through Jesus. We can use whatever resources we have and do whatever is possible to bring healing and restoration to anyone suffering from physical pain and sickness or emotional distress and anguish. We can help lead those who are bound spiritually by sin and by evil out of their old lives and into the newness and freedom of life in Christ.

Let's be faithful, like Jesus, to engage in ministering to the needs of others as the Holy Spirit leads us, so we can be used by God to touch the lives of many.

JESUS TEACHES FROM A BOAT

On one occasion, while the crowd was pressing in on [Jesus] to hear the word of God, he was standing by the lake of Gennesaret, and he saw two boats by the lake. (Lk. 5:1-2a)

WHAT JESUS DID:

Jesus' words attracted so many people that they crowded against Jesus to hear Him, pushing Him to the edge of the shore of Lake Gennesaret (another name for the Sea of Galilee). So, Jesus got into a boat belonging to Simon, had him push out a bit from the land, and continued teaching *(vv. 2b-3)*. The Lord saw the real need to instruct people in whatever way He could. Thus, when faced with the situation of a throng pushing closer and closer to Him, He creatively adapted His means of delivering His message, this time from a boat, while not changing the message itself.

WHAT HIS FOLLOWERS ARE TO DO:

Communicating the truth of God to those who would hear is a crucial aspect of being a disciple of Christ, but there is no one way to fulfill this mission. Just as Jesus did, we must be ready to adapt to circumstances in order to accomplish our task of conveying the Lord's message with others. It may mean sharing the gracious love of our Heavenly Father through speaking or writing or at times just being available to someone. And certainly, it always means caring in the name of Christ for people in need. As is said, "Preach the gospel; sometimes use words."

JESUS PRODUCES A MIRACULOUS CATCH OF FISH

And when [Jesus] had finished speaking, he said to Simon, "Put out into the deep and let down your nets for a catch." (Lk. 5:4)

WHAT JESUS DID:

Having addressed the crowds from Simon's boat, Jesus instructed him to head out to the deep waters to fish with his nets, and though Simon had fished unsuccessfully all night and must have been quite weary, he obeyed his Master's command *(v. 5)*. The result was a huge catch *(v. 6)*. Where Jesus went, He brought abundance. Through His words and deeds, people's lives were miraculously enriched. Jesus gave hope when despair had set in. He saw paucity and replaced it with plenty. He restored vigor to the fatigued.

Peter reacted to this miracle by falling to his knees before Jesus, acknowledging his own sinfulness that should not even be in Jesus' presence, and calling Him *"Lord" (v. 8)*. Thus, Jesus caused the miraculous catch of fish to create faith in Peter and the other fishermen, and the result was that they trusted Jesus and, leaving everything, followed Him *(vv. 9-11)*. We might also note that Jesus had used Peter's boat, his time, and his energy for His ministry of preaching to the crowds on the shore, and He reimbursed Peter copiously.

WHAT HIS FOLLOWERS ARE TO DO:

We who call Christ our Lord should seek to follow His guidance and in whatever way we can bring abundance, enrichment, hope, plenty, and vigor to those with whom God brings us into contact. Let us strive for relations and interactions with others that improve lives and bring greater fulfillment.

This is not to say that we are expected to perform supernatural acts as Jesus did. Our miracles occur when we are used by God to uplift souls, to help restore the brokenhearted, to feed the physical and spiritual needs of the hungry, to convert anger and hate into compassion and love. And ultimately, our actions are to create faith in the Lord and to direct people to following – NOT US – but Jesus.

And let's not forget that we are to compensate others (richly!) for the work they do on behalf of the ministry or really for any toil; as the Scripture says, **"the laborer deserves his wages"** *(Lk. 10:7)*.

JESUS TOUCHES AND MAKES A LEPER CLEAN

While [Jesus] was in one of the cities, there came a man full of leprosy. And when he saw Jesus, he fell on his face and begged him, "Lord, if you will, you can make me clean." (Lk. 5:12)

WHAT JESUS DID:

Leprosy seems to have been more prevalent in ancient times than today, and because of its unsightly and contagious nature, people kept their distance from those infected with this disease. Also, any contact with a leper would make a Jew ritually unclean. Thus, there are many instructions related to leprosy in the *Torah (e.g., Lev. 13).*

So, when this leper approached, the natural reaction would have been to separate oneself, but Jesus' response was remarkable: He reached out and touched the man, and he was immediately made well *(Lk. 5:13).* Jesus certainly had the power to speak a word of healing, as He had done before, but instead, He put His hand on the man. It was Jesus speaking nonverbally with an action of comfort, of welcoming, of warmth, of acceptance, of connection, of understanding, and ultimately, of restoration.

Wasn't Jesus concerned about His own health and wellbeing? Wouldn't He have wanted to avoid ritual impurity? I am sure the answer to both questions is, yes. But in Mark's account of this incident, we are told Jesus' motivation for His actions: He was *"moved with pity" (Mk. 1:41).* That is, He empathized with the man and felt compassion for the suffering he was experiencing, both physical and social. Jesus allowed the feelings of mercy, benevolence and kindness to trump the fear of possible contamination, and thus He put out His hand and cleansed the man of his leprosy with His touch.

WHAT HIS FOLLOWERS ARE TO DO:

Often, much of the suffering in our world is experienced by those who do not have the means to provide for themselves or to lift themselves out of their dire situations. Lacking boots, they are unable to "pull themselves up by their bootstraps." Frequently, they live in impoverished, unsanitary conditions without clean water, adequate food, or even basic medical care. They might be, therefore, dirty, poorly clothed, bad-smelling, and wracked with sickness and pain.

We who call Christ Lord must be willing, just as Jesus was, to respond to the needs of those people with compassion and mercy, and to reach out to them with hands of generosity and provision. We must allow the Holy Spirit of God to move in us to overcome our tendency to run from them, to separate ourselves from their circumstances, to keep a "healthy distance" lest we be contaminated, and instead to open and extend ourselves towards them in whatever way we can.

When we see suffering and want in others, let's seek first to understand what they are feeling – their uncertainty and worry, their despair and grief, their pain and anguish. Then, let's not turn away from them; rather, let us reach out to them in God's mercy and in the compassionate love of Jesus so that we can be used of the Lord to provide for their needs and touch their lives.

JESUS HEALS A PARALYTIC
AND FORGIVES HIS SINS

[Some people] came, bringing to [Jesus] a paralytic carried by four men. And when they could not get near him because of the crowd, they removed the roof above him, and when they had made an opening, they let down the bed on which the paralytic lay. (Mk. 2:3-4)

WHAT JESUS DID:

Jesus had returned to Capernaum where He was preaching to those who crowded around the home He was in, the throng even blocking the front door *(vv. 1-2)*. Reacting to the determined and creative faith that the lame man's friends showed by doing all they could to bring him into the presence of Jesus, He declared that the crippled man's transgressions against God were pardoned *(v. 5)*. Then, to prove that He had the authority from God to proclaim the man's forgiveness, Jesus healed him of his paralysis and made him able to walk again *(v. 12)*. It was a spiritual and a physical healing.

(Note that Jesus called the man *"Son."* This was surely just a familiar form of address, but we might also understand it in a deeper sense in that faith in Christ makes one a child of the Heavenly Father. All who have embraced the grace of God can be sure that they are His sons and daughters.)

Though we who follow Jesus do not have the power to actually forgive a person's sins against God (for God alone can do this), we do have the authority to rightfully affirm that any who present themselves in faith and repentance to the Father can receive the mercy of God and have their sins removed. It is just as the Scriptures promise:

> ▷ *As far as the east is from the west, so far does [the LORD] remove our transgressions from us. (Ps. 103:12)*
> ▷ *Though your sins are like scarlet, they shall be as white as snow. (Isa. 1:18)*
> ▷ *For I [the LORD] will forgive their iniquity, and I will remember their sin no more. (Jer. 31:34b)*

We have good news to share that God forgives sin – cleanses it, removes it, and forgets it, and when any of us trust Jesus and His message, make a profession of faith, and turn away from the clutches of our sinful life and toward the welcoming embrace of the Father in heaven, we can announce with all certainty that God has indeed graciously taken away the inequities that separated us from Him and has acknowledged us as His children. Hallelujah and Amen!

JESUS CALLS A TAX COLLECTOR TO FOLLOW

After this [Jesus] went out and saw a tax collector named Levi, sitting at the tax booth. And he said to him, "Follow me." (Lk. 5:27)

WHAT JESUS DID:

The man to whom Jesus issued this call to follow Him, named *Matthew* in his eponymous gospel *(Mt. 9: 9)*, was a Jew employed by the Romans to collect the various burdensome taxes imposed on the people of Israel and was thus despised as a weak, sycophantic collaborator and traitor. When Jesus passed by, Levi/ Matthew was engaged at that very moment in his much-reviled employ. However, Jesus, bucking popular sentiment, with a simple command to follow, chose him to become one of His disciples. Levi's response was immediate and decisive: He left everything that had to do with his old life *(v. 28)* and headed into a new one.

It is not known whether Jesus changed this man's name, but as this was something that Jesus had done previously with Simon, whom Jesus renamed

Peter, it is quite possible that Jesus gave Levi (meaning "joined") the new name Matthew ("gift from God") as a way of helping him embrace a new identity. In all of the lists of the names of the apostles, the name Matthew appears, not Levi *(Mt. 10:2-4; Mk. 3:16-19; Lk. 6:13-16; Acts 1:13).*

WHAT HIS FOLLOWERS ARE TO DO:

As Jesus did, we too are to make disciples *(Mt. 28:19).* Yet, as we think about developing relationships with people that we hope to spend time with and to mentor as followers of Christ, our inclination might be to select the popular and successful, the ones highly-esteemed in our communities, those who are leading socially-acceptable lives. Instead, let's follow Jesus' example and be open to others that God brings us into contact with who might be deemed less-than-desirable by our peers or engaged in less-than-respected fields of endeavor. (I can hear the other disciples' voices as Jesus chose Levi: *"What? That guy? Are you sure that's someone you want to be part of your ministry?"*) But as we are yielded to God's Spirit and attuned to His voice rather than the voices of others, we can trust that the LORD will reveal the ones that we are to reach out to, even those who might be considered pariahs in our society.

Also, as we see people come to Jesus and dedicate themselves to following Him, let's be active in sharing God's scriptural promises so they become aware of their new identity in Christ. In a sense, they have a new name, and we can help them to understand that. The former life can be left behind, and they can step into a new way of living, and we should participate in encouraging, strengthening, and shaping that change by reminding them that they have been born into a new life and that they have a new standing before God as one of His children.

JESUS ASSOCIATES WITH SINNERS

And as Jesus reclined at table in [Matthew's] house, behold, many tax collectors and sinners came and were reclining with Jesus and his disciples. (Mt. 9:10)

WHAT JESUS DID:

Jesus had called Matthew to become His disciple, and Matthew, whose job as tax collector for the Romans was detested by his fellow Jewish countrymen, had responded by leaving his work and following Him. He welcomed Jesus to his home with a great feast *(Lk. 5:29),* and many of Matthew's not-so-pious friends and colleagues came to eat together with his new Master. When some religious leaders chastised Jesus for keeping such sinful company, Jesus responded that His call to repentance was for sinners, not those who saw themselves as self righteous (*Mt. 9:11, 13*).

Throughout the Gospels, Jesus spends time interacting with both religious and non-religious people. His mission was to call everyone to repentance, and this of course included those involved in wrongdoing and transgression of God's law. Jesus' heart, like that of His Heavenly Father, was welcoming to all who would hear and receive His words of mercy and hope and who desired to redirect their lives toward God.

WHAT HIS FOLLOWERS ARE TO DO:

There is often a tendency among us Christians to separate ourselves from significant contact with non-Christians and to even actively shun people who do not espouse Christian beliefs or live by Christian values. This, I think, is not following the leading of the Lord. If we are to have any impact on others, we must be willing to leave our religious bubble, our zone of comfort and understanding, and to reach out to people who are far different from us. We must spend time with them, converse with them, get to know them, and perhaps share meals with them.

However, that does not mean that we should embrace a sinful lifestyle: Note that Jesus did not become a tax collector or a sinner; rather, He maintained His righteousness but received the wayward into His world, into His sphere of influence, so that He could share with them the good news of God's forgiveness.

Jesus ate with sinners. We, His disciples, should learn from His example and be open to developing relationships beyond our safe and secure gated-community of Christian religiosity.

JESUS ANSWERS A QUESTION ABOUT FASTING

Now John's disciples and the Pharisees were fasting. And people came and said to him, "Why do John's disciples and the disciples of the Pharisees fast, but your disciples do not fast?" (Mk. 2:18)

WHAT JESUS DID:

Some people, identified as John the Baptist's disciples in *Mt. 9:14*, questioned Jesus on their observation that His disciples were eating and drinking (*Lk.*

5:33) but did not engage in fasting as did other religious groups, such as the disciples of the Pharisees and of John. It seemed to have been a kind of challenge to the way Jesus conducted His ministry.

However, Jesus did not succumb to their apparent attempt to pressure Him to conform to the practices of others. Rather, He used the metaphor of a wedding feast to explain that their time of fasting would come once He (the bridegroom) was gone, but for now, it was time to celebrate His presence *(Mk. 2:19-21)*.

WHAT HIS FOLLOWERS ARE TO DO:

Other people, perhaps even religious individuals, might on occasion criticize some of our practices or how we conduct our mission for Christ, and may even go as far as calling for us to change. They may point out the ways of other Christians or other Christian groups and suggest that we follow suit. However, if our behavior and our methods are in keeping with the clear teaching of Scripture, we, like Jesus, should not allow ourselves to be compelled into fitting into their ministerial parameters. While we do need to be able to explain our reasons for the ways we choose to serve the Lord, we should be guided by God's Spirit and by Hs Word, not by the demands of others.

JESUS DEFENDS HIS DISCIPLES' PICKING GRAIN ON THE SABBATH

At that time Jesus went through the grainfields on the Sabbath. His disciples were hungry, and they began to pluck heads of grain and to eat. (Mt. 12:1)

WHAT JESUS DID:

The Pharisees were watching Jesus carefully, hoping to catch Him in some act that they could condemn. Thus, when they saw Jesus' disciples picking grain to eat (What were the Pharisees doing out in the grainfields on the Sabbath anyway?), they pounced, decrying the disciples' behavior as unlawful on the Sabbath. The religious leaders, such as the Pharisees, had rigid rules and oral traditions about what constituted "work" on the Sabbath which would result in breaking the commandment to keep the seventh day of the week as a day of rest. This included picking grain (which the religionists saw as a kind of harvesting, which was indeed proscribed in *Exod. 34:21)* or rubbing it (a detail provided in *Luke 6:1*) to remove the inedible outer husk from the edible inner kernel, so the religionists denounced the disciples' actions.

Jesus sprang to their defense, first by reminding them of the Biblical story of the hungry David and his men on the run from King Saul eating bread that was reserved for priests *(1 Sam. 21:3-6)*. Then, Jesus added that priests do their sacrificial work on the Sabbath but are not guilty of sin. He also quoted a verse from Scripture stating that God desires **"mercy, not sacrifice"** *(Hos. 6:6)* and characterized their rebuke as condemning the guiltless. Finally, Jesus proclaimed His authority as *"the Son of Man"* to have charge over the Sabbath. *(Mt. 12:3-8)*

WHAT HIS FOLLOWERS ARE TO DO:

We who seek to follow Jesus ought to also stand up for those under our care when they face unfair sharp criticism, unwarranted robust censure, or unjustified harsh scolding from others, especially from the more powerful and more authoritative. Of course, a defense assumes that the actions of those in our charge are right, fair, good, and without blame. God sovereignly brings individuals – like our children, people we mentor, and others – into our sphere of attention and supervision and puts them under our protection. We become responsible for them, and when they are wrongfully attacked, we, like Jesus, must be quick to shield, support, and preserve them.

Having said that, there are most certainly times when we need to allow the ones we nurture to fend for themselves and to stand on their own feet. But when faced with challenges from formidable intimidation (even bullying) and more influential foes, we must jump into the fray and defend them and their innocence.

Jesus, as Master and Teacher, stuck up for His students, His disciples, and we should do the same for the ones that God has placed in our care.

JESUS HEALS A WITHERED HAND ON THE SABBATH

Again [Jesus] entered the synagogue, and a man was there with a withered hand. *(Mk. 3:1)*

WHAT JESUS DID:

Jesus saw a man in need, a man whose right hand (per *Lk. 6:6*) was shriveled, disfigured, gnarled, weak, and perhaps paralyzed. Jesus' response was to have the man come to Him *(Mk. 3:3)*, to draw near Him, for He knew that He could and would heal the man.

Jesus was also aware of the accusatory eyes of the religious leaders that were watching His every move, waiting for an opportunity to indict Him for breaking any aspect of their strict, even harsh, interpretation of the Mosaic Law. So, Jesus, both sad and indignant at their callousness toward suffering, challenged them with a question that cut to their souls and for which they had no reply: Which is lawful on the Sabbath, doing something beneficial or something harmful, rescuing someone or killing them? Jesus Himself answered the query – that any time is right for doing good and saving life – by restoring the man's hand. *(vv. 2-5)*

WHAT HIS FOLLOWERS ARE TO DO:

When we who call Christ Lord see a situation of need or pain or conflict, is our first reaction to move away from it, to disassociate ourselves from it so we can stay at a safe distance? Or, like Jesus, do we bring people who are suffering closer to us so that we can minister to them and provide for their needs? Rather than erecting walls to keep out those whom society might deem less-than-desirable, let's lead lives of openness and willingness to embrace the sick and the indigent, the hungry and the oppressed, so that we are more able to show them the love and compassion of our Heavenly Father.

We are certainly called to be righteous people and to uphold the law of God, but let us never become hard-of-heart like the religionists who were so focused on "spiritual matters" that they became blind and insensitive to the physical misery that was right in front of them. We must live with open eyes and open hearts, aware of need around us and receptive to meeting those needs in any way we can. As Jesus taught on this occasion, it is always the right time to do good and to help others.

JESUS RELOCATES AND CONTINUES HIS MINISTRY

The Pharisees went out and immediately held counsel with the Herodians against [Jesus], how to destroy him. Jesus withdrew with his disciples to the sea, and a great crowd followed ... (Mk. 3:6-7)

WHAT JESUS DID:

Right after Jesus had healed a man's withered hand on the Sabbath and thus had challenged the Pharisees' misguided and calloused view of God's command to keep that day holy, they plotted to kill Him. They even conspired with the supporters of King Herod in a religious/political alliance against Jesus. Jesus was aware of their malevolent intentions *(Mt. 12:15)*, and so withdrew with His followers to the Sea of Galilee in a kind of strategic retreat from danger, probably because He still had much to do to fulfill His mission.

However, He did not let the plans of evil men change His dedication to His ministry, and continued healing those in need. People came in great numbers to Him, many of them sick, crowding around Him and understandably wanting to touch Him and be cured. So, Jesus made provision, just in case: The disciples were to have a boat ready in the event that too many people came and overwhelmed Him. *(Mk. 3:9-10)*

WHAT HIS FOLLOWERS ARE TO DO:

A few ideas come to mind regarding Jesus' actions here. First, let's not test God by putting ourselves in dangerous situations and then expect Him to get us out. We trust in our Father's protection and provision, but when we perceive that there is the likelihood of peril to life or limb, we should follow Jesus' example and pull back or withdraw. That does not mean stopping our mission, but rather relocating to a place where we can carry on the work of the Lord. We can also see in Jesus' preparations for a certain scenario (having a boat ready if the crowds swamped Him) a reminder that we too ought to look ahead as we minister and have Plan B ready if required.

And finally, notice that Jesus did not complain about the crush of people around Him. He didn't tell those in need to back off and give Him space. Jesus understood that God had sent Him to that location to minister to the needs of the people there, and He was devoted to doing God's will. We should have that same attitude. God directs us to a place where we can be used by Him to touch lives and bring about healing and restoration. Let's accept His guidance without protest and serve in every way that we can.

JESUS CHOOSES THE TWELVE APOSTLES

*And he appointed twelve (whom he also named apostles) so that
they might be with him and he might send them out to preach
and have authority to cast out demons.* (Mk. 3:14-15)

WHAT JESUS DID:

To begin with, Luke's gospel account of this event tells us that Jesus went up
on a mountain to pray and that He spent the entire night in continuous prayer
to God *(Lk. 6:12-13)* before selecting these dozen men. That shows what a
momentous decision this was for the Lord and how He approached it, namely,
through intense contemplation and communication with His Father.

Jesus had a special role for these twelve "apostles" (a word that means
"emissary, ones sent on a mission") of spreading His message and performing
exorcism. And note: Prior to being sent out, they were to be with Him. Before
they could be expected to accomplish their task, they had to spend time with
Jesus, to build a relationship with Him and get to know Him and His teaching.
Thus equipped, they would be more able to fulfill their role and complete their
assignment.

WHAT HIS FOLLOWERS ARE TO DO:

When faced with decisions, we should learn from Jesus and spend time in
prayer before God. Jesus removed Himself from possible distractions by going
alone to a mountain where He privately connected with the Heavenly Father.
And His time in prayer was not a few quick words asking for blessing; rather,
He spent many hours seeking God's wisdom to ensure that the decision He
made was in accord with God's will and plan. So, we who are followers of Jesus
ought to do the same – devote significant amount of time before God in prayer,
especially when crucial decisions are pending.

Jesus also demonstrated the importance of drawing others around us
that we can mentor and teach so that they are then better prepared to have an
effective ministry themselves. This means that we need to be open to God's
leading to bring people into our lives that are wanting to learn and grow in
faith. And as those people appear, we are to draw them near to us, to be with
us, so that we can encourage and shape their development. Ultimately, the
goal is for them to be "sent out" from us to share God's truth in Christ and to
engage in battle against wrongdoing and injustice.

That was the model set by Jesus: To pray continuously for God's guidance, to choose some to be with Him, and then to send them out to impact the world. Let us also do the same.

JESUS TEACHES ON A MOUNTAIN

Seeing the crowds, he went up on the mountain, and when he sat down, his disciples came to him. And he opened his mouth and taught them ... (Mt. 5:1-2)

WHAT JESUS DID:

Of course, what follows here in Matthew's Gospel *(Chs. 5-7)* is the magnificent compilation of Jesus' teaching commonly called "The Sermon on the Mount," which includes the Beatitudes, the Lord's Prayer, and the Golden Rule, as well instruction about relationship with God, interaction with others, religious practices like prayer and fasting, charitable giving, sin, and the Law. These words of Christ, we note, were intended for His *"disciples,"* a word that means someone who learns from another – a student. These are those individuals who chose to be with their master teacher, Jesus, to receive spiritual training and guidance from Him.

Teaching was an important aspect of Jesus' ministry, for He was able to impart to His followers the truth and wisdom of God, with a goal of making them more like Himself. Later, Jesus says that *"it is enough for the disciple to be like his teacher" (Mt 10:25a).* Certainly more than enough, Lord.

As stated previously, as we grow in our relationship with God, we should bring others into our lives so that we can develop and train them to be disciples as well. Like Jesus, we are to mentor and teach those that express and demonstrate a genuine desire to learn more about life in Christ. That often means spending time in conversation with them, sharing Scripture with them, and talking with them about what we have learned and experienced in our walk with the Lord.

That does not mean we must all be wise sages or halo-surrounded pictures of piety and saintliness. It does mean we are to become mature in Christ, to become more Christlike every day, far from perfect but moving toward godliness in our relationship with the Heavenly Father. As we do so, those people who have come close to us will see God's Holy Spirit alive in us and will be receptive to the message of Jesus. At that point, as the Lord did, when they come to us, we can open our mouths and teach them.

JESUS HEALS A CENTURION'S SERVANT

Now a centurion had a servant who was sick and at the point of death ... [He] sent to [Jesus] elders of the Jews, asking him to come and heal his servant. (Lk. 7:2a-3)

WHAT JESUS DID:

The centurion was a Roman Army officer in command of 100 soldiers. As such, he was part of the occupying and very unwelcome force in Israel at that time. So, when he sent some Jewish elders to plead to Jesus for help, the natural tendency of any Galilean might have been to resentfully, even contemptuously, ignore or deny his request; Jesus could have easily refused the man as an oppressive foreigner. However, the elders in this case interceded *"earnestly"* for the man, citing his favorable accomplishments for the Jewish people such as building their synagogue, and Jesus reacted by going with them toward the centurion's home. *(vv. 4-6a)*

The story continues with Jesus receiving a surprising message from the centurion that he was not worthy for Jesus to enter his home but that He could just speak the healing words from afar. This showed the man's humility, definitely not an attitude that would be expected from a Roman officer, and also his trust in Jesus' power to heal, even at a distance, rather than believing in Rome's pantheon of gods and goddesses. As a result, Jesus was taken aback and praised the man's amazing faith and healed his servant. *(vv. 6b-10)*

<u>WHAT HIS FOLLOWERS ARE TO DO</u>:

We are sometimes faced with a difficult decision of whether to help or not to help someone who is in distress but with whom we don't get along, or someone who has wronged us, or someone who does not share the same values as ours, or someone outside our particular societal circle. It is quite simple to focus on all the negatives and injustices and differences associated with these persons and to disdainfully blow them off when they come to us for assistance or to turn away coldly and derisively when we become aware of their need for support.

But let's follow the lead of Jesus here: When others approach us with a problem, instead of dwelling on their bad aspects and the harm they have done, maybe even to us personally, or on how alien they are to our way of life, we the disciples of Christ can make an effort to look for areas of virtue in their lives and for good that they have done and respond to that and seek ways to provide for them. And perhaps in doing so, we will be able to understand the persons more and develop a better relationship with them and have a positive effect on their lives.

We must be willing to break down the barriers of resentment, disrespect, or hate, sometimes created by our own biases or ignorance, walls which block us from interacting with or ministering to certain individuals. When we do this, we can discover more about who these people really are ... and we, as Jesus did, might marvel at what we learn.

JESUS RAISES A WIDOW'S DEAD SON

As [Jesus] drew near to the gate of the town [Nain], behold, a man who had died was being carried out, the only son of his mother, and she was a widow ... (Lk. 7:11-12a)

<u>WHAT JESUS DID</u>:

Nain was a village in the lower Galilee, about nine miles southeast of Nazareth. As Jesus approached the town, He saw the funeral procession. Once again, Jesus is moved with compassion for someone suffering, this time a widow who, having lost her husband at some point, now was grieving for the loss of her only son. Knowing what He was going to do, Jesus told the widow not to cry and stopped the funeral as He touched the bier on which the dead man had been laid. Then, He commanded the young man to get up, and the boy sat upright and started speaking. The account concludes with Jesus, perhaps helping the young man to his feet up off the bier, leading him to his mother.

Jesus' reaction in this incident showed a definite progression:

> ▷ Jesus saw the woman;
> ▷ He empathized with her deep sorrow and pain;
> ▷ He sought to console her with words of comfort;
> ▷ He approached;
> ▷ He stopped the funeral procession that was heading toward the grave by touching the bier on which the corpse was being carried;
> ▷ He commanded the young man to arise from death;
> ▷ Jesus returned the young man to his mother.

Where there was death, Jesus renewed life

WHAT HIS FOLLOWERS ARE TO DO:

We who follow the Lord can learn much from this incident and from the way that Jesus responded:

> ▷ First, let's keep our eyes open so we can become aware of people in physical pain, emotional distress, financial straits, or spiritual anguish;
> ▷ Then, we must not turn away from or ignore those who are going through hard times, but rather we ought to put ourselves in their shoes to better understand and feel what they are experiencing;
> ▷ Next, we can reply initially to these people through spoken or written expressions of consolation and encouragement;
> ▷ However, let's not offer just words while remaining aloof, but instead we need to draw closer to the persons and enter their situations;
> ▷ Additionally, if there are factors which seem to be moving toward a result that will only make matters worse or that will certainly end badly, we should take measures to stop those things;
> ▷ May we also be sure to bring the word of the LORD God so that we can speak with authority over the distressed persons and over their problems;
> ▷ And finally, let's help to restore those who are suffering or who are in want to a place of wellbeing, hope, and happiness.

Jesus took decisive and effective steps to alleviate misery and to provide for the needs of the people He met. He brought life to the dead. Let us seek to do likewise.

JESUS RESPONDS TO MESSENGERS FROM JOHN THE BAPTIST

Now when John heard in prison about the deeds of the Christ, he sent word by his disciples and said to him, "Are you the one who is to come, or shall we look for another?" (Mt. 11:2)

WHAT JESUS DID:

John the Baptist, locked in prison, perhaps not having expected things to turn out the way they did, wanted to know with certainty that Jesus was really the long-awaited Messiah. He sought affirmation that Christ had actually come. John wondered, understandably based on his current circumstance, if in fact he had found the truth or whether he should keep searching.

Jesus' response is telling: Echoing prophetic passages in Isaiah *(Chs. 35 and 61)*, Jesus cited the many great works and miracles He was performing (healing of the blind and lame, lepers and the deaf, and raising the dead) and the good news message He was proclaiming (preaching the gospel to the poor) as confirmation that indeed He was the One, and that those who continued in their belief in Him, perhaps even if He wasn't exactly what they were expecting, were truly blessed of God *(Mt. 11:3-6)*.

WHAT HIS FOLLOWERS ARE TO DO:

When Christians have professed that Jesus is Lord, people around them will question whether what they claim is truth or not. They might ask: Does Jesus genuinely transform lives? Is what Christ-followers have found in their relationship with Him the real answer to life's most pressing questions about existence and meaning? Is Jesus Christ the one that they have been searching for, or should they go on looking?

Our response, like that of Jesus, should be to point to our own lives and to the lives of many others as evidence that His claims about God and about Himself are true. But first, we must ask ourselves: Have we allowed Jesus to take away our spiritual blindness and to give us new ways of seeing things?

Have we yielded our faults and failings to Him so that He can take us by the hand and help us to walk through life confidently in His presence? Have we surrendered to Him the unclean and sickly parts of our lives so that He can make us pure and holy before God? Have we stopped listening to the voices of those that would lead us into iniquity and wrongdoing and have instead bent our ears toward the life-giving words of Christ? Have we prostrated ourselves as dead before Him so that He can lift us to a new life, a better life, one that is filled with peace and joy? Have we acknowledged our spiritual poverty before Jesus, bereft of divine wisdom and understanding apart from His gospel message? Do we hold fast to our faith and belief in Christ despite circumstances so that we can say we are indeed blessed by God?

Simply put, has Jesus Christ made a practical, visible difference in our lives? Are we different from others who do not have a relationship with Him? Not different in a weird or unseemly way, but different in terms of our words and attitudes and actions? Does knowing Christ produce in us honest and uplifting speech, goodness of character, and godly lovingkindness? If so, as Jesus did with the messengers from John, we can point to the wonderful things He has done as proof that He is in truth the One.

JESUS IS ANOINTED BY A REPENTANT WOMAN

One of the Pharisees asked [Jesus] to eat with him, and he went into the Pharisee's house and reclined at table. (Lk. 7:36)

WHAT JESUS DID:

Jesus had accepted an invitation from a Pharisee to dine at his home, but during the meal a woman entered and began to weep at Jesus' feet and then dried her tears with her hair, kissing His feet and pouring an ointment from an alabaster flask on them. The woman in this story is described as *"of the city"* and *"a sinner,"* which seems to imply that she was a prostitute. Jesus read the thoughts of the Pharisee in whose house He was dining, the man questioning and even deriding Jesus' status as a *"prophet"* because He did not rebuke the woman for her sinful ways. In response, Jesus offered a story of two debtors to show that those who have sinned greatly and are then forgiven will respond with tremendous appreciation, gratitude, and love. *(vv. 37-43)*

Jesus did not reprimand the woman for her past nor preach about her transgression of God's laws. Rather, He accepted her profound act of contrition and penitence and her acknowledgement of His status as someone worthy of being washed by her heartfelt tears and anointed with her precious oil. Jesus reacted by pronouncing the woman forgiven of her sins and by then telling her to go in the peaceful assurance that she had been cleansed and restored by her faith in Him. *(vv. 44-50)*

<u>WHAT HIS FOLLOWERS ARE TO DO:</u>

Let us never think that some people are fit to receive the grace of God while others are not. We must not sit in judgment, as the Pharisee in this incident did, over the lives of others. Before God, we all fall short of His holiness, so we need to disabuse ourselves of any notion of our self-righteousness or deservedness. None of us is better than the next person, regardless of the circumstances and conditions of our lives.

Also, when people are moved by the message of Christ and express remorse for their sins and wrongdoing and turn in repentance toward God through faith in Jesus, let's not be quick to question their contrition or to dwell on their past; instead, we should help them to understand and confidently trust the promises of God's forgiveness and new life in Christ. Though they may have felt that their past iniquities were too great to ever be completely absolved by God, let us reassure them that though their *"sins are like crimson, they shall be white as snow"* (Isa. 1:18a), and guide and redirect them to leading lives of uprightness and goodness.

Jesus accepted genuine acts of remorse, made everyone aware of their equal status before God, and reassured the penitent that they were forgiven of their sins. May we who follow Him do the same.

JESUS IS SUPPORTED IN HIS MINISTRY

Soon afterward [Jesus] went on through cities and villages, proclaiming and bringing the good news of the kingdom of God. And the twelve were with him, and also some women ... (Lk. 8:1-2a)

<u>WHAT JESUS DID:</u>

As Jesus traveled about, sharing the gospel message, neither He nor His disciples were gainfully employed. They had all given up their jobs to devote themselves fully to the ministry of healing and preaching. Naturally, they still required food and places to stay, but they trusted in God to provide for them, which He did through the support of their followers to feed and house them and to care for their needs during this time.

From this passage in Luke, we see that part of Jesus' "entourage" consisted of several women, of whom at least one – Joanna, the wife of Chuza – was somewhat well-off, being married to the head steward in King Herod's home. These women, having been healed of disease or freed from demonic bondage – such as Mary Magdalene – and others, gave Jesus and His group of disciples the financial backing they needed to engage fully in their mission (vv. 2b-3). Thus, Jesus counted these women among His disciples; in a sense, He endorsed and welcomed the women's ministry of support as a vital part of His work.

WHAT HIS FOLLOWERS ARE TO DO:

There is a common distinction made in the Christian world between those who are involved in "full-time ministry" – like pastors, Bible teachers, and missionaries – and those who are not. Also, these religious ministers are often revered more highly than those with secular jobs. However, we can see in the example of Jesus the importance not only of sharing the good news of Christ but also of providing resources toward that goal. Both can truly be considered full-time ministries. That is, there are those who devote themselves entirely to preaching the gospel and to teaching the Scripture, and there are those whose God-given task is to use their occupations to ensure that the ministry of the preachers and teachers is provided for.

These two roles, though, are by no means mutually exclusive. In other words, those who dedicate themselves fully to preaching and teaching should take part in materially supporting the ministry of others as well; likewise, those whose role is to support the ministers of the gospel also have a real responsibility to spread the message of Christ and bring spiritual healing to the world.

Obviously, support must consist of financial and material provision, without which the Christian ministry cannot survive and thrive. There are also spiritual and emotional components of support, like praying for those in ministerial jobs and befriending and embracing them and their families. We should make sure that, whatever our vocation, we are fully engaged in caring for each other and in propagating the faith.

So, let's not be quick to differentiate between clergy and laity in terms of their roles in doing the work of Christ here and now, honoring one above the other. Both are divinely-assigned, and both are essential. And one final point: God knows at all times what our needs are, and just as Jesus trusted Him for provision, let us also have faith that our Heavenly Father will take care of His children.

JESUS BINDS THE STRONG MAN (SATAN)

[The scribes] were saying, "[Jesus] is possessed by Beelzebul," and "by the prince of demons he casts out the demons." (Mk. 3:22)

WHAT JESUS DID:

A significant part of Jesus' ministry was exorcising demons – freeing people from diabolical bondage. The reaction of the religious leaders, described as *"scribes"* in *Mark* and *"the Pharisees"* in *Matthew 12:24*, was to claim that Jesus was empowered, not by God, but by *"Beelzebul,"* another name for Satan. Jesus responded, ***"No one can enter a strong man's house and plunder his goods, unless he first binds the strong man. Then indeed he may plunder his house"*** *(Mk. 3:27)*. And that is exactly what Jesus had done: He had entered the strong man's house (come into the domain of Satan on earth), had bound Him (restrained his power), and was plundering his goods (releasing possessed souls from his control). Jesus also sternly warned the religionists that their assertion was blasphemy against the Holy Spirit, an unforgiveable sin *(vv. 28-30)*.

WHAT HIS FOLLOWERS ARE TO DO:

The demonic is still at large in the world today, as evidenced by the atrocities of violence and war, the cheapening of human life, the loss of the sacred, the pursuit of selfish desire, and the disregard for the plight of others. The followers of Jesus must strive to restrict that satanic power and influence by praying, by upholding Scripture, and by being filled with and empowered by the Holy Spirit of God. As we arm ourselves with God's truth, protected by our faith in His trustworthy promises, we will be better prepared to engage in the spiritual warfare that is needed to free those held prisoner by all that is evil so they can receive Christ's call to repentance and submission to the rule of God.

JESUS AND HIS SPIRITUAL FAMILY

*And [Jesus'] mother and his brothers came, and standing
outside they sent to him and called him. (Mk. 3:31)*

WHAT JESUS DID:

Jesus' family at this time consisted of his mother, his four brothers, and at
least two sisters *(Mk. 6:3)*. (His father, Joseph, is mentioned only at Jesus' birth
and in His early years, and it is speculated that he had passed away.) Jesus had
returned to His home in Capernaum, and large numbers of people followed
Him. Told by the crowd that His family was outside, Jesus did not go out and
welcome or even acknowledge them – a reaction that may strike us as harsh
and unfeeling. However, despite the throngs that Jesus was attracting, his
family did not believe the stories they had heard of Jesus healing the sick and
casting out demons or that Jesus was a teacher now and taking on disciples.
Indeed, they thought He had lost His mind, and they had come to take hold
of Him and restrain Him *(v. 21)*.

So, when His family arrived, Jesus did not greet them with open arms.
Instead, He turned His eyes on His followers and seeing a teachable moment
proclaimed that His true, spiritual family were those who obeyed God's word
and did what God wanted *(vv. 33-35)*. For Jesus, obedience to God was more
important than family relations.

It is also important to note that Jesus did not let His family's opinions
or their attempt to intercede prevent Him from fulfilling the mission which
His Father in Heaven had sent Him to do. Jesus knew the will of God and
submitted Himself completely to it.

WHAT HIS FOLLOWERS ARE TO DO:

Jesus gives utmost significance to our relationship with our Heavenly Father.
Before family, friends, country, church affiliation, or any other entity, God
is to occupy first place. Though relatives might not accept our beliefs or
way of living, we must remain committed to the Lord. Our standing with
God is to be our primary, lifelong concern. Death separates us from all that
is temporal, including family and other persons, but our relationship with
God is eternal.

That is not to say that we should ignore or neglect our earthly relations.
Scripture tells us consistently of our solemn responsibility to love and care
for others – family, friends, community, and anyone in need. Rather, we must

continually remember that our essential identity is as spiritual beings who have been created to know God. Additionally, while we absolutely must honor our parents and love and respect our other family members, we have to first obey God and His calling; all else is secondary, and we cannot let the opinion of others prevent us from following the way of Christ and proclaiming His truth.

Jesus' point was to teach His followers that our true family goes well beyond blood relations or legal connections; our forever family is made up of those who hear God's word and lead obedient lives according to His desires. These spiritual brothers and sisters are our real, eternal family. And despite our obligations to love and provide for our earthly family, our primary relationship is with God, and we must walk as Jesus leads us. It is a lesson that we need to learn and embrace.

JESUS TEACHES IN PARABLES

*And [Jesus] told [the crowds] many things in parables
saying: "A sower went out to sow ..." (Mt. 13:3)*

WHAT JESUS DID:

Jesus had gone to the seashore and was followed by crowds of people, so He go into a boat and began teaching them *(vv. 1-2)*. Jesus often framed His message in stories, or parables, which taught central truths about God and His kingdom. Why parables? From a practical, literary standpoint, we might answer with the following:

▷ Parables keep the attention of the listener. Good story-tellers can capture and hold their audience's interest in order to eventually make a particular point.

▷ Parables are memorable. Whereas theological statements might be hard to recall or to later retell to others, a story is not so easily forgotten.

▷ Parables can incorporate the everyday circumstances of the hearers, such as their family and social relations, work, ordinary experiences, and natural surroundings, things they are well acquainted with. This familiarity lends itself to better understanding the spiritual meaning embedded in the stories.

Thus, through these instructional parables, Jesus was able to memorably and imaginatively convey understandable principles related to the Heavenly Father and to His Kingdom.

However, while the reasons given above might be true, Jesus offered a different purpose for His use of parables: to prevent understanding of those who have not embraced Him and His teaching in faith. Jesus tells His disciples that they have been given the knowledge to understand the *"secrets of the kingdom"* *(Mt. 13:11)*; in Mark's gospel, it says that Jesus explained everything to the disciples in private *(Mk. 4:34)*. But to those who had not committed themselves to following Him, Jesus' words remained a mystery. For Christ, faith comes before understanding; understanding is for those who receive His message. This is why Jesus, speaking of spiritual hearing and comprehending, ends the parable by saying, **"He who has ears, let him hear"** *(Mt. 13:9)*.

WHAT HIS FOLLOWERS ARE TO DO:

Let us remember this idea as we share the message of Jesus with others, namely, that people do not necessarily have to fully understand before they can commit themselves to receiving and following Jesus. There is a point at which upon hearing Christ's words, people must choose whether to accept or refuse His truth. Individuals do not need to grasp fully all the deep aspects of His message but just be willing to open themselves to God's promises of grace and forgiveness, despite intellectual hesitancy or skeptical reluctance. Christ's words can pierce through these barriers to faith, but we must be willing to humble ourselves as sinners before the Father in heaven and seek His mercy and forgiveness. Once that happens, once we have open and receptive ears to hear, we can trust that the clear voice of God's Holy Spirit will lead us into greater knowledge of His Kingdom.

And on a practical level, when sharing the message of Jesus, there may be times when telling a story or relating an anecdote will help someone grasp a divine reality. Explaining spiritual precepts by framing them in narratives set in our contemporary world might make them more readily understood and appreciated. Jesus used this method, and it is still a good way to convey truth.

JESUS CALMS A STORM

And when [Jesus] got into the boat, his disciples followed him. And behold, there arose a great storm on the sea, so that the boat was being swamped by the waves; but he was asleep. (Mt. 8:23-24)

WHAT JESUS DID:

Typical fishing boats of that era on the Sea of Galilee were, based on the measurements of one unearthed in 1986, about 27 feet long, 7.5 feet wide, and 4 feet deep, with space for four people to row and a single sail. Storms on this freshwater lake could produce waves large enough to easily sink a vessel of this size. We are not told how many disciples were on the boat at the time of this incident, but in any case, Jesus must have been really tired to remain sleeping during such a tempest.

Fearing for their lives, the disciples woke Jesus and in desperation begged that He save them. In Mark's account, they even frantically question Jesus' care for them as they are about to go under *(Mk. 4:38)*. Awakened to the situation and the plight of the disciples, Jesus acted decisively not only by calming the storm but also by addressing their needless fears and lack of faith *(Mt. 8:25-26)*: They didn't have to be afraid because He was with them; they had to trust in His care for them.

WHAT HIS FOLLOWERS ARE TO DO:

The metaphor of the storms of life battering us and causing us to worry and fear is apt here. At times, we certainly feel that our problems will overwhelm us and that God does not really care that we are being dragged down like a sinking ship. We cry out, understandably, in desperation, "Lord, where are you? We need help! Aren't you concerned about our wellbeing at all?" God's answer is illustrated in the life of Jesus: He's right there in the storm-battered boat with us.

While we have to do our best to bail out water and to keep the ship aright, our faith in the Lord's presence and providence must remain strong and steadfast. To be sure, fear and worry are natural responses to dire situations, as is questioning and doubting the provision of God during times of tragedy. However, may we never reach the point where we deny the Heavenly Father's great love for us. That is not to say that we will be rescued from every evil that besets us. Indeed, the Holocaust is a constant reminder of oppression and wickedness, and faithful Christians are today martyred in many places around the world. Our assurance is this: God is with us even in the worst of circumstances, and He will rescue us, either in this life or in the life to come. Let us keep that faith so that we can provide help to others.

So, as we focus on what Jesus did and how we can emulate Him, we must remember that God has placed certain persons in our care, such as family and individuals we mentor, and that He also brings into our lives people in need. And when those around us experience hardship, natural disasters, and potential destruction in life, we should, like Jesus, seek to soothe their worry and fear and to do whatever we can to resolve the situation they face. We must comfort the distressed with the many promises of God's lovingkindness and provision, and beyond words, we must take active, practical measures to help and to restore peace and security. Jesus brought calm to the raging storm; let's follow Him and strive to do the same whenever possible.

JESUS FREES A MAN POSSESSED BY A LEGION OF DEMONS

They came to the other side of the sea, to the country of the Gerasenes.
And when Jesus had stepped out of the boat, immediately there met
him out of the tombs a man with an unclean spirit. (Mk. 5:1-2)

WHAT JESUS DID:

This incident in the life of Jesus, told in all three synoptic gospels with some minor differences, unfolded in two parts: first, the healing of the man possessed by a legion *(v. 9)* of demons, i.e., 6,000 in number!; and then, the reaction of the people of that area and especially of the man healed. In both sections, there is a "sending" by Jesus.

When Jesus saw the man, He commanded the demons to come out of him, at which point the demons acknowledged Jesus as the Son of God *(v. 7)*. Jesus learned the identity of the unclean spirit – he called himself Legion, because they were so many possessing this man *(v. 9)*, and then, following their plea not to be cast into the bottomless abyss *(Lk. 8:31)* but instead to be sent into a herd of pigs, Jesus permitted them to go, which caused the animals to rush into the sea where they drowned *(Mk. 5:13)*.

When the people in the surrounding area, and presumably the owners of the swine, heard the news, they were terrified and implored Jesus to leave. However, the man from whom the demons had been cast out, now clothed and calm, his mind having been restored, begged Jesus to allow him to come with Him, but Jesus sent him back to his family and to his town to tell others of God's mercy. And indeed, the man did exactly that, proclaiming all that Jesus had done for him. *(vv. 14-20)*

WHAT HIS FOLLOWERS ARE TO DO:

The effects of the legion of demons on this poor man were many: He lived in the tombs, a place of death; he wore no clothes; he was ferocious and would not let people through; he could not be controlled by anyone; any attempts to restrain him ended in failure; he was constantly crying out and wailing; he harmed his own body by cutting himself with stones. And certainly some individuals today exhibit these same kinds of tendencies, whether due to wicked influences or emotional distress or unwise lifestyle choices. There are those who lead uncontrolled lives of excess without concern for anyone else and who refuse to be constrained by society or its norms; some people are furiously belligerent and eager to fight; certain souls are beset with constant anguish and even self-loathing that impels them to harm their own bodies; many refuse the protection offered by family and friends and expose themselves to myriad dangers, choosing roads that inevitably end in destruction and death.

What can the followers of Christ do to bring healing to those afflicted with such oppression? We must seek to understand their circumstances and to empathize with their pain. As representatives of Jesus here on earth, we should reach out to them in love and extend to them emotional and material comfort and support whenever we can. Often, we will need to commit time, energy, and resources to them, and we may be required to give counsel or a place to stay. Let's be willing to let God use us as needed to assist in their restoration. We must also commit ourselves to praying for them, speaking the promises of God over their lives that they can be freed from the bondage of sin and evil that binds them.

And if by the grace of God, they are released from their captivity and renewed in a right relationship with Him, we must encourage them to share with others, such as family, friends, and community, what God has done in their lives, to spread the good news of the healing power of Jesus. That is what Jesus told the man liberated of his demonic possession to do, and we should follow suit.

JESUS ENDS A WOMAN'S HEMORRHAGING

And behold, a woman who had suffered from a discharge of blood for twelve years came up behind him and touched the fringe of his garment ... (Mt. 9:20)

WHAT JESUS DID:

For 12 years, this woman had suffered! As recounted in the other synoptic gospels, this woman had spent all her livelihood on seeking a medical solution to her condition, but to no avail *(Lk. 8:43)*. Indeed, despite the attempts of many physicians to cure her, the bleeding had become worse *(Mk. 5:26)*.

The distraught woman was beyond the point of desperation, so, probably hearing reports of the healing power of Jesus, she sought Him out. However, maybe due to the crowd around Him or because of her humility or even fear, she did not approach Jesus directly with her plea for help; instead, she believed that just touching His garment would make her well. Her faith in Christ was rewarded (Jesus even saying that it was her faith that effected the miracle), for the moment she touched the hem of his cloak, the bleeding instantly stopped. *(vv. 21-22)*

WHAT HIS FOLLOWERS ARE TO DO:

This is definitely not a screed against medicine or doctors, for I trust in the healing powers of both. That being said, I also believe that ultimately God heals, but He uses the knowledge and skill of doctors and the curative abilities of science and medicine to restore health. We should absolutely utilize that which God has blessed us, including modern medical practice, to treat illness and care for those with medical conditions.

In this incident with the bleeding woman, we should note that Jesus didn't upbraid her for not first openly seeking His help. She had come in her own way, for whatever reasons, and had expressed her trust in Him by furtively touching His garment. We who follow Jesus can learn from His lack of chastisement of the suffering woman and His acknowledgement of her act of faith that individuals will come to Christ in different ways; not everyone will follow a set of prescribed steps to Him. Some will be public and vocal, while others will be private and silent. Let's respect those differences and remember that the important thing is that they come to Christ.

But could we Christians ever hope to be able to cure others merely through physical contact with them, as Jesus did? I am not saying that we necessarily have that power or authority. What I do desire is that we become like Jesus and lead lives of submission to God's will and be filled with the presence of the Holy Spirit, and if we do that, those who are suffering from spiritual sickness or emotional distress or feelings of hopelessness will be drawn to Christ in us and might want to come close to us, and perhaps as their lives connect with ours, they can become better and their wellbeing restored.

The Heavenly Father heals, and He may use us who follow His Son to bring about that healing in others.

JESUS RAISES A RULER'S YOUNG DAUGHTER

... a ruler came in and knelt before [Jesus], saying, "My daughter has just died, but come and lay your hand on her, and she will live." (Mt. 9:18)

WHAT JESUS DID:

From the other synoptic gospel accounts, the man who begged for Jesus' help was named Jairus and was identified as a ruler of the synagogue *(Mk. 5:22; Lk. 8:41)*. Jairus had evidently become aware of Jesus' reputation as a powerful healer and in desperation pleaded for Jesus to come and perform the miraculous raising of his recently deceased daughter. In so doing, Jairus acknowledged his faith in Jesus and in His authority over death itself.

Arriving at Jairus' home, Jesus asked the mourners (the flute players and those making a commotion by wailing and weeping) to leave because to Him, the girl was not dead but merely sleeping. Their response was derisive laughter, but despite their ridicule, once they left, Jesus held the girl's hand and restored life to her. *(vv. 23-25)* In Mark's account, Jesus raises her with the Aramaic words, *"Talitha cumi"* – meaning, *"Little girl, I say to you, arise"* *(Mk. 5:41)*. And in a charming addition that showed Jesus' practical care for the girl, He directed the parents to give her some food to help strengthen her understandably weakened body *(v. 43)*.

WHAT HIS FOLLOWERS ARE TO DO:

When faced with situations that appear beyond hope of resolution, repair, restitution, or restoration, we might be tempted to deny that God can intervene, and so we may simply give up and accept defeat. However, we can see from this incident that Jesus can bring life to even the most dire of circumstances, and we who follow Christ must be willing to be used by God to likewise offer hope to the woefully hopeless. Thus, let us ask ourselves:

- ▷ What can we provide that might solve a problem?
- ▷ What can we do to reinstate that which has been lost?
- ▷ How can our presence and actions assist in fixing that which is broken, even that which is seemingly beyond reparation?
- ▷ How can we be instrumental in bringing about restitution to that which has become impoverished?
- ▷ How can we help to rebuild something decayed or destroyed?

Any practical response to the above questions will most likely demand time, energy, emotional outlay, material resources, and certainly persistent attention and love.

And we must not be swayed or deterred by the lack of faith of others, their comments regarding the impossibility of fixing the problem, or even their mockery of our naivete in believing that God could actually intercede to reverse a fatal course and redirect someone towards goodness and righteousness. We should remove them and their negativity from the situation, keep trusting in the encouraging promises of our Heavenly Father, and proceed in the name of Christ to bring lifegiving aid to situations of apparent death.

JESUS GIVES SIGHT TO TWO BLIND MEN

And as Jesus passed on from there, two blind men followed him,
crying aloud, "Have mercy on us, Son of David." (Mt. 9:27)

WHAT JESUS DID:

The two blind men hailed Jesus as *"Son of David,"* most certainly a messianic reference, and had begged for His mercy to consider their plight. Thus, they had publicly acknowledged their belief that He was God's anointed with the power and authority to heal. When the blind men came to the house which Jesus had entered, Jesus sought to confirm their trust in Him by asking if they truly believed that He could give them sight, and their affirmative answer – an outward expression of their inward faith – resulted in their vision being restored *(vv. 28-30)*.

WHAT HIS FOLLOWERS ARE TO DO:

We are also called to bring sight to those who recognize their spiritual blindness, to those souls who are wandering through life in the dark. Separated from God's light, they lead visionless lives without purpose for the present or hope for the future. But if they are willing to acknowledge their estrangement from the Heavenly Father and to take a step of faith towards Him through Christ, we must be ready to share with them the promises of God's lovingkindness and to help them see the truth of our God who is light and in whom there is no shadow or darkness *(Jas. 1:17; 1 Jn. 1:5)*. According to their faith, He will open their eyes and reveal Himself to them and will restore their relationship with Him, giving their lives purpose, hope, and a brightened vision for things to come.

JESUS' POWER IS CALLED DEMONIC

As they were going away, behold, a demon-oppressed man
who was mute was brought to [Jesus]." (Mt. 9:32)

WHAT JESUS DID:

The religious leaders continued to oppose Jesus' mission. When Jesus responded to the need of this mute man, freeing him of the demon so that the man could speak, the Pharisees claimed that Jesus' control over spirits was actually Satanic *(vv. 33a, 34).* Their derisive and insulting comments were meant to belittle the true authority of Jesus as one sent from God and rather to portray Him as someone whose real power came from the Devil, the demonic prince. Thus, these Pharisees, instead of praising God for this miracle, reacted with scorn to Jesus' command of the supernatural. Yet, Jesus remained undaunted and persisted in the work of His ministry of healing.

WHAT HIS FOLLOWERS ARE TO DO:

We will also face opposition to our ministry, in whatever role we serve in the body of Christ. There are those who will bring up our less-than-righteous past or even our current failings as proof that what we proclaim is not true. People will question our motives for being involved in the ministry, claiming it is for our own personal gain or to fulfill our social needs or out of a desire for a sense of self-importance. Some may characterize our devotion as simpleminded or weak. But let us, like the one we call Lord, not be deterred by the statements of others. We ought not attend to their voices but instead bend our ears toward the voice of the Lord. Let us listen to God's words of encouragement, promise, and joy, and persevere in fulfilling our work in Christ so that we can be used by Him to bring healing to the infirmed and relief to the ones who are suffering.

JESUS HEALS AN INVALID AT THE POOL OF BETHESDA

One man was there [at the pool of Bethesda in Jerusalem] who had been an invalid for thirty-eight years." (Jn. 5:5)

WHAT JESUS DID:

At the beginning of this chapter, John's gospel states that Jesus was in Jerusalem for one of the Jewish feast days. It also says that there were a great number of afflicted people, including the blind and the lame, lying at this pool *(v. 3).* Yet, Jesus, surely led by the Holy Spirit of God, focused on just one of them, a paralyzed man.

Jesus knew that the man had been there for quite some time and asked him if he wanted to be healed *(v. 6).* What a puzzling question: 38 years an invalid, and Jesus asked if he wanted to be healed! Isn't the answer obvious in the extreme? However, perhaps we can view the Lord's question as more of a way to encourage the man to verbalize his situation, to specify his need, and to express his faith in God as the true healer.

Interestingly, the man did not answer, "Of course I want to be healed!" Instead, he described the superstitious belief that the pool had curative powers but only for the first person who entered its waters when they were moved (supposedly by an angelic presence), and that there was no one to help him beat the others into the pool so he could be healed (v. 7).

Jesus did not respond to the man's explanation but just cut directly to the problem and commanded the man to pick up his bed and walk. The healing was immediate, and for the first time in almost four decades, the man got up and walked off. (vv. 8-9)

WHAT HIS FOLLOWERS ARE TO DO:

Belief in superstition and "woo-woo" power can sometimes deter people stricken with illness or troubled by other difficult circumstances from seeking scientific, medical treatment or professional, dedicated assistance, and can in the end prevent them from submitting their care to God. Additionally, people in dire straits often offer excuses or cast themselves as victims of circumstances beyond their control, refusing to face their challenges honestly and courageously. There are also many who simply cannot afford to pay for the help demanded by their condition.

We who follow Jesus are called to minister to those in need, and this means, first, for us to have our eyes open and to look beyond ourselves so we can see the situation of others. But there is so much need! How can we know to whom we should reach out? Just as Jesus was led to minister to one particular man among many afflicted, we should be sensitive to God's Holy Spirit to direct us in the ways we are to be used by Him.

Then, like Christ, we can cut through layers of irrational ideas and debilitating pretexts which result in a paralysis of action, and help people to identify specifically their need and to clarify truthfully and bravely a possible, practical solution and the first step to move forward. This may involve an outlay of our time, our energy, our abilities, and our resources., but we must be willing. We must lead them as well to call on the Lord for a way out of their troubles, for He is ultimately the real deliverer.

Recovery and restoration might come miraculously, as in the incident at the pool of Bethesda, or it may occur through the loving provision and skilled care of others (or of ourselves, if we remain available to the leading of the Holy Spirit) ... or it may not happen at all. That last point is important to keep in mind as we seek to minister to the needs of those around us: God does not always bring healing or resolution in this life, but we can be sure of His promises to make us whole and bring us to a fulness of joy in His presence in the life to come.

So, let's seek to be aware of circumstances where we can show the gracious, lovingkindness of God, just as our Lord Jesus did.

JESUS CAUTIONS THE FORMERLY-PARALYZED MAN

Afterward Jesus found [the man who had been healed of his paralysis] in the temple and said to him, "See, you are well! Sin no more, that nothing worse may happen to you." (Jn. 5:14)

WHAT JESUS DID:

Jesus had healed the paralyzed man but then had slipped away into the crowd without telling the man who He was *(v. 13)*. Later, Jesus *"found"* the man, implying that He had been looking for him, to issue a stern warning: The man had been physically restored, but Jesus cautioned Him to avoid sinning so that a worse fate would not befall him.

WHAT HIS FOLLOWERS ARE TO DO:

What did Jesus mean? The man had been paralyzed for almost four decades; what worse thing could happen to him? I believe Jesus was referring to a separation from God caused by sin and, as a result, possibly suffering His judgment, whether that be physical or spiritual. Jesus had even said at a different time that it was preferrable to enter eternal life maimed or crippled rather than to be of sound body and cast into hell *(Mt. 18:8)*. For Jesus, spiritual wellbeing was of greater importance than physical health, and He wanted to redirect the man from his old life into a new relationship with the Father.

Jesus felt it was a critical message that the man needed to hear, and we who follow Him ought to convey a similar kind of warning to those who come to Christ. Once healed (i.e., forgiven) of their past wrongdoing, they are to leave their former unrighteous ways and to seek to lead lives of virtuous obedience lest they return to sin and experience spiritual separation from God and perhaps His divine judgment.

JESUS AT WORK WITH THE FATHER

The Jews were persecuting Jesus, because he was [healing] on the Sabbath. But Jesus answered them, "My Father is working until now, and I am working." (Jn. 5:16-17)

WHAT JESUS DID:

Jesus broke human religious norms time and again, but everything He did and said was in conjunction with God. Jesus saw God continually working in the lives of His creation, and He allowed God to work through and in Him, including by healing the sick and disabled every day of the week. Jesus knew God's heart and mind and will, just as a devoted child knows a loving parent., and He acted accordingly. But when Jesus acknowledged God as His Heavenly Father, the religious leaders were outraged at His blasphemous presumption to be equal with God and desired His death *(v. 18)*.

WHAT HIS FOLLOWERS ARE TO DO:

We, too, as children of God, call Him our Father in heaven. Let's seek to develop a closeness of relationship with Him to the point where we understand what a gracious Father He truly is. As we draw near to God in prayer and learn of Him through the Scripture, we will become aware of His immanent presence in all things. And as we see how He moves in the world, we can, like Jesus, work hand in hand with Him to touch the lives of many.

JESUS RETURNS TO AN UNRECEPTIVE NAZARETH

And coming to his hometown [Jesus] taught them in their synagogue, so that they were astonished, and said, "Where did this man get this wisdom and these mighty works?" (Mt. 13:54)

WHAT JESUS DID:

Jesus returned to His hometown of Nazareth. He had preached in the synagogue of Nazareth before *(Lk. 6:16ff)*. At that time, because He had said that the Scripture describing God's Anointed One was referring to Him, the townsfolk had wanted to kill Him.

Returning again, people were really surprised by His words of wisdom and presumably by the stories of His miraculous works, and yet, they still thought of Him as the boy and young man who had grown up in their village. To them, He was still Mary's son and the brother of His siblings, who still lived there. Jesus was not a prophet nor the son of a prophet; He was a carpenter and the son of a carpenter. Jesus had tried to reach these Nazarenes with His message, even despite their earlier rejection, but they could not see beyond their old ideas of Him, and their unbelief amazed Him. As a result of their stubborn lack of faith in Him, Jesus did not perform any miracles there other than healing a small number who were sick. Instead, He went to preach in other towns. *(Mt. 13:55-58; Mk. 6:1-6)*

WHAT HIS FOLLOWERS ARE TO DO:

There is a simple lesson here for those who follow Christ: Let's not give up even when the gospel is initially rejected. That dismissal may occur, as it did with Jesus, as people associate us with our past life and refuse to take seriously our current identification as Christians. But like the Lord, we need to be persistent and continue to reach out to those who disbelieve. Their hardness of heart might need multiple attempts before breaking through. And indeed, Jesus did heal some of the people in His hometown, indicating that His message had been received at least by a few.

Refusal by others can lead to discouragement, bitterness, and resentment in us, and may prevent us from sharing the good news and offer of God's gracious forgiveness. But let's not allow that to happen. The previous negative reaction to Jesus by the residents of Nazareth didn't prevent Him from coming back to give it another try, and His perseverance should encourage us to do likewise.

JESUS' COMPASSION FOR THE CROWDS

When [Jesus] saw the crowds, he had compassion for them, because they were harassed and helpless, like sheep without a shepherd. (Mt. 9:36)

WHAT JESUS DID:

Jesus was not sedentary. He did not stay where He was in his home base of Capernaum; instead, He traveled throughout the region of Galilee, teaching, preaching, and healing *(v. 35)*. Thus, He went out of his circle of familiarity, out of His proverbial comfort zone, out of His usual experience and knowledge, so that He could fulfill His mission: instructing those who hungered for righteousness, spreading His good news of the imminence of the kingdom of God, and restoring health and wellbeing to the sickly.

Looking on the crowds who were lost and without guidance, beleaguered by their diseases and powerless to treat them, He felt *"compassion"* – that is, He empathetically sought to understand what they were experiencing, He sympathetically shared their suffering, and in lovingkindness and benevolence, He demonstrated His care for them and healed them. It was the reaction of the Good Shepherd for His much-troubled flock *(Jn. 10:11).*

WHAT HIS FOLLOWERS ARE TO DO:

As followers of Jesus, we also are called to leave that which is familiar and comfortable to us, to go beyond our routine experiences and usual understanding, and to fulfill our mission of sharing God's love and forgiveness in Christ.

Let's open our eyes and our hearts to the needy world that is around us and respond with compassionate, practical action. In faith, we can teach others what we have come to know of the gospel of grace and the promises of a restored relationship with God. We can give assurances of the constant immanent presence of the King of the universe and offer the saving knowledge of access to His heavenly realm by trusting in Jesus. And, by obeying the LORD God in whatever way He leads us, we can help to bring about restoration to the lives of those beset by disease or tormented by emotional trauma or suffering from financial distress. Let's yield all that we are and all that we have to God to be used by Him however He sees fit.

Jesus left the familiar, engaged actively in His ministry, and responded with compassion to the needs of the people. We should do the same.

JESUS SENDS OUT THE TWELVE

And he called the twelve together and gave them power and authority over all demons and to cure diseases, and he sent them out to proclaim the kingdom of God and to heal. (Lk. 9:1-2)

WHAT JESUS DID:

Jesus chose these twelve individuals, men who were close to Him, to be sent by Him to expand the reach of His ministry and message. These "sent out ones," which is the root meaning in Greek of the word "apostle," had been called out of their previous lives in order to devote themselves to exercising the power of Jesus over evil and sickness and to spreading the good news of God's kingdom.

In all the synoptic accounts of this commissioning (*Mt. 10; Mk. 6; Lk. 9*), Jesus gave explicit instructions to this group, which was sent out two by two, about traveling light and depending totally on God to provide for their needs in the places where they ministered. In Matthew's account *(10:40-42)*, Jesus also promised rewards to those who carry out His work. The apostles obeyed and departed on their mission, healing disease and carrying the gospel throughout the villages of the region *(Lk. 9:6)*.

WHAT HIS FOLLOWERS ARE TO DO:

Jesus had a pattern with His disciples: Bring them near Him, develop them spiritually, and then send them out to minister. Following Jesus' lead, we can gather other believers close to us for fellowship and spiritual growth, we can offer direction and guidance, and then, when they are ready, we are to send them out to engage in ministry with those around them. Thus, we are ultimately to encourage those we have developed as "disciples" (students) to go out as "missionaries,"(from Latin, also meaning "sent out ones") into their individual areas of contact and interaction – with family and with friends, in neighborhoods and communities, at school or work or recreation. (Of course, all that is said here applies to us as well: We are to fulfill our roles as ones sent by Jesus into our own spheres of influence.)

In sending them out, we can echo Jesus' clear advice not to get bogged down with materialism nor to worry about what will happen in the future. Instead, let's exhort them to take steps of faith as they set out every day on mission that God will provide for them along the way. (I'm not decrying careful planning, which is absolutely necessary; rather, I'm simply emphasizing trust in God's provision as we walk obediently with Him.) We can also confidently convey Jesus' authority, power, and presence to fulfill their task. However, they are not to go it alone; just as Jesus sent His apostles out in pairs, we must be in close communication with each other, available to listen, to counsel, to comfort, or to assist as needed.

Being sent out doesn't mean just talking about their faith but to also show goodness and lovingkindness actively to the people that God brings into their lives. They are to care for those in need, giving physical, emotional or spiritual aid whenever they can. Where there is sickness and disease, those who are sent out are on a mission to bring healing, restoration, and wellbeing. They are also to stand in Christ's strength to denounce and oppose any wrongdoing and evil they might encounter.

We must not shy away from the responsibility placed on us by Jesus. He sent out those close to Him to be partners in His ministry and to broaden the impact of His gospel, and we ought to repeat that process, encouraging others – and ourselves – to respond in obedience and trust.

JESUS REACTS TO JOHN THE BAPTIST'S DEATH

[Herod] sent and had John [the Baptist] beheaded in the prison ... (Mt. 14:10)

WHAT JESUS DID:

Herod had arrested John at the urging of his wife, who had formerly been Herod's brother's wife, because John had vociferously condemned their relationship. She then connived with her infamous daughter Salome to have John executed. John the Baptist's disciples retrieved John's body, buried him, and then went to inform Jesus of what had happened. Jesus reacted to the news by leaving in a boat to a secluded location to be by himself. *(vv. 3-13)*

It is understandable that Jesus was greatly affected by the news of John's execution, and understandably so. Mary, the mother of Jesus, and Elizabeth, the mother of John, were kin *(Lk.1:36)*, perhaps cousins, which would have made Jesus and John related. Also, Jesus submitted Himself to John's baptism, at which time Jesus was called by God His *"beloved Son" (Mt. 3:17)*. Later, Jesus praised John as the greatest prophet to have ever lived *(Mt. 11:11)*. So, upon hearing the terrible news, Jesus went alone to a deserted place seeking solitude.

How should we react to bad or heartbreaking news? A common reaction is to seek out companions who can share the burden of the ill report with us. That is certainly a normal and beneficial reaction. But maybe we can learn something from Jesus' response.

Instead of gathering His disciples around Him for support in this difficult time, Jesus first removed Himself from everyone to be alone with His thoughts and feelings, and most assuredly to pour Himself out before God in prayer, to seek His closeness and comfort, and to be renewed in spirit. Jesus knew that all things were in the hands of the Heavenly Father, and by first drawing near to Him when saddened by John's horrific death, Jesus reaffirmed the primacy and utmost importance of His relationship with God. After His initial time of solitude and prayer, Jesus rejoined His disciples and continued His mission *(Mt. 14:14ff)*.

Considering Jesus' actions here may prove helpful to us when we are faced with similar kinds of tragedy: First, let's turn to God and seek His consolation, and then surround ourselves with family, friends, and colleagues to share our pain and lift our spirits so we can resume the work of the ministry.

JESUS DIRECTS HIS APOSTLES TO REST FOR A WHILE

And [Jesus] said to [the apostles], "Come away by yourselves to a desolate place and rest a while." For many were coming and going, and they had no leisure even to eat. (Mk. 6:31)

WHAT JESUS DID:

Jesus had sent the twelve apostles out to preach and heal in the villages throughout the region, and having completed their mission, they now returned to Him to report back on what had been accomplished for the Kingdom of God. They were obviously worn, weak, and weary from the walking and work, neglecting even to eat. Jesus could readily see their condition, so they sailed to a quiet place where they could be away from the crowds and get some much-needed food and rest. *(vv. 30-32)*

Jesus saw the physical and emotional demands that His mission had placed on the apostles, and He responded by directing them to get away and rest. We also need to be aware of times when we as followers of Christ should withdraw from the demands of our everyday lives and be together to share our experiences and simply decompress. Let's recognize when we should take a break from our individual areas of service, and set aside a time and place to meet as a group in the presence of Jesus, to reinforce and encourage one another, and to nourish our bodies and spirits. Once we have regained our strength and are spiritually reenergized, we can all go back out into our work for the Lord.

JESUS FEEDS MORE THAN FIVE THOUSAND

And taking the five loaves and the two fish, [Jesus] looked up to heaven and said a blessing and broke the loaves and gave them to the disciples to set before the people. And he divided the two fish among them all. (Mk. 6:41)

WHAT JESUS DID:

The miraculous feeding of more than five thousand *"men," (v. 44)* not including women and children, is described in each of the four gospels. The inclusion of one particular miracle by all the biblical evangelists is infrequent and perhaps suggests the significance of this event.

Hearing the news of John's execution, Jesus and His disciples had sailed to a spot where there were no other people so they could rest and reflect. However, large crowds followed, and the ever-compassionate Jesus began to teach and heal them. But as evening came, Jesus' disciples urged Him to send the hungry people away so that they could find something to eat. *(vv. 33-36)*

Jesus, though, instructed his disciples themselves to give the people something to eat *(v. 37a)*. Obediently, they gathered their meager resources of five loaves of bread and two fish, which Jesus then proceeded to miraculously multiply, and the result, of course, was that everyone had plenty to eat. There were even enough leftovers to fill a dozen baskets, the number suggesting that it was a faith-affirming lesson for the twelve apostles. *(vv. 38-43)*

Jesus saw the specific need of the crowds for food, and knowing what it was like to be hungry Himself, He responded with empathy and lovingkindness. He made use of the supplies that were available to Him, acknowledging and thanking God for His provision, and then allowed the power of the Almighty to grow the discouragingly paltry into the abundantly sufficient.

WHAT HIS FOLLOWERS ARE TO DO:

We can often be overwhelmed by the staggering level of crises all around us every day: hunger, sickness, poverty, injustice, corruption, violence, displacement, deceit, pollution ... wickedness abounds, and tremendous need is everywhere we look. The sheer numbers of issues and the immense volume of challenges we face can produce in us a sense of despair and pessimism and even lead to indifference and avoidance.

However, let's follow the lead of Jesus here and not focus on the size of the problem but on the greatness of the God we serve. Let's respond to need by taking stock of our resources, as seemingly inadequate as they may be, thanking God for what He has provided and offering it to Him to be used as He wills, and then in faith by starting actively to utilize what we have to touch the lives of others. God blesses each of us with different gifts and different possessions. Whether we are rich, middle-class, or poor, whether we have remarkable talent in some area or just everyday kinds of skills, the question is not "How much has He given us?" but "How willing are we to allow Him to use who we are and what we have?"

To simplify, we might break down this miracle lesson into the following steps:

> ▷ address the need;
> ▷ take inventory of resources to meet the need;
> ▷ thank God for His provision, whatever the amount;
> ▷ take the step of faith and start actively meeting the need;
> ▷ trust God to grow provision to meet need;
> ▷ and learn from the results.

Jesus did not succumb to discouragement when faced with a daunting problem. Instead, He trusted God to increase the little He had available to provide for the many. We followers of Jesus ought to do the same.

JESUS WITHDRAWS FROM AN ATTEMPT TO MAKE HIM KING

When the people saw the sign that he had done [feeding the 5,000], they said, "This is indeed the Prophet who is to come into the world!" Perceiving then that they were about to come and take him by force to make him king, Jesus withdrew again to the mountain by himself. (Jn. 6:14-15)

WHAT JESUS DID:

Amazed at Jesus' miraculous feeding of the multitudes, people saw in Jesus the fulfillment of the predicted prophet of *Dt. 18:15* and thus wanted to make Him king. However, their motives and their means were suspect to Jesus: They seemed to have been reacting only to the material benefits which He had given them (bread and fish) and had not responded to His teaching or His call to repentance; also, they desired to use force to create an immediate, earthly, political kingdom, whereas Jesus preached a heavenly kingdom under God's rule that God Himself would bring about in His good time. They sought a Messiah who would oust the Romans right away and provide them with their physical needs, but Jesus knew that such a plan was neither God's will nor His timing. So, He slipped away from them, going to a mountain to be alone, most certainly to spend time in prayer.

WHAT HIS FOLLOWERS ARE TO DO:

Religion often intersects with politics these days, just as it did in the past. Yet, we can learn from Jesus that our focus and mission is a spiritual one. We are not here to amass and exercise physical, political authority. Our call is to preach the good news of God's forgiveness and mercy in Christ. Like Jesus, we should be wary of those who want to bring about God's kingdom through the use of violence or injustice. Jesus' message is to open our hearts and lives to the reign of the Heavenly Father, and as we do that, He can empower us through His Spirit to strive for righteousness as individuals and as a nation.

Also, let's repeat Jesus' call for repentance and remind His followers of the cost of discipleship. Committing ourselves to the Lord does not mean that all of our material needs will be instantly met and all our earthly problems immediately resolved. We must yoke ourselves to Him, deny our selfish desires, and pick up the cross of obeying and serving Him daily *(Lk. 9:23)*, all the while trusting in God's loving provision.

And we should continually seek God's way and God's timing in all that we do. Our tendency might be to rush things or make them happen when God has not given us the go-ahead. Through prayer, meditation, studying Scripture, and yielding to His Spirit, we can attune ourselves to God's plan and know when it is time to move forward and act and when it is time to step back and withdraw, just as Jesus did.

JESUS WALKS ON WATER

Immediately [Jesus] made the disciples get into the boat and go before him to the other side, while he dismissed the crowds. (Mt. 14:22)

WHAT JESUS DID:

After performing the miraculously feeding of more than five thousand, Jesus sent the disciples ahead to sail across the lake where He would later meet them, but He stayed and personally dispersed the crowd, perhaps spending time moving among them and speaking to them as He sent them away. Then, after caring for so many – teaching, healing, and feeding them, Jesus needed some time alone to pray and went up on a mountain. However, a storm arose on the lake, and the disciples struggled against the strong wind and waves that beat against their boat. Their ordeal had apparently been lasting for several hours, because Jesus came to them, walking on the water, sometime during *"the fourth watch of the night,"* or between 3 and 6 a.m. *(vv. 23-25)*

Jesus knew the disciples were in trouble, straining to push the boat towards their destination, but we should note that He didn't quiet the sea and wind while on the mountain. Instead, He came to them, meeting them in the midst of their difficulty and distress. Eventually, as a result of His presence, calm was restored *(v. 32)*.

WHAT HIS FOLLOWERS ARE TO DO:

Let's remember the importance of personal connection. Crowds are made up of individuals, each one with a desire for acknowledgement and respect, and we can help provide that by genuinely interacting face-to-face with people.

We must also set aside time to be alone in the presence of our Heavenly Father, just as Jesus did. Involvement in ministry, in addition to all the demands of everyday living, can take its toll on us physically, emotionally, and spiritually. The antidote for such fatigue is to separate ourselves from others for a time to rest in the comfort of God, to pour out our hearts to Him, and to be regenerated by His Holy Spirit.

And just as Jesus came to the disciples during their time of trouble, we can follow His leading and go to people when they are experiencing hardship, pain, loss, or want. Let's be right there for those in need, not far away offering facile platitudes of comfort. We should draw close to them and their lives, bringing the assurance of God's love through whatever practical means we can offer to resolve the adversity they face. Our prayer is that by reaching out in the name of Christ to people who are going through difficulty or privation, we can help to provide care, assuage anxiety, and bring peace to the storms of life.

And Peter answered [Jesus], "Lord, if it is you, command
me to come to you on the water." (Mt. 14:28)

WHAT JESUS DID:

Seeing Jesus walking on the wind-tossed water of the lake greatly frightened the disciples; they even thought He was a ghost despite reassurances from Jesus that it was indeed He and that they need not fear *(vv. 26-27)*. Peter responded by asking Jesus to call him to come to Him, and when Jesus said, "Come," Peter got out of the boat and began to walk on the storm-tossed water towards the Lord *(v. 29)*.

As long as Peter kept looking at Jesus, he was able to walk on the water even though the wind and waves around him raged; however, when Peter took his eyes off Jesus and focused instead on the tempest, he started to sink and called for the Lord to save him. Jesus extended His hand quickly and grabbed Peter, preventing him from going under but also admonishing him for disbelieving and not trusting completely, and led him back to the boat, at which time the storm abated. *(vv. 30-32)*

When we, the followers of Christ, see others faltering in their faith and being dragged down by the troubles they face, we must be ready to reach out in the name of Jesus, take hold of them, and bring them to a place of safety, peace, and trust in God. This means first that we must be close enough to become aware of their need and then to react swiftly by providing whatever we can to keep them from drowning in their difficulties. If we separate ourselves from those in distress or ignore their pleas for help, we will not be able to be used by God to aid in delivering them from their hardship. Once they are restored, we can then talk about the necessity of faith in the Lord even during times of intense trial.

Like Jesus, we are to be a lifeline of support to those suffering from the many storms of this world – drawing near to them, seeing their problems, providing assistance, and encouraging their trust in God, the ultimate lifesaver.

JESUS HEALS THOSE WHO TOUCH HIS GARMENT

And when the men of that place recognized him, they sent around to all that region and brought to him all who were sick ... (Mt. 14:35)

WHAT JESUS DID:

Jesus and His disciples landed their boat at the town of Gennesaret *(v. 34)* on the northwestern shore of the Sea of Galilee, about three miles from Capernaum. The people there knew Jesus and His miraculous works, so when they saw Him, they brought to Him those who were ill. Perhaps not wanting to overwhelm Jesus with having to deal with each individual case, they begged Him just to let the sick touch the outer edge of his clothing – maybe His tunic or His cloak or His *tallit* prayer shawl – thus expressing their belief in Him *(v. 36a)*. It was not that the fabric itself had any power; rather, the people trusted that Jesus was imbued with such divine healing power radiating out from His presence that even His clothing was saturated with that energy, and everyone who touched His garment in that faith was restored *(v. 36b)*.

Think about Jesus' possessions as He went throughout Israel. What did He own? I can think of only one thing: his clothes. But when asked for help, Jesus allowed God to use even His meager belongings to minister to people.

We who follow Jesus today should also yield all of our possessions to God, whether they be many or few, so He can use them to provide for the needs of others and bring wellbeing into their lives. Let's consider all that we have as available for God's purposes. Money, homes, goods and furnishings, vehicles ... every material thing that we have been blessed with, when dedicated to the Lord, can be useful for service in the Kingdom of God. Private property? Yes, His.

JESUS OFFERS SPIRITUAL BREAD

When the crowd saw that Jesus was not there [where He had multiplied the loaves and fishes], nor his disciples, they themselves got into the boats and went to Capernaum, seeking Jesus. (Jn. 6:24)

WHAT JESUS DID:

Jesus had returned to Capernaum and began teaching in the synagogue. The people who had partaken of His miraculous feeding on the other side of the Sea of Galilee came looking for Him, but Jesus immediately understood their motive: They wanted more food. They even asked Jesus for a sign like providing manna from heaven, for it was the physical bread that they really desired. But Jesus had not come to merely fill bellies or provide for temporal, material needs; He, the Son of Man, offered spiritual food that lasts forever, namely, the bread of life which had come down from heaven, referring to Himself. All who ate of this bread would live eternally. *(vv. 25-59)*

Jesus had once before spoken to His disciples about spiritual food when He had been talking with the woman at the well in Samaria. When the disciples brought Him some food and urged Him to eat, Jesus replied that His sustenance came from doing God's will and accomplishing His work *(Jn. 4:31-34)*. Now, in the synagogue in Capernaum, Jesus explained exactly what that work was: to believe in the One whom God had sent *(Jn. 6:29)*.

We need to disavow those who come to Jesus only for material benefits, such as greater wealth or earthly prosperity. While He did provide for the basic needs of others and commanded his disciples to do likewise, Jesus' priority was spiritual, and that should be the focus of our mission as well. Let us, therefore, renounce those who preach a gospel of affluence, and let's encourage people who are lured by false pledges of worldly, materialistic abundance for believers in Christ to redirect their attention toward storing up spiritual riches in heaven *(Mt. 6:19-21)*.

And as Jesus set us an example of being sustained by doing God's will, we should in turn seek to model that in our own daily lives by not being motivated or driven by the desire for self-satisfaction, comfort, or the accumulation of fortune. Let's demonstrate to those around us a true spiritual focus, making decisions and taking actions based not on how we will profit but on how we can serve the living God.

JESUS' WORDS CAUSE SOME DISCIPLES TO LEAVE

After this many of his disciples turned back and no longer walked with him. (Jn. 6:66)

WHAT JESUS DID:

Jesus had been preaching in the synagogue of Capernaum *(v. 59)*. He had spoken of Himself metaphorically as the bread of life which had come down out of heaven, and those who ate of His flesh and drank of His blood would have eternal life *(vv. 25-58)*. This caused intense consternation among the Jews and among His disciples as well. As a result, many of Jesus' followers left Him, seemingly unable to reconcile Jesus' words with their beliefs about consuming human flesh or any kind of blood. In reaction, Jesus confronted His twelve apostles and asked them squarely if they wanted to leave as well, knowing fully that He had chosen them, even His eventual betrayer *(vv. 70-71)*. Peter, apparently answering for the group, indicated that they still believed in Him as the *"holy one"* sent by God and in His life-giving words, and that they would not be leaving *(vv. 68-69)*.

Several lessons may be gleaned from this incident, all presented here from a negative point of view of what we shouldn't do:

▷ Jesus did not become distraught at the setbacks He experienced, and neither should we. When things don't go as we plan or hope, let's acknowledge our trust in the Father and move on.

▷ Jesus didn't deny reality, and neither should we. He saw what was happening, addressed it, and continued His ministry.

▷ Jesus didn't shy away from asking His disciples directly whether they were going to stay or leave, and neither should we. Following Christ requires commitment, and if some are faltering in their walk with the Lord, we should ask them straight out if they are going to keep on the Way or go a different path.

▷ Jesus didn't beg the disciples not to leave, and neither should we. When those we have mentored in Christ decide that they no longer want to follow Christ, we must let them go, praying that the Father's grace would someday bring them back into the faith.

▷ Jesus didn't change His message because some complained and grumbled about it, and neither should we. Let's stay on course as directed by the Spirit of God, true to His word and faithful to His commandments.

JESUS OBEYS GOD'S COMMANDS NOT HUMAN TRADITIONS

And the Pharisees and the scribes asked Jesus, "Why do your disciples not walk according to the tradition of the elders, but eat with defiled hands?" (Mk. 7:5)

WHAT JESUS DID:

Once again, the religionists aimed an attack at Jesus indirectly by chastising the actions of His disciples. Previously, they had condemned the disciples' picking grain on the Sabbath *(Mk. 2:23-28)*; this time, the Pharisees and scribes went after their habit of eating without first ceremonially washing their hands. This was neither advocating hygiene centuries before germ theory developed nor was it following Mosaic Law, as there were no commandments in the *Torah* regarding the washing of hands before eating, except for the priests *(Lev. 22:6-7)*. These traditional practices had been conceived by men, had grown over time, had developed into humanly-imposed rituals to maintain ceremonial purity, and had now even supplanted the Holy Scripture.

Jesus responded with a pointed remark aimed directly at these religious leaders by quoting *Isa. 29:13* in which God denounced teaching human commandments as doctrine. Jesus went on to decry these religionists' tendency to ignore the commandment to care for one's parents by claiming self-righteously that all that they owned was dedicated to God (*"corban"*) and so could not be used to support their parents. This was blatant hypocrisy and disobedience – saying that they honored God but callously and selfishly refusing to help loved-ones in need. *(Mk. 7:6-13)*

Jesus then explained to His disciples that food did not make a person unclean; rather, sin began inwardly, in the heart, as evil thoughts and desires and manifested outwardly in immoral acts and unrighteous behavior, and that was what defiled people and made them impure before God, not washing hands or eating food *(vv. 14-23)*. The author of Mark's gospel, writing in hindsight years after this incident, added parenthetically here that Jesus thus declared all food to be clean *(v. 19b)*. I believe that, while Jesus most likely kept kosher during His life, it was later Christians who came to the understanding that dietary restrictions had been removed.

WHAT HIS FOLLOWERS ARE TO DO:

Let's make sure that we are guided by the Word of God and not by human traditions. We need to continually ask ourselves and our brothers and sisters in Christ some important questions:

▷ In our ministry and in our normal, day-to-day life, are we being obedient to His commandments or are we blindly following the practices of those around us?

▷ Do the words we speak and the expressions of our faith match our attitudes and behavior, or are we hypocritically saying one thing and doing another?

▷ Are we yielded to the move of the Holy Spirit, or do we succumb to the pressure of the ways of the world?

▷ Is our aim in how we live to please our Heavenly Father, or do we give more thought and energy to how other people think of us?

- ▷ Do our values conform to God's will, or are we molded into the image of our society?
- ▷ Do we give priority to the teaching of Jesus as to how we are to live, or are we more swayed by the many voices of the powerful, elite, rich, successful, authoritative, and famous among us?
- ▷ Are we committed to leading "clean" lives of integrity, morality, justice, decency, and goodness in accordance with the LORD's desires, or are we easily tainted by deceit, immorality, slander, corruption, greed, selfishness and pride, all of which are so prevalent today but which separate us from our relationship with Him?
- ▷ Is our inner being of greater importance than our outward appearance?

For Jesus, obedience to God's Word was paramount, and it is to be such with us as well.

JESUS IS IMPLORED BY A GENTILE WOMAN

... a [Gentile] woman whose little daughter had an unclean spirit heard of [Jesus] and came and fell down at his feet. (Mk. 7:25)

WHAT JESUS DID:

Jesus was traveling in the area of Tyre and Sidon, north of Galilee on the east coast of the Mediterranean Sea, when He encountered this Gentile woman. She is described in *Matthew 15* as a Canaanite, and here in *Mark* as of Syrian/Phoenician origin. In other words, she was not Jewish.

Despite her heritage, she had presumably heard of Jesus' authority over demonic power and in desperation begged Him to cast the evil spirit out of her daughter. Jesus' initial response to her was harsh and callous: the children (i.e., the Jews) needed to be fed (i.e., ministered to) first and that it wouldn't be right to throw their bread (i.e., Jesus' preaching and healing) to the dogs (i.e., the Gentiles). Perhaps this was Jesus' way of testing the genuineness of her faith in Him and gauging the depth of her desire to have her daughter restored, for maybe someone without sincere belief in Jesus or without a truly intense longing to see her child healed over and above her own ego might be put off by such a statement and respond with condemnation of Jesus and storm away in prideful anger. But the woman's humble reply – that even dogs eat crumbs from their masters' tables – showed both trust in Him and the true love of a mother for her child. *(vv. 26-28)*

As a result of her words, Jesus praised her faith, removed the demon, and restored the girl *(v. 29)*. Jesus' ministry was not limited to just one group of people; He came for all people of faith regardless of their national or ethnic background.

WHAT HIS FOLLOWERS ARE TO DO:

We Christians might be tempted to restrict our engagement in ministry to those who share our religious beliefs or our racial and national heritage. But let us, like Jesus, be prepared to broaden our outreach and touch the lives of people of other faiths or of other races or from other countries. We have Jesus' message of God's love and forgiveness to share, and we ought to seek to spread that to all with whom we come in contact and who have a desire to receive it.

Jesus understood the great predicament that this woman faced, and ascertaining that she was willing to trust in His power to heal despite her upbringing, He met her need. We should also do the same, helping those in need in whatever way we can with practical, specific acts of lovingkindness without regard for their citizenship or ethnic identity. God will use us freely to have an impact on people's life-situations as we bring down the walls that separate us from others and instead construct channels for His gracious love and power to heal.

JESUS OPENS THE EARS OF A DEAF MAN

And they brought to [Jesus] a man who was deaf and had a speech impediment, and they begged him to lay his hand on him. (Mk. 7:32)

WHAT JESUS DID:

In healing this man with two related conditions – unable to hear and thus unable to speak clearly – Jesus took several separate actions. First, Jesus led the man away from all the others so that He could deal with Him personally in private, one-on-one. Next, Jesus put His fingers in the man's ears, addressing His deafness. Then, Jesus spit and touched the man's tongue (presumably with His own saliva), focusing on the man's speech problem. After that, Jesus lifted His eyes toward heaven (suggesting prayer), and He also gave out a sigh – perhaps expressing externally His internal emotions of compassion, sadness, and distress for the suffering of the world. And finally, He spoke, commanding in His native language of Aramaic ("*Ephphatha*") for the man's ears to be opened. The result was that the man's hearing and ability to speak clearly were immediately restored. *(vv. 33-35)*

WHAT HIS FOLLOWERS ARE TO DO:

As we attempt to minister to people in need, we might want to keep in mind some of the steps that Jesus took when healing this deaf man.

  ▷ Often, it is a good idea to speak with people privately when discussing troubles which they are facing. This will permit greater freedom for them to share their challenges honestly and for us to offer frank advice or practical help.

  ▷ Also, we ought to always focus on obvious concerns that need attention. We can sometimes get distracted by side issues or by less prominent matters instead of concentrating on the main difficulty or circumstance.

  ▷ Let's use whatever is available to address the need. Instead of bemoaning the lack of adequate resources, we should utilize what God has given us to solve problems. At times, this will demand creativity on our part, but let's not fail to take active steps toward resolution.

  ▷ Any action we take must be accompanied by fervent, faithful prayer. Without our Heavenly Father's participation and power, our efforts will come to naught. Assured of God's commanding presence, we can confidently take appropriate measures to help bring about restoration.

  ▷ Compassion for suffering ought to move us. Let's not become hard-hearted or callous but remain empathetic towards the plight of others.

  ▷ We should speak words that those in need will understand. Forego the theological jargon and minutiae of religious debate, and communicate the simple, clear truths of God and His work in our lives.

Jesus led the way for us; let's walk in His footsteps.

JESUS' MINISTRY GIVES GLORY TO GOD

*And great crowds came to [Jesus], bringing with them the lame,
the blind, the crippled, the mute, and many others, and they
put them at his feet, and he healed them. (Mt. 15:30)*

WHAT JESUS DID:

Jesus had been in the area of Tyre toward the coast of the Mediterranean Sea where He had healed the Gentile woman *(Mk. 7:24)* but had returned to the northeastern side of Sea of Galilee in the region of Decapolis, where He had opened the ears of the deaf man *(Mk. 7:32-35)*. Jesus continued His ministry of healing there to large crowds, and the people were amazed at the miracles He was performing. Their reaction was to give praise to God *(Mt. 15:31)*.

WHAT HIS FOLLOWERS ARE TO DO:

It is noteworthy that Jesus did not object when the people thanked God for the miraculous healings they witnessed; they praised the LORD God for His power working through Jesus, and Jesus tacitly approved. A simple lesson for us who follow Jesus is that everything we do should be for the glory of God. Let's never seek our own adulation as we engage in ministering to the needs of others. Rather, as we allow the Heavenly Father to use us to provide His blessings to those around us, we must be quick to direct all thanks and praise to the One whom we serve.

JESUS FEEDS MORE THAN FOUR THOUSAND

*Then Jesus called his disciples to him and said, "I have compassion on the crowd
because they have been with me now three days and have nothing to eat. And I
am unwilling to send them away hungry, lest they faint on the way." (Mt. 15:32)*

WHAT JESUS DID:

Large crowds continued to follow Jesus, and once again, the Lord's compassion moved Him to provide for other people's needs, being averse to ignoring their condition. In both the previous account of Jesus' feeding more than five-thousand and the current account with more than four thousand hungry persons, His heart went out to those who had come to Him. Jesus was motivated to act by His feelings of sympathy and pity for their physical condition and His concern for what might happen to them in their weakened state as they went back home. As before, He took stock of what was available, in this case seven loaves and a few small fish, blessed and broke them, and then enlisted the help of His disciples in distributing the multiplied foodstuffs to the masses. And as in the prior miracle, they collected the leftovers, this time seven large basketsful. *(vv. 34-38)*

It is also interesting that Jesus did not mention His own hunger, which He must have been feeling after three days of ministering to the crowds. But we are reminded that for Jesus, His sustenance came from doing the will of the One who had sent Him and accomplishing His work *(Jn. 4:32)*.

WHAT HIS FOLLOWERS ARE TO DO:

We must first be aware of the needs of others, whether physical, material, financial, emotional, or spiritual. That means turning our gaze away from ourselves and from our own desires and opening our eyes to those around us and to their circumstances. Then, noticing areas of want, we have a choice: ignore or act. But if we do not become callous or indifferent to the difficulties of others and instead allow feelings of empathy and compassion to move us, we will take action, asking for God's blessing on our endeavors. Following Jesus' lead, as we see situations in which God can use us to provide support or resolution, let's be willing to offer whatever we can, however meager that may seem, to help out. What can I give? What do I have that can be useful? What can I do? How can I be of assistance? We can trust that our Heavenly Father will take what we yield to Him and multiply it to touch the lives of many.

Also, as we are led by God to perform deeds of lovingkindness, let's recruit other disciples of Christ to join us so that we may all participate in fulfilling His mission. We are not meant to do the Lord's work alone, but together as a body, and by uniting, we will have a greater impact.

And finally, as Jesus did, let's derive our strength, energy, and commitment to engage in ministering to others by the power that comes from knowing that we are in the will of God and doing His work. Through prayer and meditating on God's word, we can be attuned to His guidance, and by obeying His directives, we can be confident of His dynamic Spirit working in and through us. That assurance can sustain us, even in times of hardship and hunger.

JESUS REFUSES TO PERFORM A SIGN

*And the Pharisees and Sadducees came, and to test him they
asked him to show them a sign from heaven. (Mt. 16:1)*

WHAT JESUS DID:

Jesus had healed crowds of sick and disabled. He had performed miraculous
feedings of thousands of people on two separate occasions. Yet, hard-hearted
religious leaders refused to acknowledge Jesus' power or accept His authority
and kept asking for *"a sign from heaven."* Perhaps they wanted something
truly spectacular – like the clouds parting, lightning and thunder, and angels
appearing – as a proof of His identity. But Jesus refused to give them the
sign they were asking for and denounced them soundly: They could read
physical weather patterns but had no real spiritual sight and had missed the
clear presence of God working throughout His life. He characterized them
as morally wicked and unfaithful to God, and promised them just one sign,
that of Jonah, which was a reference to His future resurrection from the dead.
(vv. 2-4)

WHAT HIS FOLLOWERS ARE TO DO:

People may test us, too, just as the religious leaders did Jesus, asking to see
some kind of miraculous evidence of our claim to be children of God and
filled with His Spirit. They might say, "Let's see you heal someone" or "Let's
see you multiply food" or "Let's see you calm a storm." But our primary sign of
the truth of the gospel is demonstrated in the changed life we are leading and
in our Christlike attitudes and actions. In Christ, the old has died and we are
born again to new life, and the physical proof of that spiritual reality is shown
by what we do and say, how we act and react. As Jesus said: *"A tree is known
by its fruit"* *(Mt. 12:33b)*. The truth of God's power will be manifest in our
lives by the fruit of His Spirit: namely, *"love, joy, peace, patience, kindness,
goodness, faithfulness, gentleness, self-control (Gal. 5:22-23a)*. And as we are
yield ourselves to the Lord and are led by Him, He will use us to bring healing
and restoration to those who are suffering, to provide sustenance to those who
are needy, and to promote reconciliation to those at war. That is to be the sign
that we can offer the world.

JESUS WARNS OF FALSE TEACHING

Jesus said to [the disciples], "Watch and beware of the leaven of the Pharisees and Sadducees." (Mt. 16:6)

WHAT JESUS DID:

In response to the Pharisees' and Sadducees' spiritual callousness, Jesus' warned his disciples about them using the analogy of leaven, or yeast, a small bit of which can affect an entire loaf of bread. Jesus was rightfully concerned for the spiritual wellbeing of His disciples. The slow-to-understand disciples initially thought Jesus was talking about physical bread, but Jesus chided their lack of discernment and finally led them to comprehend that He was alerting them to the errant teachings of these misguided religionists *(vv. 7-12)*.

WHAT HIS FOLLOWERS ARE TO DO:

It is our responsibility as followers of Christ to similarly warn others who are being misled by ideas that are not in sync with the character of God or the clear ministry and message of Jesus. When we become aware of behavior or teaching, especially by religious figures, that does not accurately reflect the true nature of our Heavenly Father or His Christ, we must not keep silent but must caution those who could be swayed by such false teaching. This means that we ourselves must have a close relationship with God and be well-versed in the Scripture to be able to distinguish the real voice of the Lord from that of false teachers and preachers.

By using the metaphor of yeast and bread, Jesus warned of the powerful effect that even a small amount of bogus spiritual instruction can have on an individual's belief in God and knowledge of His true character. Thus, we must be equally diligent to care for the spiritual health of Christ's followers and call out false teaching whenever it is spread.

JESUS HEALS A BLIND
MAN AT BETHSAIDA

And [Jesus and the disciples] came to Bethsaida. And some people brought
to [Jesus] a blind man and begged him to touch him. (Mk. 8:22)

WHAT JESUS DID:

Jesus and His group of followers arrived at the town of Bethsaida on the
northeastern shore of the Sea of Galilee and again performed the miraculous.
Just as He had done with the deaf man, Jesus once more took the man aside
and used His saliva as a means of healing, though this time applying it to
a blind man's eyes. However, unlike the previous healing, which occurred
immediately, the blind man's sight was not completely restored (he said people
looked like trees) until Jesus laid hands on him a second time *(vv. 23-25)*. Thus,
Jesus' persistence prevailed.

WHAT HIS FOLLOWERS ARE TO DO:

Just as Jesus did not give up when His first attempt to heal did not accomplish
the desired effect, we who follow Him should also learn to persevere if we don't
succeed right away. It can certainly be frustrating to make endeavors to care
for someone only to see limited results; however, trusting in God, let's not be
discouraged but rather keep at it.

And we ought not settle for less-than-satisfactory outcomes. Jesus' initial try
at healing the blind man was incomplete, but He wanted a complete restoration
of sight, so He continued until the man could see clearly. If we have been led by
the Holy Spirit of God to undertake a task, let us devote our energies to it and
stick with it until the goal is reached. The Lord never gave up, nor should we.

JESUS AT THE FEAST OF BOOTHS

Now the Jews' Feast of Booths was at hand … (Jn. 7:2)

WHAT JESUS DID:

Jesus had been ministering in Galilee, avoiding Judea because some religionists
in that region wanted to kill Him *(v. 1)*, but a sacred feast day was approaching

which would require that He go there. The Jewish Feast of *Sukkot*, the Feast of Booths or Tabernacles, commemorated the forty years the Jews spent in the wilderness, living in temporary shelters before they entered the promised land. Along with *Pesach* (Passover) and *Shavuot* (Pentecost), *Sukkot* was a festival when observant Israelites would make a pilgrimage to the Temple in Jerusalem. Jesus' own brothers – James, Joseph, Simon and Judas *(Mt. 13:55)*, though members of His immediate family – didn't believe in Him, yet they urged Him to go to Jerusalem so that He could openly and publicly show Himself and His miraculous works *(Jn. 7:3-5)*.

However, Jesus was always aware of and committed to God's perfect timing, and He knew that His moment for such a public display had had not yet come *(v. 6)*. Because of Jesus' radical teaching describing Himself as *"the bread of life"* and claiming that He had *"come down from heaven"* *(Jn. 6:35, 38)*, the religious leaders sought His death, but Jesus still had much to do in His ministry. So, He sent His brothers and most likely His disciples as well to Jerusalem without Him, maybe fearing that His entourage would attract hostile attention. Jesus finally made the journey, though privately without telling anyone, waiting until the middle of the weeklong festival to appear in the Temple and speak publicly. *(Jn. 7:8-14)*

In this incident, Jesus exercised courage tempered by prudence. He knew God's timetable for His life, so He did not recklessly act in such a way that would certainly have provoked an untimely and aggressively negative reaction on the part of the Jewish religious leaders. In the end, by teaching openly in the Temple, not changing or diluting His message despite His awareness of the enmity of the religious leaders, He proved to be fearlessly committed to His mission, though not rash in its fulfillment.

WHAT HIS FOLLOWERS ARE TO DO:

We who call Jesus Lord often need to learn to balance enthusiasm for our ministry with judicious behavior. Let's not dash headlong into something simply because it is part of our mission, justifying our actions as trusting in God's providence to protect and deliver us. We must be circumspect, even (and especially) when it comes to the "things of the Lord." We should not always be hurried to leap into the lions' den without seeking the Lord's will first. Our timing and God's timing are not necessarily the same, and certainly there will be occasions when God tells us to wait. Then, when the light goes green, we should be willing to bravely step out in faith and to confidently walk the path that God has laid out for us, proclaiming the word of the Lord in the fulness of its power.

Jesus was sensitive to God's timing, so He was not imprudent. He was sensible, even in His mission, but ultimately, He acted with a fearless trust in His Heavenly Father. We Christians ought to do the same.

JESUS CAUSES DIVIDED OPINIONS

There was a division among the people over [Jesus]. (Jn. 7:43)

WHAT JESUS DID:

Jesus made radical statements about who He was and why He had come. He had performed great miracles to prove His identity and authority, and yet, opinion about Him was still divided. Some said He was a good person, while others condemned Him for misleading people *(v. 12)*. Some who heard His words cited the Scripture to support why they did or did not accept Him *(vv. 40-42)*. There was even dissent among the religious authorities: The chief priests and the Pharisees sent temple guards to arrest Jesus, but these Levitical officers did not do so when they heard His words *(vv. 45-46)*. And even a leading Pharisee, Nicodemus, whom Jesus had met with in the past at night, criticized the other religious leaders for their unlawful attempt to seize Jesus but was denounced and arrogantly and incorrectly (for Jonah was also from the area of Galilee) told to search the Scripture to see that no prophet ever came from Galilee *(vv. 50-52)*.

Jesus had explained that this division would happen, saying that He had not brought peace but a sword *(Mt. 10:34)*. His words and actions were (and still are) constantly the source of disagreement, disputes, rifts, and major schisms among people, including family members, friends and religious leaders. And yet, some people did come to believe in Him *(Jn. 8:30)*.

WHAT HIS FOLLOWERS ARE TO DO:

We Christians must be aware that the message we convey about Jesus, our beliefs about Him, and our desire to lead lives in accordance with His principles will not always be well-received by everyone, even by our loved ones. Those with strong religious ideas may be especially vocal in their opposition, and the plethora of denominations and sects at large today is evidence of the many differences caused by the words and actions of Jesus. Of course, we ourselves need to be sure that our understanding of Christ's teachings are soundly based on the truth of Scripture.

We ought not to seek separation and dissent, but it may come. And if it does, let's continue to reach out in lovingkindness to the ones who disapprove of our faith and our lifestyle choices. Perhaps by doing so, as happened with Jesus, some will put their faith in Him and accept Him as Lord.

JESUS AND THE ADULTEROUS WOMAN

The scribes and the Pharisees brought a woman who had been caught in adultery ... (Jn. 8:3)

WHAT JESUS DID:

Jesus had spent the night on the Mount of Olives; early the next morning He had returned to the Temple and had begun teaching the people when some Pharisees brought this woman to Him *(vv. 1-2)*. This was a kind of religious test, a trap really, as they hoped to ensnare Jesus, who preached forgiveness, and denounce Him for countering Mosaic Law. However, though the woman had been *"caught"* in a sin for which the *Torah* commanded death by stoning, Jesus was not quick to condemn her. Rather, His censure would be directed at those who sought to kill her, and He bent down and began to write in the dirt with His finger. *(vv. 4-6)*

Many theories have been proffered regarding what Jesus wrote in the ground that day – from a verse in Scripture, to the sins of the accusers, to just doodling while He gathered His thoughts. Speculation aside, we can see much in what Jesus did NOT do: He didn't demand a rigorous application of the law when He deemed that mercy and forgiveness were merited.

The story (which does not appear in the oldest manuscripts of John's gospel) ends with Jesus' well-known words that the one without sin should throw the first stone, and when the humiliated accusers departed, Jesus pronounced the woman freed from judgment and redirected her life by exhorting her to change her sinful ways *(vv. 7-11)*. Jesus didn't tell her that she had not done anything wrong, as she had openly transgressed the command of God; rather, He refused to condemn her and urged her to lead a different life.

WHAT HIS FOLLOWERS ARE TO DO:

We who strive to follow Jesus ought also not be so ready to pronounce judgment on those who disobey the commandments of God. That is not to say that we should not strongly oppose evil and wrongdoing. But let us, like Jesus, see the power of compassion and clemency over a blind and heartless application of the letter of the law.

Just like the woman's accusers, we are all sinful individuals and do not have the right or authority to execute sentence on one whom we judge to be guilty of sin. We can certainly make others aware of the iniquity or immorality in their lives which separates them from their holy Father in heaven, but in doing so, we should also extend our hands to them in lovingkindness, offering the forgiveness that Jesus gives and the hope of restoration of their relationship with God.

It is always good to remember that when we point a finger at someone, there are three fingers pointing back at ourselves. Jesus was not compelled to enforce the law when mercy proved more judicious. Let's seek to have the same mind as our Lord and allow it to direct our every attitude and behavior.

JESUS HEALS A MAN BORN BLIND

As [Jesus] passed by, he saw a man blind from birth. (Jn. 9:1)

This man, born blind, had never seen anything in his whole life. As such, he was unable to see Jesus; however, Jesus was able to see him and responded to the man's condition by giving him sight. Using His saliva once again, this time mixed with dirt, He applied the mud to the man's eyes. As part of the miraculous process, all meant to display the work of God *(v.3b)*, Jesus sent the man to wash in the pool of Siloam, and the man did as he was instructed and received the ability to see. *(vv. 6-7)*

(Note: The writer of John indicates that Siloam means "sent" (v. 7), perhaps a play on words in that the man was sent by Jesus to this pool. Also, the water from this large pool was ritually poured out on the altar in the Temple during the Feast of Booths.)

The story continues that the formerly-blind man was taken by people who knew him to the Pharisees to show them the miracle that had been performed, but their response was to revile Jesus as a sinner for healing the man on the Sabbath and to throw the man out of the synagogue, suggesting perhaps a kind of excommunication from the congregation. When Jesus heard about this, He went and found the man and revealed Himself to him as the Son of Man, and the man believed. Thus, he was healed physically and spiritually as well. *(vv. 13-41)*

WHAT HIS FOLLOWERS ARE TO DO:

We who follow Jesus must keep our eyes open so we can be sensitive and receptive to all those in need that the Lord brings across our life paths, and then respond in lovingkindness. We ought to react to both physical and spiritual need by providing practical help to meet material demands and by sharing the good news of the gospel – all in the name of Christ for the glory of our Heavenly Father.

And we should not be dissuaded from extending ourselves to seemingly lost causes, people who for their entire lives have been indifferent or even hostile to the things of God. There are no hopeless cases. It must be remembered that we are all afflicted with spiritual blindness, unable to see or know the works of the one true God. But He sees us and is continually reaching out to us, offering spiritual sight so that He may reveal Himself to us and that we may see Him clearly and know Him personally. Let's join the LORD in this good work, even with the hardest of individuals.

Also, just as Jesus was sent from the Father, and the blind man was sent by Jesus to wash the mud from his eyes, we should realize that God has sent us to minister to others. And as people respond positively and become spiritually healed, let's send them out to share what God has done for them in their lives.

Finally, sometimes when people give their lives to Jesus, there is a negative reaction from those around them – such as family, friends, colleagues, neighbors, employers, colleagues, classmates, and religious leaders – and these new believers may be ridiculed, rejected, shunned, excluded, or ostracized. When we become aware of such a situation, let's be quick to reach out to the ones suffering this kind of emotional and psychological pain and isolation, to embrace them with the love of God, to share His promises of salvation, and to do whatever we can to restore their sense of wellbeing.

JESUS' COURAGE IN PROCLAIMING TRUTH

[Jesus said,] "I and the Father are one." The Jews picked up stones again to stone him. (Jn. 10:30-31)

WHAT JESUS DID:

Jesus' life had been threatened several times. As a babe, recognized by the Magi as the coming King, Herod had ordered His slaughter *(Mt. 2:16)*. At His hometown, when He had preached the fulfillment of prophecy in His person, the enraged Nazarenes wanted to throw Him off a cliff *(Lk. 4:29)*. Having described Himself as the Bread of Life whose flesh and blood would give eternal life, infuriated Jewish religionists sought to kill Him *(Jn. 7:1)*. Speaking in the Temple at the Festival of Booths, many believed in Jesus, but the chief priests and Pharisees reacted by sending guards to arrest Him *(Jn. 7:32)*. He had said that He existed before Abraham, using the divine term *"I am"*, and they wanted to stone Him to death for blasphemy *(Jn. 8:58-59a)*. However, despite all of these threats, Jesus never backed down from His message. And here, back in Jerusalem for the Feast of Dedication or *Hannukah (v. 22)*, people once again wanted to kill Him, this time for claiming oneness with God. Jesus must have known that His words would provoke an intense and even violent reaction, yet He did not hesitate to proclaim truth.

We might ask, how did he escape every time? A simple, direct answer is: *No one laid a hand on Him, because His hour had not yet come. (Jn. 7:30).* Jesus had trusted His Heavenly Faith; He knew that His life at every moment was in the Father's hands. Filled with this conviction, though aware of the danger, He bravely spoke the words that people needed to hear.

WHAT HIS FOLLOWERS ARE TO DO:

We should follow the example of Jesus in not being afraid to share His good news of God's love and forgiveness in Christ. Certainly, not everyone will accept it. There may also be strong, negative reactions to the message we bring, and that can definitely be intimidating and lead to silence. But we can confidently rely on the Lord's power to give us the courage to speak. We might not know what to say or how to say it, but Jesus promised that, even when we are brought before hostile opponents of the gospel, the Holy Spirit would give us the right words *(Lk. 12:12)* So, let's be trusting, even as Jesus was, in God's providential plan, and boldly declare the gospel to our world.

JESUS ASKS THE DISCIPLES
ABOUT HIS IDENTITY

[Jesus] said to [his disciples], "But who do you say that I am?" (Mt. 16:15)

WHAT JESUS DID:

Jesus and His followers were in the area of Caesarea Philippi, some 25 miles north of the Sea of Galilee, when Jesus asked his disciples what other people thought about who He was. Their answers ranged from John the Baptist reborn to one of the Jewish prophets come back to life. But that question was just a precursor to His more pointed query of what the disciples themselves thought about Him. And when Peter responded that Jesus was the Messianic Son of God, Jesus pronounced him blessed, having received favor from the Heavenly Father in this divine revelation of Jesus' identity. *(vv. 13-17)*

However, in a somewhat mystifying end to this incident, Jesus commanded that they not disclose His true identity to anyone *(v. 20)*. Theories seeking to explain this "Messianic secret" are varied, but I believe it was just not yet Jesus' time to declare Himself openly as He still had much preparatory work to do in spreading His message, teaching His disciples, and performing miraculous healings, all of which would substantiate His eventual claim to messiahship.

WHAT HIS FOLLOWERS ARE TO DO:

That same question that Jesus posed, **"Who do you say that I am?"**, should be a primary question that we followers of Jesus ask others as they consider their relationship with Him. Is He just someone who lived long ago, or does He have a real, guiding presence today? Is He a great sage, or is He Lord of our lives? Are our ideas about Him based solely on reasoning and logic, or have we had a revelatory faith encounter through the Holy Spirit of God illuminating Christ's true nature in our hearts? Jesus' question still needs to be considered and answered by everyone of us.

JESUS BEGINS TO REVEAL HIS DEATH AND RESURRECTION

From that time Jesus began to show his disciples that he must go to Jerusalem and suffer many things from the elders and chief priests and scribes, and be killed, and on the third day be raised. (Mt. 16:21)

WHAT JESUS DID:

Jesus openly told His disciples what would happen to Him in the near future in Jerusalem, namely, suffering and death at the hands of the religious leaders, but also resurrection. Peter, the very one who had recently confessed his belief that Jesus was the Messiah, seemed not to have heard the part about resurrection and reacted to Jesus' prediction of suffering and death with an emphatic denial that they would ever happen to Him. Jesus, in turn, rebuked Peter and identified his flawed thinking as something diabolical and an impediment to fulfilling His mission. *(vv. 22-23)*

WHAT HIS FOLLOWERS ARE TO DO:

When God reveals to us our mission here on earth, we should not be dissuaded from it by the opinions of others. Those around us, even family and friends, might encourage us to seek a different path from the one that our Heavenly Father has set before us, especially if our direction involves hardship or moves in unexpected ways. That is not to say that we should never hear the wise counsel of others as we make important decisions about our life in Christ or our specific areas of ministry; indeed, we should actively seek out the advice of godly people whom we know and trust *(Prov. 15:22)*. Yet, as Jesus did, once we have set our minds on the Lord and have heard His clear voice telling us His will, let's not be swayed from it by the faulty ideas of others.

We can also thankfully remember that, though serving Christ will in all likelihood bring with it difficulties, adversity, privation, estrangement, and at times even torment, there is always the promise of resurrection. In the end, despite circumstances, God gives life.

JESUS' TRANSFIGURATION

And after six days Jesus took with him Peter and James, and John his brother, and led them up a high mountain by themselves. And he was transfigured before them, and his face shone like the sun, and his clothes became white as light. (Mt. 17:1-2)

WHAT JESUS DID:

Jesus selected His three closest disciples – Peter and the brothers James and John – to witness this event. He wanted them to see with their own eyes His true nature as one filled with the radiant light of God's glorious presence and to hear with their own ears the Heavenly Father's laudatory appraisal of Him. The account continues, describing the appearance with Jesus of Moses and Elijah, confirming His fulfillment of the law and the prophets, and a heavenly voice affirming Jesus as His *"beloved son"* with Whom He was well-pleased and commanding that the disciples *"listen to Him."* The three apostles were understandably struck with fear, but Jesus comforted them with His touch and reassured them not to be afraid *(vv. 3-7).*

We who follow Christ should allow those with whom we are in close relationship to see how we really are. Unlike Jesus, this will not always be something bright and shining, but it is better to reveal our true selves to those we trust rather than wear a false-faced mask to impress others or to cover up our deceptive hypocrisies. While it can be anxiety-inducing at times to give others access to our inner beings, we need to let the Spirit of Christ assuage our fears and to take great comfort in the declaration by our Father in Heaven that we are His children.

It is also of great importance that others are able to see true change in our lives. While we can talk about how Christ has transformed us, our attitudes and actions speak much more loudly toward reality. So, as we yield to the Lord daily and continue to grow spiritually in His presence, we will become more like Him, and perhaps the light that illuminated Christ on the mountain of transfiguration will start to shine out in our lives as beams of lovingkindness, goodness, and grace.

JESUS HEALS A BOY WITH AN UNCLEAN SPIRIT

And they brought [a boy with an unclean spirit] to [Jesus]. And when the spirit saw him, immediately it convulsed the boy, and he fell on the ground and rolled about, foaming at the mouth. (Mk. 9:20)

WHAT JESUS DID:

A father had brought his afflicted son to Jesus, begging him for healing. Jesus responded to the heartfelt cries for help made by the father for his son who had been under the control of demonic power since his childhood. This spirit made the boy suffer epileptic-type seizures and rendered him deaf and mute. (*vv. 17-21*). So, it was not the boy himself who sought Jesus' healing but the loving and justifiably distraught father.

The father confessed that he was not a person of great faith as he pleaded with Jesus to help him despite his nagging unbelief. But Jesus, filled with compassion and perhaps even impressed by the man's brutal honesty, answered his plea for healing and cast the spirit out of the boy, commanding it never to return. Fittingly, Jesus then took the restored boy's hand to help him off the ground where the spirit had thrown him. *(vv. 22-27).* And as told in Luke's gospel *(9:42),* Jesus returned him to his father

At times, people in tremendous need do not themselves seek the help they require. This may be due to pride and a desire for self-sufficiency or fear of being exposed as needy, or perhaps confusion about whom to contact or even a disability that impedes a request for assistance. In any of those cases, they must rely on the good will of others who see their plight and compassionately aid them in finding care.

Like the father in this story, we who are followers of Jesus can take on an active role of bringing the troubles of others before the Lord to ask for his gracious succor. And like Jesus, when people request our help in dealing with a problem, regardless of the strength of their faith in Christ (or lack thereof), let's be open and willing to do whatever we can to take practical measures toward utilizing our own resources and those of other individuals and organizations to accomplish healing and restoration in the lives of persons suffering hardship. Jesus responded to need; let's follow suit.

JESUS REMINDS THE DISCIPLES OF HIS FORTHCOMING DEATH

But while they were all marveling at everything he was doing, Jesus said to his disciples, "Let these words sink into your ears: The Son of Man is about to be delivered into the hands of men." (Lk. 9:43b-44)

WHAT JESUS DID:

Jesus had miraculously fed crowds of people. He had been transfigured before the eyes of three of His apostles. He had performed amazing healings of many sick, disabled, and demon-possessed. People could readily see the magnificent divine power at work in Him *(v. 43a),* and without doubt, they were filled with excitement and perhaps anticipation for greater things to come. However, Jesus wanted His disciples to grasp the reality that was before them, so He emphatically repeated what He had already told them about what lay ahead: His arrest and death at the hands of evil men, but also His resurrection *(Mt. 17:23; Mk. 9:31).*

As followers of Jesus, we need to be aware that there will be times of great joy and spiritual success as well as times of intense trial and discouraging defeat. Even when we are experiencing tremendous spiritual growth and can see the power of the LORD at work in the lives of many around us, we ought to remind each other that things will not always go as we would hope for and that we must be prepared when difficult days arrive. It is the responsibility of mature Christians to help those new to the faith to grasp this truth so they can be ready when hardships come and not fall away from their trust in our Heavenly Father. Let's also remember that Jesus' resurrection followed His death, and that ultimately, in this life or in the next, God will bring us out of dark times of trouble and distress and into the light of peace and comfort.

JESUS PAYS THE TEMPLE TAX

When they came to Capernaum, the collectors of the two-drachma tax went up to Peter and said, "Does your teacher not pay the tax?" (Mt. 17:24)

WHAT JESUS DID:

A tax collected by fellow Jews to help fund the maintenance of the Temple and its services was required of every male Israelite over the age of twenty. Interestingly, this incident is reported only by Matthew, who of course had himself been a tax collector, though his job was collecting taxes for the Romans.

When Peter came to the house where Jesus was staying, Jesus immediately engaged him in dialog: He didn't necessarily agree with the payment of these taxes; however, to not needlessly upset others or give them reason to reject His message, He humbly instructed Peter to pay the tax – a half shekel for each of them – miraculously provided for in the mouth of a fish. *(vv. 25-27)*

WHAT HIS FOLLOWERS ARE TO DO:

While we may grumble about taxation in general and even oppose some particular taxes, Jesus' example is clear and simple: We should pay up lest we unnecessarily put an obstacle in the way of people to receive the gospel. The greater issue is not payment of taxes but communicating the saving message of Christ without creating pointless resentment or prejudice.

Does this mean that we who seek to follow Jesus should never stand up against certain specific taxes or actively refuse payment of taxes that conflict with our Christian values and beliefs? Absolutely not! Jesus here acquiesced to paying a Temple tax, originally inaugurated in the wilderness for the support of the Tabernacle (Exod. 30:11-16), so it was in keeping with God's commandments. However, when taxes are imposed that directly go against what we as believers in Christ hold to be true, we should peaceably, rationally, and conscientiously oppose them in whatever way we can. By doing this, it will not be a stumbling block to others but instead will perhaps attract them to the conviction of our faith.

JESUS USES A CHILD TO EXPLAIN GREATNESS IN GOD'S KINGDOM

At that time the disciples came to Jesus, saying, "Who is the greatest in the kingdom of heaven?" (Mt. 18:1)

WHAT JESUS DID:

The disciples had been arguing about who was greatest among them *(Mk. 9:34; Lk. 9:46)*, so they posed a question to Jesus, framing it in Matthew's account about greatness in the Kingdom of God. Jesus understood what they were really asking: Which of us is the greatest? So, He put an innocent and unassuming child in front of them to make a point which was so contrary to their way of thinking: The greatest is the most humble *(Mt. 18:2-4)*. For Jesus, greatness was measured in terms of simple, unassuming service to others *(Mk. 9:35)*.

WHAT HIS FOLLOWERS ARE TO DO:

As Christians, we need to continually remind each other to develop and maintain an attitude of humility and unpretentiousness. The Lord does not care how we are viewed by the world – successful, powerful, authoritative, popular, famous ... in a word, great; rather, He is interested in our embracing His teaching and obeying His command to be a servant to others. That is being truly great in God's eyes.

Also, when people ask us questions pertaining to God, we should follow Jesus' example and make use of the physicals things around us to teach spiritual truth. He illustrated His teaching with plants and animals, the land and the weather, and a variety of characters in His parables. And here, Jesus used a little child to teach a lesson of immense importance. We can often help others to understand more clearly the things of our Father in Heaven by offering comparisons to our everyday, earthly life.

JESUS ENDORSES OTHERS MINISTERING IN HIS NAME

[The apostle John said,] "Master, we saw someone casting out demons in your name, and we tried to stop him, because he does not follow with us." (Lk. 9:49)

WHAT JESUS DID:

Nicknamed one of the "Sons of Thunder" along with his brother James, John seemed like someone who would want to impose His will on others. *(See the segment below on the Samaritan village that refused to receive Jesus.)* Here, he and other unnamed disciples had tried to stop someone not from their group who was performing exorcisms in Jesus' name. However, Jesus corrected John's wrong intent, saying that those who were not enemies were actually allies *(v. 50).* Thus, Jesus gave approval of the ones outside His immediate band of followers to do the work of God in His name and said they would even be rewarded for their ministry *(Mk. 9:41).*

WHAT HIS FOLLOWERS ARE TO DO:

We Christians should follow Jesus' lead and admonish other believers not to be quick to criticize or condemn those who differ from us and our specific beliefs but who are involved in ministering to people's needs in the name of Jesus. We can often become so convinced of our own self-righteousness and specialness, so certain of the correctness of our way of doing things that we feel empowered to exercise authority over people who are not part of our ministry, and to denounce or even try to stop their way of serving the Lord. We must not become inbred and enclosed in our tight circle of creedal uniformity and ministerial methods to the exclusion of anyone outside of our particular group. Instead, we should exhort one another to emulate the accepting and inclusive love of Jesus for all who serve in His name.

JESUS HEADS TOWARD JERUSALEM

When the days drew near for him to be taken up, he
set his face to go to Jerusalem. (Lk.9:51)

WHAT JESUS DID:

Jesus was absolutely committed to the completion of His mission. And so, while aware of His impending death but certain of His eventual ascension, He headed toward Jerusalem.

His determination to complete the task set before Him is described in various ways in the many translations of Scripture: *steadfastly; deliberately; determinedly; made up his mind; resolutely; settled himself fully; moved steadily onward; gathered up his courage and steeled himself; nothing would stop him; intently; strong with resolve; set fast his face; fixed his face on.* But perhaps the most poetic rendering of Jesus' resolve harkens back to the words of the prophet Isaiah describing one who endured tremendous suffering and yet set his face like a piece of hard flint toward obeying God, trusting in God's help and confident that he would ultimately be vindicated *(Isa. 50:6-7)* Jesus was determined to see His mission through to the very end.

WHAT HIS FOLLOWERS ARE TO DO:

First, we who call Jesus our Lord need to know our own particular mission. Our general task is to spread the gospel of God's love in Christ through our words and actions. But we have each been called to a specific spiritual work that can make best use of our individual gifts and resources. Taking stock of what we are good at or what our bents are or what we possess in relation to the needs around us can help us understand what God wants us to undertake. The Holy Spirit can also reveal this to us as we seek divine guidance.

Then once we know what we are to do, let's follow the lead of Jesus and set our faces resolutely to its accomplishment. Through God's grace and in His strength, our mission should be our priority and central focus; all else should be secondary. Let's apply some of those words mentioned earlier to our own lives and our pursuit of mission: steadfastly; deliberately; determinedly; resolutely; intently; with minds made up; moving steadily onward; fully settled on; with faces fixed fast; our courage gathered up and steeling ourselves for what lies ahead so that nothing can stop or sway us ... like Jesus, with faces set like flint toward the goal.

JESUS IS REJECTED IN A
SAMARITAN VILLAGE

And [Jesus] sent messengers ahead of him, who went and entered a
village of the Samaritans, to make preparations for him. (Lk. 9:52)

WHAT JESUS DID:

In this incident, we can see something that Jesus did and something that He
did not do.

First, Jesus sent some of His disciples into a Samaritan village ahead of
Him to act as messengers and to prepare the people in the village to receive
Him. The job of this advance-party would have certainly been to tell the
people that Jesus was coming to share His message of the Kingdom of God
with the villagers, and to preach, teach, and heal. These disciples would also
have arranged for things like food and lodging during their stay.

However, they were not well received. The long-standing, historical
enmity between Jews and Samaritans must have surely played a part in the
village's refusal to welcome Jesus, but it was also because He wasn't planning
to stay too long as He resolutely headed toward Jerusalem, and perhaps the
villagers felt slighted. In reaction to this rebuff by these Samaritans, two of
Jesus' apostles, James and John, whom Jesus had fittingly nicknamed *"Sons
of Thunder" (Mk. 3:17)*, asked for the Lord's approval to pray that God would
destroy the villagers with heavenly fire. Jesus' response was swift and decisive
as He turned to face and scold them, for their request was not at all in keeping
with His purpose: His mission was not seek-and-destroy but search-and-
rescue. Without lingering, they simply continued on toward another village,
hoping this time for a more welcoming reception. *(vv. 53-56)*

WHAT HIS FOLLOWERS ARE TO DO:

Jesus sent His disciples ahead of Him to prepare for His arrival, and we
Christians should also send out "messengers" to prepare the hearts of
spiritually lost souls. Our messengers can be gracious words of kindness and
active deeds of love that will help make people more receptive to the gospel
of Jesus. By reaching out to those in need with practical, thoughtful, and
compassionate actions, we can make people more ready to hear the message
of how Jesus can transform lives. May our comforting and encouraging speech
and our loving and caring behavior be sent out like an advance-party for the
coming of Christ.

We should also keep in mind that Jesus did not condone violence against those who did not receive Him. We need to rebuke anyone who wants to harm a religious opponent or who prays for God's vicious judgment on those who want nothing to do with the gospel. That conduct and that attitude have no place in the ministry of Christ. If the message we bring of God's love and forgiveness is refused, we must not respond in condemnation, but instead just move on.

What did Jesus do? He sent messengers ahead to prepare for His arrival. What didn't He do? He didn't approve hurting those who refused to hear His message. Let's follow our leader.

JESUS CHALLENGES THREE
WOULD-BE DISCIPLES

As they were going along the road, someone said to [Jesus],
"I will follow you wherever you go." (Lk. 9:57)

WHAT JESUS DID:

Three people are mentioned here who had accepted the call of Jesus to become His followers, but Jesus strongly challenged their level of commitment. The first person, identified as a scribe in Matthew's gospel *(Mt. 8:19)*, pledged to follow Jesus wherever He went, to which Jesus responded by reminding him of the sacrifice that He, the Son of Man, had made in fulfilling His mission: He had given up the happiness and security of family and homelife as He dedicated Himself to ministering to the needs of others. By extension, He seemed to imply that such as degree of sacrifice was necessary for His followers as well. The second person heard the call to discipleship but needed to first take care of family matters. For Jesus, however, spreading the good news of God's Kingdom was a greater priority and demanded an immediate response. The third person wanted one last time to go back to his old life, but for Jesus, His disciples were not to look back longingly at or return to the lives they led before. They were to be forward-looking, keeping their eyes on the mission of bringing about God's reign over their own lives and over the entire world. *(vv. 58-62)*

WHAT HIS FOLLOWERS ARE TO DO:

Though somewhat harsh in tone, Jesus' replies to these three would-be followers were meant, I believe, to emphasize the real demands of becoming a committed disciple of Christ. We preach a message of love, forgiveness, and salvation, Hallelujah! But to those who accept God's grace we must also make known the cost of serving the Lord and obeying His teaching. To walk with the Lord is a joy and brings great fulfillment, yet let's never sugarcoat the challenges and demands that He makes of us as we seek to follow Him. As Jesus did, we must clearly explain to those considering dedicating themselves to Christ that it will mean sacrificing worldly things, giving priority to the spiritual aspects of life, and breaking away from our past lives.

JESUS SENDS OUT THE SEVENTY-TWO

After this the Lord appointed seventy-two others and sent them on ahead of him, two by two, into every town and place where he himself was about to go. (Lk. 10:1)

WHAT JESUS DID:

Until this time, Jesus had delegated His twelve chosen apostles to represent Him and to assist in spreading His message to a broader audience. As His reputation and fame escalated, Jesus attracted more and more disciples to Himself, and seeking to multiply the extent of His ministry, He sent out seventy-two trusted individuals to act as a kind of advance team to prepare the places where He intended to eventually go and to help meet the growing demands of His work. As Jesus told them, using an agricultural metaphor, the crop was indeed abundant, but there were few workers to harvest it *(v. 2)*.

In commissioning these seventy-two, Jesus warned them to be careful of those who would seek to do them harm; He told them to travel light; He issued instructions on where to stay and what to expect as compensation for their ministerial work; and He specified their task as preaching the Kingdom of God and healing the sick. *(vv. 3-9)* Jesus also endowed them with special authority, saying that whoever heard their words actually heard Jesus speaking *(v. 16)*. When they later returned from their mission, they reported joyfully that even the demonic world was subject to them in Jesus' name *(v. 17)*.

WHAT HIS FOLLOWERS ARE TO DO:

The main point that we as Christ-followers may take from this event in Jesus' life is the realization that we can't accomplish the goals of our mission alone.

We love being the Lone Ranger in our ministry in the world, but even he had his loyal partner Tonto (not to mention his magnificent horse Silver).

Let's gather those around us who have demonstrated strength of character and faith and who are willing to collaborate with us in spreading the good news of God's grace in Christ Jesus and in reaching out in lovingkindness and compassion to touch a needy world. As we join forces with likeminded individuals who are devoted to serving God and humanity, we can through the power of the Lord's Holy Spirit broaden and increase the influence and impact of the gospel.

In His wisdom, Jesus opted not to go it alone, but rather He selected reliable and committed people to help Him in His mission. Let's take that as a model in our own ministering as well.

JESUS CONDEMNS UNREPENTANT CITIES

Then he began to denounce the cities where most of his mighty works had been done, because they did not repent. (Mt. 11:20)

WHAT JESUS DID:

When Samaritan villagers refused to welcome Jesus (described in an earlier segment from *Lk. 9*), two of His apostles wanted to call down lightning from heaven on them, but Jesus rebuked the apostles for their desire to destroy those who rejected Him. However, Jesus made no attempt to soften the reality of the consequences for all who did not heed His message and repent: Judgment awaited them.

Jesus singled out the three Galilean cities where He spent most of His time ministering – Chorazin, Bethsaida, and Capernaum. He had preached the gospel and had performed miraculous deeds in each of these places, and yet, the people there did not change their ways in preparation for the coming Kingdom of Heaven. As a result of their hardheartedness, they were under God's judgment and one day would face His wrath. *(vv. 21-24)*

WHAT HIS FOLLOWERS ARE TO DO:

We are called to preach the good news of God's love and gracious forgiveness in Christ Jesus. However, we must also not fail to present the complete truth as we understand it, and that includes the judgment of sin by a holy God. Our unrighteousness separates us from a relationship with the LORD, and because of this, He calls us to confess our sin to Him and in repentance to change our ways (our thoughts, our words, and our actions) so that we might enjoy the fullness of being a child of the Heavenly Father. But if we reject His offer of forgiveness and refuse to turn from evil and wrongdoing, we remain distant from God and risk His judgment.

Jesus shared the gospel of His Father's love, but He warned of divine judgment as well to those who would not receive His message. Let us who follow Jesus make known the entire truth of God.

JESUS REJOICES

In that same hour [Jesus] rejoiced in the Holy Spirit and said, "I thank you, Father, Lord of heaven and earth, that you have hidden these things from the wise and understanding and revealed them to little children; yes, Father, for such was your gracious will." (Lk. 10:21)

WHAT JESUS DID:

Jesus is sometimes depicted as dour and depressing, but we can see here an entirely different portrayal. The seventy-two disciples sent out by Jesus to prepare His way and to reach more people with His ministry and message had returned with glowing reports of their success. In response, Jesus was filled with such inner joy at seeing God working His pleasure in those who trusted with innocent faith that He was moved by the power of the Holy Spirit and outwardly spoke words of praise and thanksgiving to His Heavenly Father.

We can picture the Lord Jesus here, like the psalmist who sang words of praise with his lips and lifted his hands in blessing to God *(Ps. 63:3-4)*, with His hands raised, perhaps smiling, and offering up exuberant acclaim to God – a dissimilar picture indeed from what we are used to seeing.

WHAT HIS FOLLOWERS ARE TO DO:

We Christians, too, can sometimes be seen as mean-faced penitents who move through our daily lives ever-so somberly and without joy. But we ought to look at Jesus as He enthusiastically praised the Heavenly Father and seek to mirror that same delight. Rather than doom-and-gloom prophets all the time, let's be the happy souls who exude the reality of God's active presence.

We must also be mindful to acknowledge God for His constant provision and to thank Him for dynamically bringing about His will in our lives and in the lives of others. God desires that we worship Him *"in spirit and truth"* *(Jn. 4:23)*, so we need to freely offer to the LORD our words of praise, just as Jesus, did.

JESUS REPLIES TO QUESTIONS IN DIFFERENT WAYS

And behold, a lawyer stood up to put [Jesus] to the test, saying,
"Teacher, what shall I do to inherit eternal life?" (Lk. 10:25)

WHAT JESUS DID:

People often made statements to Jesus or posed questions to Him, and He responded in a variety of ways: Sometimes He quoted Scripture, as during His temptation by Satan *(Mt. 4:1-11)*; at other times, before answering, He rebuked the questioners for their lack of understanding, as He did with the Sadducees who were trying to test and trap Him *(Mk. 12:24)*; and sometimes He chose not to answer, as He did with Herod *(Lk. 23:9)*. In the incident with a lawyer, Jesus answered his questions in two other ways, both of which He commonly used throughout the gospels: 1. He answered a question with a question, and 2. He told a parable.

His purpose in the first seemed to have been to allow the ones asking the questions the chance to reflect and find the answers on their own. In His exchange with the lawyer, Jesus' question – how would the man answer according to Scripture – turned the responsibility back on the man, who indeed came up with the right solution himself, namely, loving God and loving one's neighbor as commanded in the *Torah*. In the second, Jesus used stories to illustrate His response, which would have made it easier for the questioners to grasp the truth of His answers. When the lawyer asked who was to be considered one's neighbor, Jesus told the wonderfully memorable and instructive parable of the Good Samaritan as a way of explaining that we are to be compassionate and show active lovingkindness for anyone in need, regardless of his or her lack of familiarity or similarity to us. *(vv. 26-30)*

How are we to emulate Jesus' ways of responding in our own lives? I believe that when someone poses a question to us as Christians, we can follow Jesus' lead and draw from His different methods of answering. (Let's not think that quoting verses from Scripture will always be the sole way to respond.) Choosing the best way to reply will depend on who is asking and the circumstances in which the question is asked. There are times when quoting Scripture is indeed most effective, while at other times it may be better to ask a follow-up query to help the questioners think more deeply about how to answer, and sometimes relating a germane anecdote will enable those asking the questions to clearly understand the response. Realizing how to answer is not always easy, and we should certainly ask the Holy Spirit to guide us as we seek to represent Christ to others.

Let's just be aware that there is no one correct way to answer questions regarding God and Jesus; rather, responses can be as varied as the people who pose the questions. So, we must consider the questioners and their situations and also the reasons for their particular inquiries. And let's pray for the Lord's wisdom to know what to say and how to say it, for His glory.

JESUS WITH MARTHA AND MARY

Now as they went on their way, Jesus entered a village. And a woman named Martha welcomed him into her house. (Lk. 10:38)

WHAT JESUS DID:

When Jesus entered Martha's home, He went about His mission of teaching. Her sister, Mary, chose to sit and listen while Martha busied herself with perhaps cooking their meal or drawing water to wash with or preparing a place for Jesus to stay. And Jesus initially neither commended nor reprimanded either woman for their individual choices as they were both actively engaged in their relationship with Him … that is, until Martha complained that Mary was not helping her, at which time Jesus pointed out Martha's worry and anxiety about many (relatively unimportant, material)things and Mary's choosing the one necessary (and most significant, spiritual) thing, and He would not deprive her of it. *(vv. 39-42)*

<u>WHAT HIS FOLLOWERS ARE TO DO:</u>

A lesson for us as Christ-followers might be taken from what Jesus did not do in His visit to Martha's home. As stated above, at first Jesus did not praise Mary or chide Martha for what they were doing. Each had opted to do what suited them best. So, we must learn to accept that different people will show their devotion to Jesus in different ways according to their gifts and natural tendencies. Some who enjoy studying and reading will prefer to spend a great deal of time in poring over Jesus' life and His words, while others may be gifted with organizational and logistical skills and serve by arranging things to go smoothly and accommodating the needs of others. Both have a vital role in the ministry of sharing Christ, and it is important for us to keep that in mind.

Also, let's not be quick to criticize how others go about fulfilling their call to be disciples of Jesus. Note that it is Martha's criticism of her sister that elicits Jesus' rebuke: She was bothered by fussing over too many small, insignificant details, and Mary had directed her attention to His words, the one thing that is really needed. His response to Martha's complaint is a good example of His teaching not to judge others so that we won't be judged (Mt. 7:1), something we all certainly need to learn and practice. So, when believers disparage others for how they minister and serve the Lord, as long as it is a ministry and service in keeping with the clear teaching of Jesus, we must call the complainers on it and remind them of the value of different methods of showing devotion to Christ.

JESUS TEACHES HIS DISCIPLES TO PRAY

Now Jesus was praying in a certain place, and when he finished, one
of his disciples said to him, "Lord, teach us to pray ..." (Lk. 11:1)

WHAT JESUS DID:

Jesus responded to the disciple's request with the words of what is called "The Lord's Prayer." It is Jesus' instructing his disciples how and what to pray, and it has a wonderfully simple structure:

▷ offering praise;
▷ expressing a desire to see God's rule on earth;
▷ asking for God to meet physical needs;
▷ seeking forgiveness for wrongdoing and reminding us to be forgiving;
▷ and requesting divine help in avoiding sin *(vv. 2b-4)*.

Note that the request to be taught how to pray came after Jesus had been praying. The disciples saw this practice of Jesus, and they wanted to learn how to do it, as well. Jesus responded *not* by telling them to figure it out themselves or to seek guidance through their own spiritual experiences with God; rather, He gave them a specific outline to follow and even particular words they might say when praying. And the fact that Christians have prayed the "Our Father" since the 1st century CE is a testament to its power and importance.

WHAT HIS FOLLOWERS ARE TO DO:

Jesus modeled behavior and spiritual practice to His disciples, and when they sought to emulate Him, He taught them how. We who follow Christ today should also be exhibiting righteous behavior and joyful obedience, walking in the way of the Lord in such a way that attracts people to Jesus and the fulness of spiritual life in Him. Thus, as we lead godly lives that affirm our relationship with our Heavenly Father, others – both Christian and non-Christian – will want to learn how they too can develop a closeness to God and enjoy a life of spiritual purpose and fulfillment, and it will then be our privilege and responsibility to teach them.

We should also be actively engaged in spiritual practices like praying, studying and meditating on God's word, fasting, giving charitably, and sharing the gospel – practicing what we preach, right? Then, we can teach those who are drawn into our lives and want to learn from us about a deeper life in Christ.

Jesus gave to His disciples a pattern for life in the Spirit, including prayer, and they followed His lead. Let us do the same with those around us, setting a daily example that they can emulate and instructing them in the ways of knowing, loving, and serving God more and more each day.

JESUS AND HIS MOTHER ARE PRAISED BY A WOMAN

As [Jesus] said these things, a woman in the crowd raised her voice and said to him, "Blessed is the womb that bore you, and the breasts at which you nursed!" (Lk. 11:27)

WHAT JESUS DID:

Jesus had just cast a demon out of a mute man, which resulted in the man being able to speak and in the crowd marveling at Jesus' authority over the spiritual realm. However, He was immediately denigrated by some who claimed that Jesus' power came not from God but from the Devil. Jesus countered by explaining that Satan's kingdom would fall if it were divided against itself but that if His power was truly from heaven, then God's kingdom had come into their midst. *(vv. 14-23)*

A woman responded to Jesus' works and to His words by blessing His mother, an indirect way of praising Jesus Himself. It is like someone saying, "Your parents must be so proud of you," which commends a person's greatness by referencing that person's family. But Jesus didn't politely thank the woman in the crowd for her kind sentiment; instead, He turned her praise and attention away from Himself and toward God and the true blessedness in obeying His word *(v. 28)*.

WHAT HIS FOLLOWERS ARE TO DO:

Does this mean that we as Jesus-followers should never accept a compliment, whether for our accomplishments or for our work in the ministry of reaching others for Christ? I think that would be extreme. Still, I believe there is a principle that can be drawn from Jesus' action here: Seek to turn focus away from ourselves and from what we do and say and direct attention toward God and the need to obey His commands. Thus, when we do well and that is recognized by others, we can be politely thankful, but we ought not to bask in the adulation; rather, let's acknowledge the Lord whom we serve and the necessity to submit to His demands on our lives which will result in the real assurance and enjoyment of His favor.

Jesus deflected praise directed at Him toward the Heavenly Father and emphasized the need for obedience to Him. We should do the same.

JESUS – AN UNWASHED DINNER GUEST - DENOUNCES THE RELIGIOUS LEADERS

While Jesus was speaking, a Pharisee asked him to dine with him, so he went in and reclined at table. (Lk. 11:37)

WHAT JESUS DID:

When Jesus accepted the invitation of a Pharisee to come to his home and eat, there was bound to be a confrontation of some kind given the many hostile interactions that had already taken place between Him and the religious leaders. So, why did Jesus agree to join the man, certainly realizing it would be a volatile situation? Perhaps Jesus was offering the man a chance to hear and genuinely respond to His message, or possibly Jesus was modeling His command to embrace one's opponents in love, or maybe Jesus anticipated such a criticism and knew it would be an opportunity to teach God's truth. Whatever the reason may have been, a predictable clash occurred.

Jesus did not wash His hands before eating, something which modern-day hygiene would recommend. But in the time of Christ, the washing of hands was more of a ritual observance rather than a physical cleansing or sanitizing of the skin. It seems, then, that Jesus might have purposedly chosen not to wash because He sought to visibly demonstrate His teaching about inner versus outer purity. He must have known that it could provoke a negative reaction from the Pharisee, and when it happened, though a guest in the man's home, He delivered His biting criticism of tradition as opposed to true godliness *(vv. 38-52).*

WHAT HIS FOLLOWERS ARE TO DO:

The issue here is not if we should wash our hands before a meal; knowledge of germs, viruses, and bacteria has made that simple action a good health practice. The greater question here is whether we who follow Jesus are willing to openly make a stand for divine truth, even if it means defying customary ideas and social practice. I'm not encouraging impolite behavior or discourteous action, but if something is contrary to God's Word, we must be willing to speak up. Our lives, including what we say and how we conduct ourselves, must candidly exhibit what we believe, both in public and in private.

So, while we must reach out in lovingkindness to everyone as Jesus instructed, even to those who oppose us and deride our message and our way of life, we must also be prepared to denounce that which is wrong and that which goes against the clear, righteous teaching of Scripture. Regardless of whether those false ideas come from the religious or the secular, we must be courageous in God's spirit and proclaim the truth, sometimes even to the powers that be. In His interaction with the religionists, Jesus showed the need to confront erroneous beliefs and practices. Let's follow Him.

JESUS REFUSES TO MEDIATE A TEMPORAL MATTER

Someone in the crowd said to [Jesus], "Teacher, tell my brother to divide the inheritance with me." (Lk. 12:13)

WHAT JESUS DID:

An unidentified person, presumably a man given that social milieu, brought a matter before Jesus involving a family inheritance and asked Him to order the person's brother to split it with him. Perhaps the man's brother was the elder son and thus allotted a greater portion of the inheritance, and the younger son wanted part of it. Jesus, however, was not a legal judge and refused to mediate in this temporal matter. His was a spiritual mission, so Jesus used the man's request to warn against greed and to communicate the truth that death awaited us all and that we should be rich toward God and store up treasure in heaven. *(vv. 14-34)*

WHAT HIS FOLLOWERS ARE TO DO:

Justice is of great importance, and fairness should always be a goal that we seek. But following the example of Jesus, let's not get bogged down in temporal affairs, especially those involving money and material possessions. Our priority is to be on the things of the Spirit of God, not on earthly matters.

Yes, we are commanded to meet the physical and emotional needs of those around us in whatever way we can, and we must dutifully and diligently obey. We should avoid, though, becoming mired in the myriad avenues of worldly pursuit to the detriment of striving for godliness and righteousness. Instead, just as Jesus did, let's retain our focus on the Kingdom of Heaven.

Also, we need to be open to moments when a question or situation might provide us with an opportunity to share spiritual truth. That is not to say that we should constantly be on a soapbox madly preaching to everyone or poised to pounce with a Bible verse at every moment. Rather, as occasions arise that seem appropriate for us to offer spiritual insight or explain our understanding of the nature of life and the afterlife, let's be ready and willing to speak up and convey God's good Word.

JESUS RESPONDS TO SOME VIOLENT NEWS

There were some present at that very time who told him about the Galileans whose blood Pilate had mingled with their sacrifices. (Lk. 13:1)

WHAT JESUS DID:

News was brought to Jesus of the death of His fellow Galileans at the hands of Pilate while they were offering up sacrifices to God. Though there don't appear to be any historical references to this particular incident in Josephus or elsewhere, it is in keeping with what we know of Pilate's brutal character and violent tactics – he had done this kind of thing before.

Jesus' response is informative, I believe, for perhaps it would have been expected for Him to mourn the death of these worshippers or to condemn the ruthlessness of Pilate and the oppression of the Roman occupation. However, Jesus reacted first by sternly disavowing the notion that these slain Galileans were perhaps killed due to their excessive sinfulness compared to others *(v. 2)*. Jesus then used the news to refocus the attention of its deliverers to what was of greater importance and more in keeping with His mission, namely, repentance from their sinful ways. Jesus demanded a radical change in their thoughts, words, and deeds, a turning from practicing the ways of pride, selfishness, and wrongdoing to leading lives of humility, compassion, and righteousness. Without this change, they would remain spiritually dead, separated from God and under His judgment *(v. 3)*.

We are bombarded daily by the 24-hour news cycle with stories of cruelty, injustice, greed, and self-centeredness. There is a constant stream of information about warfare, crime, political deceit, ecological destruction, etc. And while all of these are areas which we must work hard toward correcting and eradicating, they can easily distract our attention from the real mission that Christ has given His followers to share His message and to live according to His teaching.

Let's do what we can to make this world a better place for all people by standing against evil and promoting good; yet, in so doing, we must not neglect our true commission to spread the gospel. Jesus did not allow news of current events to move His primary focus from preaching a call to repentance and announcing the good news of the Kingdom of God, nor should we.

JESUS HEALS A DISABLED WOMAN ON THE SABBATH

Now [Jesus] was teaching in one of the synagogues on the Sabbath. And behold, there was a woman who had had a disabling spirit for eighteen years. She was bent over and could not fully straighten herself. (Lk. 13:10-11)

WHAT JESUS DID:

Some of the religious leaders of Jesus' time condemned healing on the Sabbath as a violation of God's commandment to keep that day holy and to do no work on it. However, when Jesus saw need and suffering, regardless of the day, He responded to a higher principle of lovingkindness and compassion.

In this incident, a woman had been demonically afflicted for eighteen long, arduous years by a condition that bent her back so that she could not stand up straight. Jesus was teaching in the synagogue on the Sabbath Day, as was His custom, when He noticed the woman. Women were permitted in synagogues, though they were separated from the men, but Jesus called her to come over to Him, perhaps going against the custom of segregation of the sexes. Then, after pronouncing her freed of her disability, He put His hands on her, which certainly broke ancient norms of propriety, and she was immediately able to straighten up. For this wonderful, long-awaited healing, she praised God. *(vv. 12-13)*

The predictable reaction of the head of the synagogue, probably with the approval of other religious leaders in attendance, was to angrily denounce this Sabbath healing as a transgression of Mosaic law. But Jesus in turn decried their hypocrisy by pointing out that they don't hesitate to take care of their animals every day of the week, so why shouldn't He also act even on this special day to end the suffering experienced by this child of God? *(vv. 14-16)*

<u>WHAT HIS FOLLOWERS ARE TO DO:</u>

As followers of Jesus, we too are called to respond to God's command to do what we can to meet the needs of others and to end suffering. Let's not be inhibited by cultural norms or by social customs that might prevent us from fulfilling our mission. When we see those in need, we should not turn away from them for fear of rocking the boat of tradition and disturbing the status quo of accepted common practice. Rather, we must reach out in compassion and let our lives touch others, drawing those facing hardship close and offering words of comfort and practical actions that will help to alleviate their problems. That is the way of Christ.

Also, we ought to be courageous in calling out hypocrisy when it appears. Of course, before we focus on the behavior of others, we must reflect on our own lives to ensure that we are not guilty of the same issue. Once that is done, however, we must denounce hypocrisy, especially in those who claim religious affiliation.

Jesus showed us how to respond to need with empathy and love and how to react to hypocrisy with courage and conviction. Let's take note and do the same.

JESUS IS WARNED ABOUT HEROD

At that very hour some Pharisees came and said to [Jesus], "Get away from here, for Herod wants to kill you." (Lk. 13:31)

<u>WHAT JESUS DID:</u>

It is interesting that some Pharisees, normally portrayed as the dogged opponents of Jesus, should warn Him about this threat to His life. Did the warning express a genuine concern for Jesus' safety, or was it an attempt by these religionists to scare this upstart yet popular preacher away? Whatever their motivation, Jesus did not react as they might have hoped, that is, they failed in persuading Him to change His course and leave that area. Rather than heeding the warning, Jesus responded by characterizing Herod as a fox, a sly predator bent on His demise and by expressing His unwavering determination to continue His ministry of exorcism and healing and to fulfill His mission, even to the point of death, while perhaps hinting at His eventual resurrection on the third day *(v. 32)*.

WHAT HIS FOLLOWERS ARE TO DO:

There will be times when we who follow Jesus are cautioned by others, both friends and opponents alike, to not be so devoted to Christ and to the ministry. They may advise us to take a more sensible approach to life, balancing our religious convictions with secular points of view. We might also be ridiculed as Jesus fanatics in an attempt to deter us from our dedication to serving the Lord. But if we do succumb to these admonishments, it could result in a kind of compromise of our commitment to Christ and the gospel.

God has given each of us specific tasks in ministry; we all have a particular mission to fulfill. So, regardless of our ministerial assignment, when the counsel of those around us conflicts with God's call and the direction which He sends us, we must not be persuaded to take a different tack; instead, we need to always pay attention to God's voice and to yield to the leading of His Holy Spirit. Jesus was dedicated steadfastly to seeing his mission through, regardless of the warnings or opinion of other people. Let's learn from Him.

JESUS HEALS A MAN WITH DROPSY IN THE HOME OF A LEADING PHARISEE

One Sabbath, when [Jesus] went to dine at the house of a ruler of the Pharisees, they were watching him carefully. And behold, there was a man before him who had dropsy. (Lk. 14:1-2)

WHAT JESUS DID:

Once again, Jesus was invited on the Sabbath to share a meal with the religious leaders, this time at the home of one of the head Pharisees. Present were both members of the Pharisees and experts in *Torah* law *(v. 3a)*, and they had their eyes on Jesus, waiting for Him to do something that they could condemn.

We don't know who the ailing man was: one of the guests or possibly one of the household servants, or perhaps a beggar hanging out near the home wanting some food or someone who had heard of Jesus' healing power hoping for His attention. In any case, the man was suffering from the condition of edema (*"dropsy"*), a swelling especially of the limbs and joints due to an accumulation of water in the body, which, besides being unsightly, causes tenderness, pain, and limited mobility. Jesus saw the hardship this man was facing and was moved by compassion to heal him. However, Jesus understood, most likely from His previous dealings with them, the religionists' opposition to such an act which in their thinking would break the Sabbath law. The Pharisees were constantly attacking Jesus with the recurring charge of transgressing the rules governing the Sabbath, and in most cases, Jesus gave a response repeated for its effectiveness in silencing their familiar criticism – namely, by contrasting acts of lovingkindness with narrow-minded interpretation of Mosaic regulations.

So, rather than waiting for them to openly express their hostility, Jesus went on the offensive and challenged them with a question meant to show how misguided they were in their intolerant attitudes toward suffering and their unrighteous attempts to abide by Sabbath restrictions. And when they were either unable or unwilling to respond to His question, Jesus healed the man, showing once again that mercy and compassion superseded unfeeling religious law, and sent him on his way. *(vv. 3-4)*

WHAT HIS FOLLOWERS ARE TO DO:

Sometimes, the best defense is a good offense. Jesus demonstrated this as He confronted the religious leaders, and we who follow Him should learn from it. When we face opposition to our beliefs, our actions, or our way of life, we need not always sit quietly waiting to be condemned. Instead, let's be prepared to strongly voice what we hold to be God's truth and to clearly state how we are instructed to conduct ourselves. There ought to be good reasons for all that we do and say, and let's be courageous in explaining what they are. In so doing, our goal should not be to confound our critics or to win a spiritual debate, but to clarify our motivations and perhaps to cause the opponents to our faith to reflect more deeply on their own lives and possibly see the truth in what we do and why we do it.

We also need to keep in mind that we should seek to minister to the needs of those going through difficulty and pain, just as Jesus did, and not simply strive to comply with religious rules or expectations. Compassion and lovingkindness are to be what compel us rather than blind and heartless obedience to pious platitudes and religious mandates. Let's allow the spirit of God's law of love to constantly guide our words and actions.

One other comment: When people are healed of the spiritual sickness (sin) that had once separated them from God, we should "send them away," that is, encourage them to move away from their old life and engage in a transformed way of living, to leave previous, unrighteous habits and develop new, virtuous customs and behaviors, and to distance themselves from those former friends or acquaintances who might inhibit spiritual growth and enter into the company of others who will promote a closeness to God.

Jesus took the offensive in His interactions with those who actively opposed Him and used proven responses to counteract their criticism, always championing love and doing good over strict adherence to human-made traditions and the letter of the law. And having healed the man, He directed him to a new life. Let us who call Jesus our Lord act in similar ways.

JESUS INSTRUCTS THOSE WHO SEEK TO BE HONORED

Now [Jesus] told a parable to those who were invited, when he noticed how they chose the places of honor ... (Lk. 14:7a)

<u>WHAT JESUS DID:</u>

Jesus was aware of went on around Him. At this dinner in the home of a prominent Pharisee, He saw how the guests were jockeying for the prized spots near the head of the table. These invitees sought to be seen by others as occupying the *"places of honor"* which would signify their importance and elevated social status.

Despite unspoken rules of propriety and politeness when a guest in someone's home, Jesus did not ignore the self-aggrandizing behavior of these people. A vital aspect of His mission was to instruct others about truths that went deeper than social norms – in this case, about the importance of humility. Thus, Jesus did not hesitate to seize this teachable moment to make the others conscious of their prideful, selfish actions and to explain that the best way to be honored was by being humble *(vv. 7b-11)*.

First, the fact that Jesus noticed and chastised this self-honoring conduct should lead us Christians to remind each other to adopt a more self-denying, unpretentious attitude. That is not say that we must always refuse to receive any recognition for our work, but it does mean that we are not to seek being honored or put in the spotlight so we can bask in the accolades and applause of others. Receiving honor is not to be the motivating factor in our engaging in ministry or in any good activity, and we need to communicate and model that to one another. Let our goal be to please God, not other people; let us seek His acclaim for our actions, not the praise of others.

Additionally, just as Jesus did not refrain from admonishing those exhibiting selfishness and unrighteous behavior, we ought to also pray for the same kind of boldness to point out wrongdoing and offer advice on how to lead more godly lives. (Of course, this means that we ourselves are leading godly lives of righteousness; Jesus was able to make His comments on humility because His life was characterized by a humble spirit.) When we see misconduct or sinfulness, let's not turn a blind eye to it but rather call it out and use it as an opportunity to teach a better way that accords with the person and character of God. Jesus did that, and so should we.

JESUS DEFINES THE COST OF BEING HIS DISCIPLE

Now great crowds accompanied [Jesus], and he turned and said to them ... (Lk. 14:25)

WHAT JESUS DID:

Jesus' preaching and miraculous healing power kept attracting more people, but rather than reveling in the adulation of the throngs, Jesus explicitly delineated to them the exacting requirements to be a true disciple. While He sought to reach more people with His message of the arrival and presence of the Kingdom of God and need for repentance, Jesus did not merely seek to increase the number of His followers, especially if that meant compromising His teaching in any way. He desired people who were genuinely devoted to Him and always spoke words of truth even at the possible expense of alienating some would-be followers.

So, Jesus turned to face those traveling with Him and set forth stringent, even harsh, prerequisites of being His disciple. These involved dying to self and serving Him without reservation, putting Him and His God-ordained mission ahead of any other worldly relationship, including family. Tough, to be sure, but something that needed to be considered before committing to following Him. *(vv. 26-27)*

WHAT HIS FOLLOWERS ARE TO DO:

As we seek to spread the gospel of Jesus, let's be mindful that Jesus was more about quality than quantity. Though it is important for us to share His life and words with as many as possible, we should also be greatly concerned with the spiritual growth of those who respond positively to Him. That means stating in no uncertain terms the demands placed on all of us as His followers.

Also, we should remember that Jesus was definitely not a crowd pleaser. There might be a tendency on our part to limit an explanation of the gospel to the wonderful promises of forgiveness and assurance of the Father's love, as glorious as they are. However, we would not be true to Jesus' message if we taught that discipleship was without any personal cost. That would be what some would call "cheap grace." No, to follow Christ means to let go of the earthly and embrace the heavenly, to prioritize our relationship with Him above all else, and to give up our own desires and accept and shoulder the burden of ministry to others. As Jesus did, let's make that clear from the start.

JESUS ILLUSTRATES GOD'S LOVE FOR THE LOST

Now the tax collectors and sinners were all drawing near to hear [Jesus]. And the Pharisees and the scribes grumbled, saying, "This man receives sinners and eats with them." (Lk. 15:1-2)

WHAT JESUS DID:

Jesus came to seek those who were spiritually lost, the ones who were separated from God but who wanted to be reunited with Him, the people who were willing to acknowledge their sinfulness and turn in repentance back to their Heavenly Father. These are the ones who were drawn to Jesus and His message, and the Lord welcomed them all.

Jesus received social outcasts and even broke bread with them, associating with the worst of the worst in their community. This, of course, was noted by the piously religious of that time who saw themselves as morally superior to all others. Their reaction? Grumbling, complaining, criticizing, and condemning when they should have been reaching out in love and compassion as Jesus did.

In response to their grousing about whom He was socializing with, Jesus used the analogy of a man looking for his lost sheep, something which even these religionists could comprehend and relate to. Jesus gave them further illustrations of the all-embracing love of God, telling them stories of a woman searching for a lost coin and of a father welcoming back his wasteful, self-indulgent but ultimately repentant son. Yet, the hardness of their hearts, like that of the older brother in the story of the prodigal, prevented them from supporting Jesus' mission to the lost. *(vv. 8-32)*

WHAT HIS FOLLOWERS ARE TO DO:

We Christians tend to be very selective with whom we associate. We prefer to socialize with those we deem to be morally pure and who share our values and beliefs. We normally spend time with people of our same race, socio-economic status, and political ideals. We often move entirely in Christian circles of church and like-minded believers, rarely venturing outside our well-constructed religious walls.

However, we can learn much from Jesus' seeking and open-armed reception of anyone who was attracted to His person and to His teaching. He embraced all who longed for a place in the Kingdom of Heaven and were willing to turn from their sinful ways and accept the forgiveness offered by God, and that should be our attitude as well: welcoming to anyone who genuinely is searching for the truth, regardless of past unrighteousness and ungodly life choices. We are in no way spiritually or morally better than anyone else; all of us are merely sinners saved by God's grace. So, let's not separate ourselves from non-Christians or even from the social pariahs of today's world. Instead, like Jesus, let's go beyond the bubbles of our comfortably familiar lives and reach out to all for the sake of the gospel.

And if others around us grumble about whom we associate with, let's keep hearing the voice of the Lord who calls us to seek and save lost souls. That was Jesus' mission then, and it is still our mission today.

JESUS ANSWERS THE LOVERS OF MONEY

[Jesus said], "No servant can serve two masters ... You cannot serve God and money." (Lk. 16:13)

WHAT JESUS DID:

Jesus was very clear about the danger of money becoming our master rather than God. The reaction of the Pharisees, who are described as holding money in highest esteem, was to mock His teaching *(v. 14)*. However, Jesus was not about to backtrack on account of their derision; instead, He explained that their imbalanced reverence for all things monetary was absolutely detestable in God's eyes *(v. 15)*. As always, Jesus boldly spoke divine truth to those with earthly power.

WHAT HIS FOLLOWERS ARE TO DO:

Jesus did not value financial success the way we often do, as we fawn over those who have material wealth. So, let's follow the Lord's stance that God is to be our sole master and that anything usurping God's place on the throne of our lives is to be dealt with decisively and rejected outright.

Jesus did not budge from His opinion about money and serving God, even when ridiculed by others, and we also ought to be strong and unafraid to express what is truly precious in God's Kingdom, namely, spiritual riches and hearts filled with compassion. We may face opposition to this idea, even from those who name Christ as Lord but whose actual primary focus is striving for personal worldly prosperity. However, as evident in the life of Jesus, priority must be given to serving God as He leads us and not simply to amassing material wealth and monetary power. We as Christians today need to embrace that notion unequivocally and espouse its principles openly and forthrightly, just as Jesus did.

JESUS HEALS TEN LEPERS

And as [Jesus] entered a village, he was met by ten lepers ... (Lk. 17:12a)

<u>WHAT JESUS DID:</u>

Jesus was headed toward Jerusalem, in an area between Samaria and Galilee. Ten people (maybe just men, maybe both men and women), all afflicted with the disease of leprosy and therefore keeping their distance, called on Jesus to show mercy on them. They called Him *"Master,"* which could have been either a respectful form of address or an acknowledgement of their awareness of His power to heal and their submission to His authority. Even though they did not directly ask Jesus to heal their disease, Jesus could readily see their miserable condition, and He responded to their plea for help with compassion and lovingkindness. However, the healing was not immediate: They had to, in faith, follow His instruction to show themselves to the priests, and as they obediently acted, while on their way, they were healed. *(vv. 11-14)*

It is interesting that at times, when Jesus healed people, He instructed them to tell no one, while at other times He directed them to openly proclaim what God had done for them. In the incident, Jesus told these lepers to show themselves to the Jewish priests in obedience to the command in *Leviticus 14* for those cleansed of their leprosy. Perhaps as well, Jesus wanted the religious leaders to see direct testimony of His power to heal so that they might acknowledge His God-ordained mission and receive His message of love, forgiveness, and the coming of the Kingdom of Heaven. It is possible, too, that Jesus wanted these cleansed lepers to be reintegrated into the society from which they had been cruelly ostracized due to their condition, and this would be facilitated by a pronouncement from the priests showing that they had indeed been made well again. Once back in their social circles, these former lepers could also witness to others about the healing power of God through Jesus.

The story concludes with one of the lepers, a Samaritan, returning to Jesus to thank Him and to praise God for having been cleansed of his disease. Jesus commended the man for his restorative faith, but only after pointing out with very apparent displeasure that just one of the ten healed lepers, a foreigner at that, had expressed his gratitude. *(vv. 15-19)*

<u>WHAT HIS FOLLOWERS ARE TO DO</u>:

We can glean some principles from this incident in the life of Jesus that we, His followers, should seek to incorporate into our own lives today. First, when others, especially those in dire circumstances, call on us for help, let's be ready and willing to provide for them in whatever way we can to alleviate their suffering and lift them out of their troublesome situation. Our attitude must be one of compassion and empathy, and we should take active steps of lovingkindness to meet their needs.

Additionally, while we Christians tend to focus on the New Testament scriptures, we also need to understand the teaching of the *Tanakh*, the canon of the Hebrew Bible, i.e., the Old Testament. Jesus knew the word of God of His time in its entirety and sought to abide by its righteous commands, and we today, though not bound by the ritual law, ought to live by the truth of the moral values that we find in Scripture.

And finally, we should encourage those rescued from their sinful life to express gratitude to God for saving them. Thankfulness is a desirable trait for every child of the Heavenly Father, and let us openly and freely offer up our praise in appreciation for all He has done for us.

In sum, let's continually take our cues on how to speak and behave from Jesus, for He is Lord.

JESUS BLESSES LITTLE CHILDREN

And [people] were bringing children to [Jesus] that he might touch them, and the disciples rebuked them. (Mk. 10:13)

<u>WHAT JESUS DID</u>:

During the height of His ministry, Jesus must have had exceptionally long days with people constantly crowding around Him to hear and touch Him. He probably had very little time to Himself, but He did not complain about it – He was selflessly on mission and His focus was firmly fixed on accomplishing what God had sent Him to do.

The disciples were certainly aware of the demands put on Jesus as an increasingly public figure, and they seemed here to have been attempting to give Him some space and perhaps some downtime by preventing people from bringing their kids to receive a blessing from Him. However, Jesus was angered by the disciples' actions as they were obstructing His objective of reaching people (even young ones) with His message of the real presence of God's Kingdom and touching them with His healing power and His life-changing words. So, He gladly welcomed these innocent, trusting children to come to Him, embraced them in unconditional love, and prayed for the Father's abundant favor on their little lives. *(vv. 14-16)*

WHAT HIS FOLLOWERS ARE TO DO:

We Christians should not only admire Jesus' strength and determination to stay on task and to constantly give of Himself to those around Him; we should also follow His lead as we engage in our own God-ordained ministries, never griping about not having enough "me-time" or grumbling about how tired we are or grousing about how needy everyone is. Let us instead continually welcome all the people that are divinely led into our lives, including children, so that the Lord can use us to bring them into a closer relationship with Him. And let's not neglect praying that God would bless and keep them in His constant care.

We need to learn from Jesus as well that there is a time for righteous anger: Indignation and outrage are appropriate reactions to that which impedes true knowledge of the Heavenly Father or hinders the spread of Jesus' message of lovingkindness and forgiveness. We must not meekly accept human-imposed obstacles to receiving the promises of God but rather stand and speak out against anything that is contrary to the Almighty's wishes.

And certainly, an obvious application of this incident from Jesus' life is His desire for us to bring our children to Him so they can know Him and experience through Him the all-encompassing love of our Heavenly Father. These innocent ones can readily understand and accept the unnuanced good news of God's grace *(vv. 14-15)*, so let us introduce our kids even at an early age to the Lord.

Jesus welcomed everyone, old and young, with open arms, and chastised those who placed impediments in their way. Let's emulate Him.

JESUS RAISES LAZARUS FROM THE DEAD

Now a certain man was ill, Lazarus of Bethany, the village
of Mary and her sister Martha. (Jn. 11:1)

WHAT JESUS DID:

As recorded in John's gospel alone, in response to the news of His sick friend, for whom and for whose sisters, Mary and Martha, He had great love*(v. 5)*, Jesus eventually did make His way to Bethany. Jesus showed tremendous courage in going there because the Jewish religious leaders of that region wanted to arrest or even kill Him *(10:31, 39)*. His disciples warned Jesus not to go *(11:8)*, but Jesus understood that this was part of God's plan, and He was determined, despite the possible danger, to do the will of His Heavenly Father. Does this mean that Jesus was not afraid? I don't believe so. I'm sure He felt fear, just as we all do, but He did not let that dread control His actions; instead, He was motivated by His immense love for humanity and by His overwhelming sense of mission to relieve suffering whenever possible and to present Himself as the Messiah. He chose those feelings of love and awareness of mission to override any anxiety He might have been experiencing.

Surprisingly, when Jesus received the news of Lazarus' illness, He did not immediately set off to Bethany; rather, He waited two days before heading there, and by the time He arrived, Lazarus had already been dead and buried for four days *(vv. 6, 17)*. (Jesus was on the other side of the Jordan River *[10:40]* when the messengers reached Him.) Why the delay? Jesus certainly knew the miracle He was about to perform, so perhaps Jesus waited so that there could be no question that this was truly a resurrection from the dead, not merely Lazarus' recovering naturally from his illness. All of this was for God's glory *(11:4b)*, and Jesus was attuned to the Father's perfect timing.

Arriving in Bethany, Jesus saw Mary and others weeping loudly, and Jesus was Himself overcome with emotion. To think of Jesus as a cold, unfeeling individual, stoically accepting the events around Him and callously ever-resigned to divine providence, would be misguided, indeed. Here in this incident with Lazarus, Jesus publicly expressed His deep feelings at the death of His dear friend and at the pain of loss being experienced by Lazarus' sisters and by others in the community. Thus, Jesus was profoundly affected and cried openly. *(vv. 33, 35)*

Standing at Lazarus' tomb, Jesus was greatly moved with emotion once more, and He looked toward the sky and began to thank God for hearing Him. Jesus had evidently already prayed in His heart for His Heavenly Father to perform a miracle, but then He spoke His prayer aloud so that those around Him knew it was God who had sent Him and who was working in and through Him. Jesus then showed the power of His prayer to God, confident that His Father always heard Him, by commanding the dead man to leave his tomb, and wrapped in his burial clothes, Lazarus emerged. Finally, Jesus instructed those around Him to remove the linen strips that bound Lazarus' limbs and the cloth covering his face so that he could move about freely.. *(vv. 38-44)*

WHAT HIS FOLLOWERS ARE TO DO:

Just as Jesus bravely went to Bethany in spite of the very real threats against His life, we who seek to follow our Master must also show courage in engaging in our areas of ministry. Not all will go smoothly for us; difficulties and troubles are sure to arise as we share the gospel of Christ and reach out in love to those in need. This will undoubtedly create anxiety and apprehension in us; yet, we ought not be deterred from our mission because of fear of what might happen. Let's trust in God's care and boldly do our work for the Lord.

We must realize, too, that although we have a restored relationship with our Heavenly Father, it doesn't mean tragedy will never strike our lives. Jesus had devoted Himself entirely to doing God's will, and yet, a very close friend, someone He loved deeply, passed away. Our lives, even while we are committed to serving Christ, will not be immune to shock or heartbreak.

Let us as well avoid knee-jerk reactions to every situation. There are times when an immediate response is called for, but on other occasions we should seek God's clear timing of when to act. By staying in tune with God's Holy

Spirit, we can learn to clearly discern His voice and know when He says "Go," when He says, "No," and when He says, "Wait."

We need also to remember that God created us with a capacity for emotional response and that our feelings are an integral part of being human. While I am not advocating for a constant display of demonstrative outbursts, we should not be afraid to show our true feelings when circumstances are appropriate, including at times crying openly.

Additionally, prayer should be a continual part of our Christian life, whether it be done silently in our hearts or spoken out loud in the presence of others. Jesus has promised us that our Heavenly Father always hears us, so let's lift our needs to Him, asking Him to do great things, and if they do come to pass (or even if they don't), we ought to be sure to give Him praise, just as Jesus did.

And lastly, when persons have been raised from the spiritual death of sin into the renewed life in Christ, they will need our support and assistance in removing that which formerly bound them. They must cast off any encumbrances to righteousness, such as old attitudes and habits, before they can be expected to walk in the freedom of the Spirit, and this will perhaps be much more readily done with the help of other Christians around them.

JESUS EXERCISES CAUTION

From that day on [the Pharisees] made plans to put [Jesus] to death. (Jn. 11:53)

WHAT JESUS DID:

In the last segment, we saw that Jesus chose to go to Bethany to raise Lazarus despite the threats against His life. This was a commendable display of trust in God's care and yielding to mission rather than allowing fear to dominate His actions. However, even Jesus at times exercised caution so that He could successfully complete His objective of spreading His good news message of the Father's love and of the immanent presence of the Kingdom of Heaven.

This was the case following the Scripture cited above. The Jewish religious leaders, especially the Pharisees, having seen the power of Jesus in raising Lazarus from the dead, were afraid that He would gather such a large following that the Romans would intervene and take complete control of the land and even their special *"place,"* presumably referring to the Temple *(vv. 45-52)*. So, they sought His death. As a result, Jesus chose the better part of valor, and discreetly removed Himself for a time from His very public ministry, going with His disciples to a remote town some twelve miles northeast of Jerusalem near an uninhabited desert region *(v. 54)*.

<u>WHAT HIS FOLLOWERS ARE TO DO:</u>

Let's not be foolish in the choices we make regarding our own mission. We should recognize that there is healthy balance between trusting in God and undertaking ventures that may result in our demise or in the termination of our ministry. We need to stand for our faith, yes! We need to openly declare our allegiance to our Heavenly Father and to Jesus Christ, yes! We need to reach out in love to alleviate suffering in the world, yes! But we must not simply throw caution to the wind and plunge blindly into the fray, expecting the hand of the Almighty to keep us from harm or to prevent any calamity from striking us or our loved ones.

How to know when retreat is preferrable to advance? Certainly, we must seek the Lord's will as we engage in ministry and listen attentively for His orders. When faced with the possible destruction of our work for the Kingdom of God, we ought to tread carefully and to prayerfully consider the best actions to take, guided by the voice of the Father and the leading of His Holy Spirit.

Just like Jesus, we should be cautious to make prudent decisions so that we can fully accomplish the mission God has given us.

JESUS AND THE RICH YOUNG RULER

And as [Jesus] was setting out on his journey, a man ran up and knelt before him and asked him, "Good Teacher, what must I do to inherit eternal life?" (Mk. 10:17)

<u>WHAT JESUS DID:</u>

Jesus was back on the road again when this man came to Him. Identified in other synoptics as *"young," "rich,"* and *"a ruler" (Mt. 19; Lk. 18)*, this man ran to Jesus, perhaps expressing some urgency, and reverently kneeling before Jesus and acknowledging Him as a respected rabbi, posed a question to Him, seemingly quite sincere in hoping for a definitive answer as to how he might be granted life without end. Jesus responded to the question in different ways.

First, Jesus answered the question with a question of His own to the man, asking him why he had called Jesus good? *(Mk. 10:18)* The Lord thus wanted the man to engage in some self-reflection so that the man might clarify in his own mind whom he was addressing and the authority of His response.

Next, Jesus quoted scriptural commandments *(v. 19)*, perhaps as a way of asking the man to genuinely appraise how obediently he had followed God's demands on his life. When the man responded that he had kept all these mandates, even since he was a boy, Jesus looked into his eyes and felt love for him, maybe at the honesty of his answer *(vv. 20-21a)*.

After that, Jesus gave the man a series of even greater challenges: to sell all that he owned, to give the proceeds to the poor, and to come follow Him as a disciple *(v. 21b)*. Possibly the man's clothes or jewelry indicated his wealth, but Jesus knew the one thing that obstructed the man from leading a truly godly life, namely, his quest for material possessions and his desire to accumulate more earthly riches. The man, sad and dejected as he was aware of this deficiency in his life, realized that he could not meet the requirements set by Jesus, and he turned and walked away *(v. 22)*.

Jesus then used this occasion to teach His disciples, warning them about the spiritual dangers of materialism and how a pursuit of wealth can be a real impediment to a life of submission to the rule of God, the King *(vv. 23-25)*.

WHAT HIS FOLLOWERS ARE TO DO:

We who seek to follow Jesus can learn several principles from this incident.

When people come to us with questions, let's consider various ways to answer them, such as by posing questions to them that will lead them to do some soul searching in order to find answers on their own or by quoting Scripture, which can act as a mirror by which people may evaluate their lives.

Also, as we ourselves train disciples and they begin to grow spiritually, we ought to challenge them further to develop an even deeper relationship with the Lord. We can do this by encouraging fellow believers to fully obey God's commandments and to surrender all that they have to Him to be used in serving the less fortunate.

Additionally, let's not neglect to show love and compassion to those who honestly seek after God, despite their doubts and failings. We should truly seek to see people and to know them and their circumstances, just as Jesus did with the rich young man, and we must always remember that we are all in need of God's mercy and forgiveness and that all of us are recipients of our Heavenly Father's grace.

Finally, we should look for events in life which can be illustrative of a spiritual truth. That is not to say that everything needs to be spiritualized or turned into a Bible lesson; however, we would do well to make use of both significant and ostensibly insignificant occasions as teachable moments to instruct those around us in their walk with Christ.

JESUS AGAIN FORETELLS HIS DEATH

And they were on the road, going up to Jerusalem, and Jesus was walking ahead of them. And they were amazed, and those who followed were afraid. And taking the twelve again, he began to tell them what was to happen to him. (Mk. 10:32)

WHAT JESUS DID:

Jesus and His group of disciples were heading toward Jerusalem. Jesus was fully aware of the rendezvous with death that awaited Him there, and yet, we see Jesus in the lead, walking ahead of the others, absolutely intent on fulfilling the mission for which He had been sent by His Heavenly Father.

Jesus' disciples, because of their trust in Him, followed after Him, filled with a mixture of wonder and fear at what they were doing. Jesus understood their puzzlement and their apprehension of the unknown and again clearly explained to His twelve chosen apostles exactly what was going to happen once they reached the Holy City – that He would be condemned and killed by the chief priests, but that three days later He would rise from the dead *(vv. 33-34)*. This was actually the third time that Jesus told them of His impending death and resurrection, but despite Jesus' candid declarations, His disciples still had a hard time grasping and accepting the fate He predicted.

WHAT HIS FOLLOWERS ARE TO DO:

Jesus led, and His disciples followed. We in turn should lead those that the Lord brings into our lives as we all seek to become closer in our relationship with God. Our attitudes, our speech, our behavior, our interactions with others, all that we say and do and are should be worthy of emulation by other believers. In a way, we can provide a present-day, flesh-and-blood model of Christlike behavior.

Like Jesus, as we engage in the ministries that the Father has assigned us, let's keep our faces turned toward the goal of fulfilling our mission, even when difficulties and obstacles lie in our path, knowing and trusting that everything is part of God's perfect plan. We should be honest with others, though, about problems that we experience or that we are likely to encounter. Jesus promised that there would be trials and tribulations for Christians; it is the inevitable cost of genuinely following Him, and we ought to be candid when hardships and obstacles confront us.

If we are true to our commitment to serving Jesus, others will be drawn to His presence in our lives and to the character that the Holy Spirit is working to develop in us. We will then have the responsibility to teach those around us about the person and ways of God and of Christ. However, let's not be discouraged or upset if the concepts we try to convey to others are not immediately understood. Jesus had to repeat Himself several times in an effort to teach His disciples about God's Kingdom and about the sacrifice that He was called to make ... and they still didn't quite get it.

In brief, we who follow the Lord must be exemplary in our lives, committed to our mission, and patient with those around us ... even as Jesus was.

JESUS DEALS WITH HIS
SELF-SERVING APOSTLES

And James and John, the sons of Zebedee, came up to [Jesus] and said to him, "Teacher, we want you to do for us whatever we ask of you." (Mk. 10:35)

WHAT JESUS DID:

Two of Jesus' twelve chosen apostles, the brothers James and John, approached Jesus with a rather extravagant request to let them sit in positions of power on either side of Him when He reigned in His glorious kingdom. Jesus responded, not by rebuking them, but first by questioning their commitment to His mission and its rigorous demands and then by explaining that such a request was not His to grant, perhaps suggesting that only the Heavenly Father had such authority *(vv. 36-40)*.

This exchange did not go unnoticed by the other ten apostles, and their reaction was anger directed toward the sons of Zebedee. But Jesus did not permit their resentful attitude to go uninstructed; instead, He used this moment to teach all His disciples that true greatness was achieved by humbly serving others. *(vv. 41-44)*

The Lord has placed certain individuals under our care. We have family, friends, and fellow believers whose growth in godly character and whose development in spiritual maturity we can directly impact and shape. So, let us learn from Jesus and not allow sinful attitudes and conduct like selfishness and unrighteous indignation to go unchecked. When such an outlook or behavior is exhibited, whether by ourselves or by those around us, we must deal with it by naming it for what it is (un-Christlike) and by teaching a more godly way to think and act.

Jesus didn't hesitate to correct His misguided and self-serving apostles, a group of special men that He Himself had chosen as His representatives and emissaries. We too need to be ready to deal with un-Christian thoughts and comportment by anyone within our circle of influence and to provide guidance toward the mind of Jesus and His righteousness.

JESUS HEALS A BLIND BEGGAR

As [Jesus] drew near to Jericho, a blind man was
sitting by the roadside begging. (Lk. 18:35)

WHAT JESUS DID:

Jesus was on mission, heading toward Jerusalem for His final days. As He approached the town of Jericho, a blind beggar called out for Jesus to have pity on him, addressing Jesus as *"Son of David,"* thus perhaps expressing his belief that Jesus was the long-awaited Messiah. (In *Mk. 10:46*, we are told his name, Bartimaeus; in *Mt. 20:29*, there are two beggars, and this incident occurs on Jesus' way out of town.)

Jesus responded to the cry for help: He stopped and ordered that the blind man be brought to Him. Then, as He often did, Jesus asked the man what He wanted, possibly requesting that the man verbalize specifically what he needed from Jesus. When the man replied that he wanted his sight restored, Jesus healed the man and explained it was the man's faith that had made him well, which is to say, because the man had expressed his trust in Jesus's mercy and power, he was given his sight. As a result, the formerly blind man praised God, as did the witnesses to this miracle, and began to follow Jesus. *(Lk. 18:41-43).*

When people cry out for help, we who love the Lord and seek to follow His ways must stop what we are doing and attend to their needs.

We are often so busy and so intent on accomplishing our own goals that we fail to hear others' heartfelt pleas for help or ignore their expressed grief and pain. So, let's keep our eyes and ears open and be receptive to the conditions of those around us, and when we do become aware of a particular hardship, we should turn our focus from our own lives and redirect it toward the lives of those facing difficulties. Let's be moved with compassion, just as Jesus was, and then do what we can to alleviate suffering, to provide solutions to problems, and to restore wellbeing, just as Jesus did, always remembering that it is all for God's glory.

JESUS AND ZACCHAEUS

[Jesus] entered Jericho and was passing through. And behold, there was a man named Zacchaeus. He was a chief tax collector and was rich. (Lk. 19:1-2)

WHAT JESUS DID:

Jesus' fame as a teacher and healer had preceded Him; also, He had just restored sight to a blind man, which certainly must have caused a stir with news of the healing spreading fast. A rich tax collector in Jericho named Zacchaeus wanted to see Jesus, but being short, Zacchaeus' view was blocked by the crowds, so he ingeniously and perhaps unceremoniously climbed up a sycamore tree for a better vantage point. As Jesus entered town, Jesus noticed the short man who had climbed a tall tree to catch a glimpse of this renowned wonder-worker. Although Zacchaeus was employed by the hated Romans to collect taxes from their Jewish subjects, and was thus himself despised by his countryman, Jesus went against most accepted social norms and invited Himself to eat and stay at his home. Zacchaeus happily accepted this privilege, but others in town grumbled at Jesus' choosing to lodge at the house of such a sinful man. *(vv. 3-7)*

Being present with Jesus for a time had an immensely positive affect on Zacchaeus, motivating him to pledge greater charity to the poor and to compensate *"fourfold"* any financial misconduct. Jesus reacted by announcing that Zacchaeus' change of heart had brought salvation to his home, which was exactly the focus of His mission – seeking and saving lost souls. *(vv. 8-10)*

Jesus specifically chose Zacchaeus to host Him while He was in Jericho as a way to honor an individual reviled by many, to elevate his status in their society, and to preach his message of the need for repentance as preparation for the Kingship of God. Jesus expressed, in essence, his acceptance of Zacchaeus as a person while not necessarily approving of his profession. For Jesus, Zacchaeus was a lost soul that needed salvation, just like all others. The Lord reached out to him in lovingkindness and compassion, and Zacchaeus responded with a vow to redress past wrongdoing and to have mercy on the less fortunate.

We Christians should follow Jesus' example and be ready and willing to display active love to everyone we encounter, even those who are rejected by society. When God brings into our lives someone who has experienced revulsion or shunning by others, let's be the ones who go against the stream of social refusal and open our arms to welcome them. All of us are merely lost souls who need God's gracious forgiveness, and by offering ourselves to the pariahs of our society, we are extending the loving embrace of our Heavenly Father. By showing respect to the disrespected, by treating with kindness those who have experienced maltreatment, by drawing close to those cast out from their communities, we can demonstrate the true character of the God who is love. And perhaps they will respond positively and receive the spiritual salvation found in Christ and devote themselves to leading lives of righteousness. If so, we will have done our work as missionaries of Jesus.

JESUS ADDRESSES AN INCORRECT EXPECTATION OF THE KINGDOM'S ARRIVAL

[Jesus] proceeded to tell a parable, because he was near to Jerusalem, and because they supposed that the kingdom of God was to appear immediately. (Lk. 19:11)

WHAT JESUS DID:

Jesus had preached a message of the coming of the Kingdom of God and had performed miracles of healing and exorcism to substantiate His claims. His disciples and other followers who heard Him expected God's Kingdom to arrive right away, so Jesus, rather than letting people continue believing incorrectly, told a parable to address this misconception. In Jesus' story, a nobleman gave his servants money *("ten minas"* each or about 30 months in wages for a worker) to use wisely as he left for a foreign country, and on his return, he called each one into account. Jesus' point was to explain that before the Kingdom would arrive, work had to be done by those who served Him, using the resources that their Master had given them *(vv. 12-26)*.

WHAT HIS FOLLOWERS ARE TO DO:

We, too, like the Lord, must address incorrect and false beliefs. We must be prepared and active in disavowing wrong ideas regarding God, Jesus, and, as the Scripture quoted above shows, about the coming of the King to rule over all. This requires that we be well-versed in the life and teachings of the Lord (which means we have to spend time in study of and meditation on the Holy Word) so that we have a clear understanding of His mission and His message.

Let's not allow the dissemination of false preaching to go unchallenged. When we hear something spoken which we know is an incorrect portrayal of our faith, we must confront it and explain the truth clearly and succinctly. Jesus showed us the importance of maintaining a right understanding of God and His Kingdom, and we need to do our best to uphold all that He taught us.

JESUS SENDS FOR A DONKEY COLT

[Jesus] said to [two of his disciples], "Go into the village in front of you, and immediately as you enter it you will find a colt tied, on which no one has ever sat. Untie it and bring it. (Mk. 11:2)

WHAT JESUS DID:

Drawing near to Jerusalem, Jesus was about to begin His final days on earth. All His life had led to this moment; this was the start of the completion of His mission. So, at the Mount of Olives, to fulfill the Scripture that describes the King riding on a donkey into the holy city *(Zech. 9:9)*, Jesus sent His disciples to commandeer a never-ridden colt so that He could enter Jerusalem as a triumphant king. In anticipation of the beast's owners' questioning what the disciples were doing and to assuage the owners' understandable apprehension, Jesus instructed His disciples to tell them that the Lord needed it and would return it right away. *(vv. 1-3)*

A simple lesson that we who follow Jesus can learn from these verses is that we should also encourage other Christians to use their resources to spread the gospel and to bring about God's righteous kingdom. (Of course, all of this applies to us ourselves as well.) Jesus requested support from others in order to accomplish His goal of bringing about our salvation and ushering in the Kingdom of Heaven. We Christian believers also have a mission given to us by Jesus to spread His gospel of God's mercy and forgiveness, and that takes giving of our time, talent, and treasure to accomplish.

So, though it might be somewhat difficult to ask others for material support of the ministry, we should follow the lead of Jesus and not be ashamed or intimidated to do so. Rather, when a need arises and we or some people we know have the assets to meet that need, or even in making a general request for assistance and provision to the body of Christ at large, we ought not hesitate to ask for help in doing God's work. The basis of our appeal should always be that the Lord has need of it along with the promise of the return of immediate blessing for all we invest for the Kingdom.

JESUS' TRIUMPHAL ENTRY

And they brought the colt to Jesus and threw their cloaks on it, and he sat on it. (Mk. 11:7)

WHAT JESUS DID:

Jesus entered Jerusalem triumphantly but humbly. He did not come in a pretentious fashion on a white stallion proclaiming Himself as king. Rather, He rode the colt of a donkey – small, lowly, and unassuming ... hardly a splendid display of power or self-aggrandizement. Nonetheless, the people received Jesus joyously, laying their cloaks and leafy branches on the road before Him, and welcomed Him with cries of blessing for the one who had come in the LORD's name and with shouts of supplication for salvation. *(vv. 7-9)*

<u>WHAT HIS FOLLOWERS ARE TO DO:</u>

As we look to Jesus for guidance in our own lives today, let's see that He did not puff Himself up arrogantly or try to impress others with exhibitions of magnificence. Though the crowd praised Him, He remained unpretentious in His demeanor. Thus, we Christians should also seek to maintain an attitude of humility even in our moments of triumph. Let us resist the temptation of the prideful desire to be applauded or to be honored for our accomplishments. The meekness of Christ should ever be our mien.

JESUS REFUSES TO RESTRAIN THE PRAISE OF HIS DISCIPLES

And some of the Pharisees in the crowd said to [Jesus],
"Teacher, rebuke your disciples." (Lk. 19:39)

<u>WHAT JESUS DID:</u>

As Jesus drew near to Jerusalem, His disciples praised God and welcomed Jesus with loud shouts and enthusiastic voices as the King who had come in the LORD's name. In reaction, the religionists told Jesus to reprimand His disciples for their display of such intense emotion and their words of worshipful, messianic exclamation. But Jesus refused to restrain the disciples, for if humans did not offer praise, the walls of Jerusalem and perhaps even nature itself would. *(vv. 37-40)*

WHAT HIS FOLLOWERS ARE TO DO:

Believers around the world choose to worship in a variety of ways. Some show their reverence with silent prayer, while others engage in lively song. Some bow their heads and close their eyes, while others lift their hands and shout out acclamations of praise. Let's follow Jesus' example and not criticize or restrict anyone in their particular form of adoration as long as it is in keeping with the clear teaching of the Scriptures. It is between individuals and God how they choose to acknowledge and worship Him.

JESUS WEEPS OVER JERUSALEM

And when [Jesus] drew near and saw the city, he wept over it … (Lk. 19:41)

WHAT JESUS DID:

As Jesus rode in triumphant procession toward Jerusalem, the holy city came more clearly into view. Jesus knew of the destruction of the city that would happen in the near future and the loss of life that would occur, all preventable had the people repented of their sinful ways and embraced the arrival of the King of the peaceful Kingdom of God *(v. 42)*. In response to this heavy awareness of the terrifying, pending calamity that faced Jerusalem, Jesus broke down and cried.

WHAT HIS FOLLOWERS ARE TO DO:

We who follow Jesus should not be cold, indifferent, or calloused to what is happening in the world around us. When tragedy strikes, let us feel deeply for those affected and allow those strong emotions to move us into action to provide help and alleviate suffering. We can all be so caught up in our own lives that we have no time or no room for empathy toward others undergoing extreme hardship. But that is not the way of our Lord. He was constantly moved by compassion to do what was necessary to relieve pain, to resolve difficulties, and to restore wellbeing. That is what Jesus did, so that is also what we should do.

JESUS LOOKS AROUND THE TEMPLE

*And [Jesus] entered Jerusalem and went into the temple. And
when he had looked around at everything, as it was already late,
he went out to Bethany with the twelve. (Mk. 11:11)*

WHAT JESUS DID:

Upon entering Jerusalem, Jesus went directly to the Temple. He saw what was happening there, especially the money being exchanged, and while the scene must have angered Him greatly, He did not act rashly or impetuously but left for nearby Bethany with His apostles. Jesus certainly must have been planning what He was going to do on the next day when He once again would come back to the Temple.

WHAT HIS FOLLOWERS ARE TO DO:

Following Jesus' lead here, though there are times when immediate and swift engagement is demanded, there are also other occasions when it is wiser to carefully and prayerfully plan a course of action. In those latter cases, we should not rush headlong into a situation in a reckless attempt to ameliorate or rectify it; instead, we need to peruse circumstances and wisely consider how best to address whatever is before us.

Rely on God moment-by-moment? Definitely yes. But let's not behave impulsively or react in unrighteous anger to something. We must seek God's wisdom and His timing in all that we do. Godly planning is an essential part of our Christian life today just as it was for Jesus.

JESUS CURSES A FIG TREE

*On the following day, when they came from
Bethany, [Jesus] was hungry. (Mk. 11:12)*

WHAT JESUS DID:

Having spent the night in the neighboring village of Bethany and now headed back into Jerusalem, Jesus felt hungry, so He went to a leafy fig tree but could find no fruit because it was not the right season for figs. Reacting to this, within the hearing of His disciples, Jesus pronounced a "curse" (as it is later called in *v. 21b*) on the tree that it would never again bear fruit. *(vv. 13-14)*

Why would Jesus curse a fig tree and cause it to wither and die because it did not have any fruit despite not being the right season? We might consider the fig tree as a representation of the nation of Israel, and its cursing was a symbolic way of showing God's judgment of the Jewish people due to their rejection of Jesus as Messiah. But there might also be another way of viewing Jesus' action.

Perhaps Jesus was using this incident to teach His puzzled disciples about faith, for in the verses that follow, when Peter expressed amazement at this miracle, Jesus explained that faith can make even mountains move *(vv. 20-25)*. Thus, the shriveling and death of the tree was meant by the Lord as an object lesson to the still-unbelieving and slow-to-understand disciples of the power of faith.

WHAT HIS FOLLOWERS ARE TO DO:

Let's seek to emulate Jesus by acting in faith at all times, expecting the miraculous to occur while ever trusting in God's perfect plan. With even the smallest amount of faith, like the size of a tiny mustard seed, we can remove huge obstacles of hatred and injustice and heal people of their despair and anger. As we call upon the Lord and take action in faith to address the many challenges in our lives, the extraordinary can happen through God's almighty Spirit. And when that does take place, we should use it as a way to teach others around us about the enormous value of faith, even as Jesus did.

JESUS "CLEANSES" THE TEMPLE

And Jesus entered the temple and drove out all who sold and bought in the temple, and he overturned the tables of the money-changers and the seats of those who sold pigeons. (Mt. 21:12)

WHAT JESUS DID:

(Note: John's gospel places this event early in Jesus' ministry [Jn. 2]. The synoptics record this as happening during the last week of His life [Mt. 21; Mk. 11; Lk. 19]. Some commentators see these as two separate occurrences.)

The sacrifice of animals, such as sheep or pigeons (for those who couldn't afford a sheep), was constantly being performed in the Temple.

According to the Mosaic Law, the animal had to be without any defect or blemish (*Exod. 12:5; Lev. 1:10*), so worshippers, especially those traveling from afar and unable to bring any sacrificial animals with them, were obligated to purchase unblemished animals to offer up a religiously acceptable sacrifice. However, they could not use the Roman coins commonly in circulation to buy these animals because Roman currency bore the likeness of the Emperor, which, for religiously strict Jews, was a transgression of the commandment to not make any carved image (*Exod. 20:4*). Therefore, Roman coins needed to be exchanged for Temple coins, with interest, a slick and convenient way for the Temple's ruling elite to maintain control and make a healthy profit.

Jesus reacted in righteous anger to this practice and perhaps to the deep-rooted corruption of the entire system under the command of powerful religious elites, upset that His Father's house had been turned away from its real purpose as a place of worship, prayer, and comfort, and had become instead a business-oriented operation. Quoting *Isa. 56:7*, which describes God's Temple as a house of prayer, Jesus forcefully condemned the place of unscrupulous commerce that it had become. Thus, Jesus' zeal moved Him to act, and He drove out the animals and the currency-changers (*John 2:15* says with a whip of cords) and toppled the tables of money. Having "cleansed" the area by expelling those with unrighteous motives, Jesus then restored the Temple to its rightful intent by healing those in need. (*Mt. 21:13-14*)

In the evening, Jesus left Jerusalem and returned to nearby Bethany to spend the night (*v. 17*).

Jesus was zealous when it came to the things of God. He vigorously exalted His Father in all that He did and said, and He ardently opposed that which was against His Father's will. Let us Christ-followers devote ourselves with the same fervor and passion as we do our God-ordained work. We should dedicate ourselves to leading lives of righteousness and compassion, even in our everyday activities. And we must also stand firmly against all that is not in keeping with the character of our Heavenly Father's holy nature of justice, integrity, and lovingkindness. If we become aware of that which is contrary to the true God, we must not be silent but must take an active stand against it, including against so-called Christian ministries that are merely a religious front for the accumulation of material wealth and the support of an extravagant life-style – those who might be seen as today's money-changers.

Having said that, let us also vow to eschew extreme forms of violence and fanaticism. Yes, Jesus overturned tables and drove people out of the Temple, but He did not actually injure anyone in the process. We too must not seek to inflict bodily harm on individuals even for the sake of the gospel. Our clear message, though spoken with boldness, is one of mercy, forgiveness, peace, and love.

One final point: While we are called to oppose evil and wrongdoing, we must also seek to bring about restoration. It is not enough just to tear down and block that which is wicked; we have to build up and create access to that which is good, as well. Our mission is as sure as our message: to bring healing and hope in Christ to a needy world.

JESUS' AUTHORITY IS CHALLENGED

And [Jesus and His disciples] came again to Jerusalem. And as [Jesus] was walking in the temple, the chief priests and the scribes and the elders came to him ... (Mk. 11:27)

WHAT JESUS DID:

The opposition Jesus faced throughout His ministry was primarily from religious figures, and this again was the case as He reentered Jerusalem to teach and to preach His message of the Kingdom of God. Having condemned the unrighteous practices in the Temple the day before, He was challenged by the religious elites as to His authority to perform such dramatic actions *(v. 28)*. Jesus was not taken by surprise by their question; He seemed to have anticipated it and was ready with a response.

Jesus said He would answer them if they first replied to His question of what they thought about John the Baptist. This posed a serious dilemma for the religionists, and they contemplated their possible answers: If they said John was sent by God, Jesus would ask them why they hadn't submitted to his baptism, but if they said John did not have the spiritual authority to preach his message, the people would denounce them. Having considered their options, neither of which was good, they refused to reply, so Jesus also did not answer their initial question. *(vv. 29-33)*

WHAT HIS FOLLOWERS ARE TO DO:

Jesus was well-prepared for this test and was thus able to quiet His detractors. We, too, should be ready to counter opposition from those who question our beliefs and actions. Just as in Jesus' time, disapproval of our ministries may indeed come from ostensibly religious sources.

If we are in God's will and guided by His word and Spirit, we can speak and act with His authority and thus be strong in our convictions as we react to confrontations about what we say and do. We need to think about what kind of questions and challenges will be made against us and develop appropriate responses. Yes, we should trust God to give us the right words at any given time *(see Mt. 10:19 for a related promise)*, but we ought to also anticipate certain scenarios and be prepared to respond in truth and in love. And if we do have clear, concise answers inspired by the Holy Spirit of God, they will silence our critics, just as Jesus did.

JESUS THWARTS ENTRAPMENT CONCERNING CAESAR'S TAXES

Then the Pharisees went and plotted how to entangle [Jesus] in his words. (Mt. 22:15)

WHAT JESUS DID:

Jesus had been teaching using parables, and the religionists understood that some of the parables were directed against them and their arrogance and their spiritual ignorance *(Mt.21:28-22:14)*. So, the Pharisees and supporters of Herod conspired and set a kind of verbal trap for Him. But first, they sought to butter

Jesus up with false flattery as bait for the trap, dishonestly praising His godly teaching and His determined commitment to truth. Then, the trap was set: They asked Him whether it was right to pay taxes to the Roman Emperor. *(vv. 16-17)*

Jesus was quite cognizant of their motives, as the different gospel accounts clearly express: *"aware of their malice" (Mt. 22:18)*; *"knowing their hypocrisy" (Mk. 12:15)*; *"perceived their craftiness (Lk. 20:23)*. Jesus, as we have seen previously, seemed to have been prepared for this question and had a ready answer: He noted that Caesar's image was displayed on Roman coins, therefore, one should give to Caesar that which belonged to him but to give to God that which was His. Jesus' detractors were confounded. He had evaded their sly trap, so they could do nothing more but leave. *(vv. 18-22)*

WHAT HIS FOLLOWERS ARE TO DO:

What can be learned from Jesus' actions in this exchange? First, as stated in earlier segments, we will face opposition to our mission for Christ, just as He did, so we have to be aware of those around us who will actively seek to disprove or discredit His message. Jesus put it so well when He told His disciples to be *"wise as serpents but innocent as doves" (Mt. 10:16)*. As followers of Jesus, we must lovingly and guilelessly reach out to all, but we also need to be on guard against those who seem bent on trying to subvert the gospel.

Additionally, as explained before, we must be prepared to respond well to challenges that will be made against the teachings of Jesus. Jesus certainly knew that He would be questioned about paying taxes to Rome since it was a topic of heated debate at that time, so He had a ready answer. We Christians can also think of specific issues – such as evolution, abortion, gender and sexuality, and warfare – that we might anticipate will come up in our interactions with nonbelievers. Let's study, then, and be prepared to give a sound defense of what we believe.

Finally, we should never succumb to honey-dripping words of flattery. We all love to have our egos stroked, but we must not allow praise and acclamation to distract us from leading lives of righteousness and integrity. As I have said before, this is not a call to never accept a compliment or a commendation for work well-done. The point is not to let the praise of people become our motivation or objective rather than the approval of our Heavenly Father.

There will be traps set for us and for our ministry, just as there were for the Lord Jesus. Let's do our best to be ready for those snares so that we are not caught in them.

JESUS AFFIRMS THE GREATEST COMMANDMENTS

And one of the scribes came up and... asked [Jesus], "Which commandment is the most important of all?" (Mk. 12:28)

WHAT JESUS DID:

A scribe, whose job it was to make meticulous copies of the Sacred Writ, was impressed by Jesus' interaction with the religious leaders, so he asked Jesus to name the most important commandment. In response, Jesus fell back on the fundamental teaching of the *Torah*, quoting well-known verses from *Deut. 6:4-5* and *Lev. 19:18b* to love God and to love other people. Jesus was thoroughly Jewish and remained Jewish throughout His life, thus Jewish Scriptures were His lifeblood. By citing these verses from Holy Scripture, Jesus was affirming these two commandments as being the greatest of all and a kind of summation of the entire Law. *(vv. 28-31)*

Then, when the man responded well to Jesus' reply by stating that he agreed that loving God and loving others were even greater than offering animal sacrifices, Jesus commended him for being very close to the Kingdom of God *(Mk. 12:32-34a)*, i.e., that the man's understanding would lead him on a clear path to the rule of God in his life and would ultimately give him access to the heavenly realm.

After that exchange, so impressed were the religious leaders at Jesus' answers that they asked Him no more questions *(v. 34b)*.

WHAT HIS FOLLOWERS ARE TO DO:

When asked what we as Christians believe to be the truth, let's follow Jesus and base our answers on what is clearly taught in the Scriptures. We should not respond with our own theories or notions, nor should we focus on the minutiae of biblical doctrine; rather, we ought to lean on the foundational precepts of Holy Writ and its presentation of the simple, most clear-cut teachings of Jesus. To do so will oblige us to be well-versed in Scripture, which will require some dedication to study and meditation on God's word. When we are equipped with such knowledge, we will be able to respond correctly to questions about our faith and lifestyle.

Also, when those we teach or mentor display a good grasp of spiritual truth, we should, like Christ before us, commend them and encourage them to keep advancing in the Kingship of God over their lives.

JESUS QUESTIONS THE PHARISEES ABOUT THE CHRIST

Now while the Pharisees were gathered together, Jesus asked them a question, saying, "What do you think about the Christ? Whose son is he?" (Mt. 22:41-42a)

WHAT JESUS DID:

The religious leaders had been constantly asking Jesus questions, often in unsuccessful attempts to trap Him in some kind of incorrect teaching or to induce Him to making some heretical statement or to expose Him as an incapable teacher. Now, Jesus turned the tables on these hypocrites and asked them questions of His own.

First, He asked them what they thought about Christ (the Greek word for the Hebrew term *"Messiah"*) and whose son He is. When they responded that He was David's son, Jesus pressed them with a deeper question: If Christ was the Son of David, why did David call Him Lord (as is written in *Psalm 110:1*)? Jesus' point was that the Messiah, while of the Davidic line and therefore his son, was greater than King David and was in fact affirmed by God to be his Lord. Unable to muster an adequate reply, these religionists once again asked Him no further questions. *(Mt. 22:42b-46)*

WHAT HIS FOLLOWERS ARE TO DO:

As stated previously when discussing earlier incidents in Jesus' life, sometimes we need to go on the offensive against those who openly disparage our beliefs and ways of life. If we sheepishly just allow our spiritual opponents to continually bully us with their critical remarks, our failure to respond will be seen as a sign of weakness, and the attacks will only intensify. We are to follow Christ in an attitude of meekness in terms of our conduct, but when it comes to defending our faith, we need to be vigilant and strong, just as Jesus was, and at times we must confront our detractors with God's truth and reasoning.

So, let us learn from Jesus that, if we want to stop the criticism being continually directed at us, on occasion we must not merely defend our ideas but also strike at the false understanding held by others. Beyond that, we ought to be able to clearly explain who we are, what we do, how we think … and why. This may help those who belittle us to know us better and perhaps even to soften their antagonism to the message of Jesus and, God willing, to receive the good news of our Heavenly Father's love and forgiveness.

JESUS WARNS OF RELIGIOUS HYPOCRISY

[Jesus said]: "The scribes and the Pharisees sit on Moses' seat,
so do and observe whatever they tell you, but not the works they
do. For they preach, but do not practice." (Mt. 23:2-3)

WHAT JESUS DID:

Jesus had previously on several occasions warned those who followed Him about the hypocrisy of the religious leaders, and He did so once more here, indicating that it was an important issue that needed to be addressed again. These scriptural scribes and members of the Pharisaical branch of Judaism taught adherence to the Mosaic Law while they themselves did not uphold it. Jesus acknowledged their positions of respect but also rebuked them and told His disciples and the others around Him to heed their teaching on the *Torah* but not to imitate their unrighteous and hypocritical behavior.

WHAT HIS FOLLOWERS ARE TO DO:

Jesus cautions us today as well to beware of hypocrisy, whether in our own lives or in the lives of others. As we are led to make disciples, we must take daily stock that our words and deeds are in line with what we believe and what we openly preach. If there is an obvious discrepancy between what we say and what we do, we have become the hypocrites that Jesus warned of, and we either need to change our ways or stop teaching and mentoring.

Let us also be bold in pointing out any hypocrisy among the leaders of the Church. We are to hold them to high standards of speech and conduct because they are the more visible representatives of Christ on earth. If there is blatant inconsistency between their words/message and their actions/lifestyle, we must, as Jesus did, denounce their hypocrisy and encourage others not to emulate their behavior.

JESUS AND THE POOR WIDOW'S OFFERING

And [Jesus] sat down opposite the treasury and watched the
people putting money into the offering box. (Mk. 12:41a)

WHAT JESUS DID:

Jesus was in the Temple in Jerusalem close to the treasury where the funds for the maintenance and operations of the Temple were kept. This money came from both taxes and voluntary contributions. Nearby was an offering box into which people – both rich and poor – could make donations for the Temple, and Jesus observed what they put in. Thus, He was aware of how much each person was giving, some wealthy ones offering a great deal more than the tiny amount of an impoverished widow. Jesus then used what He had seen to teach His disciples the importance of sacrificial giving, explaining that the rich had given from their abundance while the widow had given from her poverty. *(vv. 41-44)*

WHAT HIS FOLLOWERS ARE TO DO:

Do Jesus' actions here mean that we should keep an eye on how much people give for the support of the ministry and mission of Christ? Well, perhaps. First, however, we must remember the clear teaching of Jesus to give in secret so that we are seen only by our Father in Heaven and for His approval alone and not for the applause of others *(Mt.6:1-4)*. Note that in this incident at the treasury, Jesus did not openly praise the widow as she dropped in her donation, nor did He deride the rich on the spot for what they gave. It was not until after the gifts had been given, and presumably the givers had left the area, that Jesus spoke to His disciples. His purpose, thus, was not so much to focus on the givers but rather to teach about sacrificial giving.

So, how do we apply what Jesus did? From a fiscal standpoint, there is certainly a requirement in any ministry to know where the funding comes from, and that would include how much each individual contributor is giving. This is not so that we can single out certain donors for their magnanimity or others for their lack of generosity, as that would go against the principle of giving in secret and might encourage unrighteous pride or produce human-induced guilt; instead, as good stewards of all with which the Lord has blessed us, our purpose should be to maintain oversight and accountability and to facilitate prudent distribution of resources and judicious planning for the future.

We should also exhort our brothers and sisters in Christ (and ourselves as well) to maintain an ongoing commitment to share, even sacrificially, what we have been given by God to provide for the needs of others. Our hands and our wallets are to be open so that they can be used by the Lord as He leads. Jesus spoke often about the wise and godly use of money, and we who follow Him need to pay careful attention to His teaching and to His actions regarding it.

JESUS IS TROUBLED WITHIN HIS SOUL

[Some Greeks] came to Philip ... and asked him, "Sir, we wish to see Jesus." (Jn. 12:21)

WHAT JESUS DID:

We are not sure why these "Greeks" (Greek-speaking Jews in Jerusalem for Passover) wanted to meet with the Lord, but the disciples Phillip and Andrew conveyed their request to Jesus *(v. 22)*. However, having come so far, Jesus did not want to be distracted from the mission which His Father in Heaven had sent Him to fulfill. Jesus knew He would be here on earth for only a few more days, so rather than entertaining the Greeks' request for an audience, He began explaining to His disciples the great significance of the time they were entering. When He, the Son of Man, would receive His honor and glory *(v. 23)*.

WHAT HIS FOLLOWERS ARE TO DO:

We Christ-followers must also discern occasions when we need to focus solely on our God-given ministry and not be preoccupied by other things going on in our lives. Of course, this does not mean that we can neglect our essential responsibilities related to family, work, or community (though, seemingly, these are duties which Jesus during His time of ministry did not share); yet, we must give priority to our spiritual mission. We are all allotted a certain number of days, months, and years in our earthly lives, and we must be prudent in how we use that time, just as Jesus was.

> *"Now is my soul troubled. And what shall I say? 'Father, save me from this hour'? But for this purpose I have come to this hour."* (Jn. 12:27)

WHAT JESUS DID:

Jesus had put His trust totally in the providence of His Heavenly Father, but He could clearly see what lay ahead of Him – a time of intense trial and suffering., and this caused Him real distress. Yet, He understood that He had been sent by God to complete a mission of sacrifice, one that He had willingly accepted. Now that the time had come for Him to lay down His life, He would not refuse it and seek to be spared.

However, He was still in turmoil and shaken by the looming specter of agony and death. So, Jesus openly shared with those close to Him what He was feeling deep within His very being. He bared His soul to them, possibly to ease His burden and to help them understand what He was going through.

<u>WHAT HIS FOLLOWERS ARE TO DO</u>:

Do we trust God only during times of comfort, success, and happiness? If we say we are always in our Father's hands, that means also during hardship, failure, and dejection, and as Jesus did, we should acknowledge and accept that which God brings into our lives. This doesn't mean that we will never be worried, disheartened, sad, or afraid; these are normal human reactions to tough and tragic situations. Nor is this a kind of fatalism or passive tolerance of every bad thing that happens to us. We need to strongly oppose wrongdoing and work for what is good and right. It is, rather, a continued faith in our loving Heavenly Father even as we experience difficult circumstances and an abiding belief in His perfect plans.

But when we do experience serious trouble in our souls and spirits, let's not close down or shut up; instead, we should be transparent and open in our feelings. This will let others know what is causing our distress, and by sharing, it will perhaps help to alleviate our anguish and to get us through it. Being honest in this way can also allow others to support us in carrying our emotional load and maybe bring us into a closer relationship with them.

When Jesus had said these things, he departed and hid himself from them. Though he had done so many signs before them, they still did not believe in him. (Jn. 12:36b-37)

<u>WHAT JESUS DID</u>:

Jesus was discouraged by the lack of response to His message despite all the miraculous signs He had performed. To deal with the disappointment, He temporarily withdrew from everyone, even hiding from them, most likely for prayer and for baring His soul before God. Once encouraged and reenergized by spending time with His Heavenly Father, Jesus returned to the public realm to complete the divine task which He had been given *(v. 44ff)*.

<u>WHAT HIS FOLLOWERS ARE TO DO</u>:

When we get disheartened by the lack of fruit in our ministry or maybe even in our own lives, let's follow the example of Jesus and retreat to the intimate presence of God for a time of inspiration and strengthening. As we express our heartfelt emotions to the Lord God and our need for Him, He will refill our drained souls and recharge our depleted spiritual batteries so that we, like Jesus, can reemerge to do our sacred work of sharing the gospel.

JESUS PREDICTS THE DESTRUCTION
OF THE TEMPLE

And as [Jesus] came out of the temple, one of his disciples
said to him, "Look, Teacher, what wonderful stones
and what wonderful buildings!" (Mk. 13:1)

WHAT JESUS DID:

The disciple was apparently in awe of the grandeur of the magnificent Temple buildings built by King Herod and expressed their wonderment to their Rabbi. Jesus, however, had a different point of view and began to describe in detail the structures' ultimate demolition *(v. 2)*, which eventually occurred under the Romans in 70 CE. This did not mean that Jesus had no appreciation of beauty; He admired and spoke affectionately of the splendor of the natural world (e.g., *Lk. 12:27*). Rather, He wanted to warn His disciples about placing too much value on physical, temporal things that would eventually be gone. His constant desire was that they focus on that which is spiritual and eternal.

WHAT HIS FOLLOWERS ARE TO DO:

Let us who call Jesus Lord seek to develop His perspective about material things versus the things of the spirit. The former is temporary and will, in time, disappear, like everything in this earthly life; the latter will exist without end in the heavenly realm. Let us prize and strive after the things of God far above things made by people. Yet, as in Jesus' case, this does not require us to disregard or disparage the loveliness that we see in our world, whether natural or made by humans. Instead, while acknowledging beauty, we should remember that it is fleeting, and thus we ought to value more highly and endeavor to attain with greater determination that which will last forever.

Once we ourselves have the mind of Christ regarding the impermanence of worldly things, we will be able to teach and mentor others as well to develop an eternal viewpoint rather than a temporal one. Let us, as Jesus demonstrated in His own life, always remain devoted to the Heavenly Kingdom and to godly righteousness over and above the kingdoms and things of this earth.

JESUS DESCRIBES THE END OF THE AGE

As [Jesus] sat on the Mount of Olives, the disciples came to him
privately, saying, "Tell us, when will these things be, and what will be
the sign of your coming and of the end of the age?" (Mt. 24:3)

WHAT JESUS DID:

Jesus had foretold the coming destruction of the Temple, and as they settled in for the night on the Mount of Olives, the disciples wanted to know when this would occur and more than that, when the end times would happen. Jesus did not ignore their question or tell them not to worry about the future events and rather focus on the problems they were facing today. No, He did not want them to be deceived or misled *(v. 4)*, so He addressed their question with a rather lengthy discourse (two full chapters in Matthew's gospel, *Chs. 24-25*) describing the signs preceding the end of the age and the events that would culminate in the arrival of the cosmic figure *"the Son of Man"* and the final judgment.

WHAT HIS FOLLOWERS ARE TO DO:

Following Jesus, we too cannot ignore eschatological questions about the ultimate destiny of our world and humanity. We should seek to know and understand the Scriptural depiction of what lies ahead for us. Jesus described general signals that would indicate the proximity of the last days, so I believe it is valid for us to look at the events in our world today to see how they might play a role in the end times.

Yet, having said that, let me offer a couple of caveats. First, we need to remember well that no one knows the exact time when the Son of Man will arrive, not even Jesus, but only the Father in Heaven *(Mt. 24:36)*. Believers throughout the centuries since the time of Christ have predicted the specific date of His return … all woefully incorrect.

Also, let's not allow a preoccupation with the end of the world to subvert our mission of bringing the message and love of Jesus to the world in the here and now. Yes, we need to be aware of the Lord's life and the entirety of His teachings, including those about the last days, but our focus should be on growing in our relationship with God, yielding to the guidance of His Holy Spirit, and leading lives of righteousness and compassion so that we can minister to the countless needs of the world around us – feeding the hungry, giving drink to the thirsty, welcoming the stranger, clothing the naked, visiting the sick or imprisoned – for in doing so, we are ministering as to Christ *(Mt. 25:31-46)*.

JESUS ONCE MORE TELLS OF
HIS IMMINENT DEATH

*[Jesus said]: "You know that after two days the Passover is coming, and
the Son of Man will be delivered up to be crucified." (Mt. 26:2)*

WHAT JESUS DID:

As He had done several times before, Jesus once again spoke of his impending
death. There had been resistance among His disciples to the idea that Jesus
would be taken from them, so apparently to continue to disavow His followers
of their misguided belief, Jesus not only told them He would soon die but
also how it would occur – through the ignominious and torturous ordeal of
crucifixion.

WHAT HIS FOLLOWERS ARE TO DO:

As mortal beings, we need to accept the indisputable fact that all our lives,
without exception, end in the same way: We all die. To paraphrase a popular
saying, no one gets out alive. As hard as it may be, we must, as Jesus did,
remind our loved ones that we will not always be with them, nor they with us.
That is the way of life, and we must embrace it.

I'm not encouraging a morbid obsession with death but a healthy
recognition of the impermanent nature of our flesh. Will that help to assuage
the grief of the loss of a loved one? Perhaps not. Yet, it is the truth, and denial
only tends to prolong anguish. So, like Christ, let's neither hide nor avoid
addressing the reality of death. We must be open and forthcoming about it,
especially with those close to us. Our time will come, and we must trust that
we are ever in the good and providential hands of our Heavenly Father.

JESUS' PRE-BURIAL ANOINTING IN BETHANY

*It was now two days before the Passover ... And while [Jesus] was at
Bethany in the house of Simon the leper, as he was reclining at table, a
woman came with an alabaster flask of ointment of pure nard, very costly,
and she broke the flask and poured it over his head. (Mk. 14:1a, 3)*

WHAT JESUS DID:

(Note: John's gospel, Ch. 12, puts this event six days before the feast of Passover as Jesus was moving ever closer to Jerusalem. In John's account, it presumably takes place in the home of Lazarus and his sisters, Martha and Mary; the woman is identified as Mary; and she anoints Jesus' feet. Mark's and Matthew's telling of this incident, Chs. 14 and 26, respectively, seem to differ somewhat from John's in time, place, participants, and manner, though some commentators harmonize the three gospel stories.)

Jesus was in the village of Bethany, on the outskirts of the capital city. A woman honored Jesus as a special guest by pouring a flask of nard, an aromatic and expensive ointment made from a flowering plant, on His head as a way of showing great respect.

However, some disciples who witnessed this became upset and angry at what they deemed to be a waste of resources which could have been used to help the less fortunate *(v. 4-5a)*. Though their motives may have been good, they nonetheless openly reprimanded the woman *(v. 5b)*, and that is when Jesus stepped in, questioning their response and defending the woman for her beautiful act of devotion *(v. 6)*. They could always help the poor, but He wouldn't always be with them *(v. 7)*. Jesus further explained that her action was an anointing in preparation for His burial, and that she would be remembered as this story spread with the gospel *(vv. 8-9)*

It is unfortunately common in Christian circles to hear criticism of others who are seeking to serve the Lord in a way that some holier-than-thou individuals disagree with. Fault is found in how they live for Christ and carry out their ministry in His name. But let's follow the Lord's lead when it comes to the methods that others use in service to God, first by refraining from being so critical of any Christian ministry that may be different from the way we might like, and also by not allowing others to engage in that kind of malicious censure.

Everyone serves the Lord in his or her own way, led by the Holy Spirit, and as long as it does not blatantly contradict His clear teaching, we do not have the right to disparage how others dedicate themselves to Jesus. Thus, we must step up when we hear Christians bad-mouthing the work of fellow believers, strongly oppose such un-Christlike attitudes and behavior, and come to the defense of any true servant of God. Perhaps the way they demonstrate their love for Jesus and the way they are involved in ministry are not particularly our way; however, let's stop being so judgmental of how they serve the Lord.

Jesus challenged those who publicly disapproved of one person's form of dedication to Him and spoke up in her defense, and we should learn from this.

JESUS SENDS APOSTLES TO PREPARE FOR PASSOVER

Now on the first day of Unleavened Bread the disciples came to Jesus, saying, "Where will you have us prepare for you to eat the Passover?" (Mt. 26:17)

WHAT JESUS DID:

In response to the disciples' question, Jesus instructed them to go into Jerusalem and tell an unnamed someone that Jesus would be celebrating Passover at his home. The disciples did just as they were told and made preparations for the holy feast day. More details of this incident are given in Mark's and Luke's accounts: The disciples are to follow a man carrying a water jar who will lead them to the right house; also, the room in which they are to prepare the meal is a large, furnished guest room in the upper part of the house *(Mk. 14:13-15; Lk. 22:10-12).*

As we have seen before, Jesus was thoroughly Jewish and therefore kept the religious festivals prescribed in the *Torah*, even up until His death. Additionally, Jesus made use of the resources of His disciples: The man who apparently owned the home with the upper guest room was most likely a follower of Jesus because he would accept the request of his *"Teacher"* to celebrate Passover there.

WHAT HIS FOLLOWERS ARE TO DO:

I think there is something to be said for Christians to observe religious commemorations as part of the calendar year. While not encouraging the distorted, commercialized versions of such holidays as Christmas and Easter, I believe that designating special "holy days" to remember and celebrate has the valuable effect of reminding us of Jesus. The dates, of course, do not necessarily reflect when the events actually happened; however, it is not the specific timing that we honor but the One in whose life they occurred.

From the actions of Jesus in utilizing the room of one of His disciples, we can also see the importance of encouraging His followers today to use their assets for the work of spreading the gospel. When believers have the wherewithal to fund or provide for a particular need in sharing Christ's love, we should not be remiss or ashamed in requesting such support. This, naturally, applies to everyone, regardless of our economic or social status. All that we have been blessed with, whether through genetics or material success, must be made available in the service of the Lord, and when called upon, we should willingly and joyfully give of our hearts, our hands, our homes, and our resources.

JESUS' ENDURING LOVE

*Now before the Feast of the Passover, when Jesus knew that his hour
had come to depart out of this world to the Father, having loved his
own who were in the world, he loved them to the end. (Jn. 13:1)*

WHAT JESUS DID:

Jesus knew that He was going to die and go to his Father in Heaven; He knew that He was about to be betrayed by someone He had trusted; He knew that He would be denied by one chosen to lead His church after His death; He knew that He was going to be deserted by those with whom He had spent much time engaged in ministry and who had seen His miraculous works. And yet, His love for them never ceased. He had committed Himself to them, completely and unconditionally, and He would not allow circumstances to change that.

WHAT HIS FOLLOWERS ARE TO DO:

We who follow Jesus need to embrace His total dedication to caring for those around Him and to devote ourselves, regardless of situations that arise, to continue showing active and often sacrificial love for the persons in our lives. We may be faced with dire hardships; our trust may be abused; some, even those closest to us, might openly reject us; we may give our time and energies to people who ultimately will disparage us and remove themselves from us. Despite all these possibilities, our commitment to loving them must be firm, undeterred, unwavering, not focused on circumstances but on the Christ who showed us the meaning of true love.

JESUS WASHES THE DISCIPLES' FEET

[Jesus] rose from supper. He laid aside his outer garments, and taking a towel, tied it around his waist. (Jn. 13:4)

WHAT JESUS DID:

Nearing the end of His life, Jesus was aware that He had little time left on earth. So, while He and His disciples were sharing their final meal all together, the Master got up to teach them a crucial object lesson. Removing His outer clothing and wrapping a towel around His waist, He filled a basin with water and proceeded to wash the disciples' feet and to wipe them with the towel *(v. 5)*. He did this to all of them, including to one who would deny Him, and to those who would desert Him in His time of need, and even to His betrayer. Thus, He provided for them a valuable lesson in unconditional love, humility, and service.

WHAT HIS FOLLOWERS ARE TO DO:

Explaining His action, Jesus said that He had given them an example that they should follow *(v. 15)*. We who call Jesus Lord, Master, and Teacher need to take this lesson to heart. Jesus came in humility to love and to serve, and we are called to follow His lead and do the same. Let us not see others as less important than ourselves; instead, we ought to humbly consider how we can meet their needs, realizing that it might require sacrifice on our part. And we should extend this sort of lovingkindness even to those who are against us or who betray our trust. These are the ways of Jesus, and with them come His promise that we will be blessed if we walk in them *(v. 17)*.

JESUS OFFERS BREAD TO HIS BETRAYER

After saying these things, Jesus was troubled in his spirit, and testified, "Truly, truly, I say to you, one of you will betray me. (Jn. 13:21)

WHAT JESUS DID:

Jesus shared the startling news with his disciples that one of them would betray Him. When one disciple asked Him – apparently in a whisper – who it was, Jesus told him that it was the one to whom He would give a dipped piece of bread *(vv. 25-26)*. So, as Jesus ate this final meal with all His disciples, in an act of love (for He always acted in love), He took a piece of bread, dipped it in a sauce, and shared it with Judas, the one whom He knew would that night betray Him and deliver Him into the hands of evil men. And later, even as His betrayer kissed Him to identify Him to the arresting soldiers, Jesus called him *"Friend" (Mt. 26:50)*. Jesus displayed in His life and in His words what it truly meant to love one's enemies.

WHAT HIS FOLLOWERS ARE TO DO:

This point may seem repetitious, but it cannot be stressed enough. Quite simply, we are commanded to love everyone, even those who would oppose or deceive or betray us. However, obviously, this is more easily said than done. It is only as we yield our wills to the Spirit of the God who is love that we can hope to show concern and care for our enemies. God's mercy and forgiveness have been extended to us, and we in turn are to reach out to others with that same kind of grace. Jesus did that even to Judas; can we do any less?

JESUS INSTITUTES A MEMORIAL

And [Jesus] took bread, and when he had given thanks, he broke it and gave it to them, saying, "This is my body, which is given for you. Do this in remembrance of me." And likewise the cup after they had eaten, saying, "This cup that is poured out for you is the new covenant in my blood." (Lk. 22:19-20)

WHAT JESUS DID:

At the same meal, Jesus gave His disciples a special way to remember Him and His sacrifice. Using two of the elements of the Passover supper, Jesus took some bread and broke it to symbolize how His body would be broken. He also took a cup of wine as a symbol of His blood which would soon be shed for the forgiveness of sins *(Mt. 26:28)* and of the *"new covenant"* relationship between the Heavenly Father and His children. Jesus thanked God for the bread and wine and gave them to His disciples to eat and drink and share with each other, instructing them to do this as a memorial to Him.

WHAT HIS FOLLOWERS ARE TO DO:

First, obviously, we who follow Jesus are to obey His command to remember Him ritually with bread and wine. However we do this – with little crackers and tiny cups of grape juice or loaves of unleavened bread and actual wine; once a week, month, or year; at home with family, outdoors with other believers, or in a church with members of the body of Christ; whether we call it "Communion" or "The Lord's Table" – the focus is to be on Jesus, His sacrifice and our forgiveness, and the new promise of a restored relationship with God.

Beyond our basic observance of Christ's directive to *"do this in remembrance of me,"* how can we incorporate Jesus' actions at this "last supper" into our lives? I am not going to encourage believers in Jesus to institute new rites or observances, but I think we can apply the way He used the things around Him, such as the elements present at the Seder meal, to remind His disciples of all He did and said.

What I mean is that we can also bring to mind (and encourage other Christians to do so as well) His words and life as we move about and encounter things in our everyday world. Thus, when we view a bird, we might recall Jesus' saying that not even a sparrow alights without the Heavenly Father willing it *(Mt.10:29)*, and let that produce in us feelings of comfort and security; or perhaps seeing a refugee on television can evoke the image of Jesus and His family fleeing from the persecution by a tyrant monarch *(Mt. 2:13)*, and that can generate greater empathy and compassion within us; or if we are experiencing conflict with family members or colleagues, we could recollect how Jesus also faced adversity from people who were close to Him *(Mk. 3:21)*, and that may give us the strength to continue to love them; or when we become discouraged or we fail, we can think about how Jesus seemed disheartened at times by His disciples' lack of understanding and faith, by people rejecting His message, and by opposition from religious leaders, but chose to carry on, and that might help us to do likewise.

So, let's recall and celebrate with bread and wine Jesus' sacrifice by which we have entered into a new relationship with our Father in Heaven. Also, we can use the things we see and touch and what we feel and experience to remember Jesus' life and teachings.

JESUS INFORMS THE APOSTLES OF A LOOMING SATANIC ATTACK

[Jesus said,] "Simon, Simon, behold, Satan demanded to have you, that he might sift you like wheat, but I have prayed for you that your faith may not fail. And when you have turned again, strengthen your brothers. (Lk. 22:31-32)

WHAT JESUS DID:

In a scene reminiscent of *Job 2:1-6*, where Satan was given permission by God to test Job, Jesus here informed Peter and the other apostles (the first reference to *"you"* in the Greek here is plural – *"all of you"*) of the Devil's desire to attack their lives and their trust in Christ.

"Sift like wheat" refers to the way a farmer would remove the external husk, or chaff, surrounding the inner, edible kernel of wheat. This threshing process was accomplished by spreading out the grains on a hard floor and beating them to loosen and separate the husk and the grain. Perhaps Jesus here was implying a separation from Him, but it certainly suggested being subjected to a time of great adversity and trial.

At any rate, Satan had apparently been granted access to Peter and the others by God, and they would temporarily falter as they would soon desert and deny Him. However, Jesus indicated that despite this hellish assault, He had prayed specifically for Peter so that the apostle would return in faith to Him and give renewed vigor to the others to continue in the work of the ministry.

WHAT HIS FOLLOWERS ARE TO DO:

What kind of application can believers in Jesus make from this incident? I first want to say we should in no way freely allow demonic influences to affect those around us, and especially those closest to us. We need to stand and oppose evil with prayer and the power of God's Word, and we must take active measures against that which is anti-God and anti-Christ, steadfastly blocking any attempts to derail the ones in our care from leading lives of faith and righteousness.

However, there is a definite role in life for administering "tough love" as we interact with family, friends, and community. That is, when others, even our kids, make poor choices that do not reflect our own personal beliefs, we should resist our natural tendency to intervene so that they won't have to experience any suffering. But if there is not the danger of permanent physical or emotional damage to themselves or to harm to other people, there are times when we ought to step back and let those we love to go through troubles and feel pain as part of learning difficult life-lessons.

In any case, we must be diligent to lift up in prayer to the Heavenly Father those under our supervision and care, so that even though they may turn away from Him for a season, they may be granted grace to one day repent and return to His welcoming embrace, like the proverbial prodigal *(Lk. 15:11-32)*. Having grown even stronger spiritually, they can encourage others and serve God more faithfully with greater commitment to attend to and provide for those in need.

Jesus allowed Peter and the other apostles to undergo a period of testing, torment, and sorrow but prayed for their restoration. We who follow Jesus need to do the same.

JESUS' TWOFOLD PROMISE: A HELPER AND HIS RETURN

[Jesus said to His disciples]: And I will ask the Father, and he will give you another Helper, to be with you forever, ... I will not leave you as orphans; I will come to you. (Jn. 14:16, 18)

WHAT JESUS DID:

Jesus knew what lay ahead for his disciples, namely, persecution and death. The world would reject the Master, and it would do so to His servants as well. It would be a very tough road for them, one that they could not walk without help. They would feel like children who had lost their parents, all alone to face the challenges of life. So, He made two promises to them to encourage them and to give them hope and strength: first, that He would ask the Heavenly Father to send the Holy Spirit of truth as another helper – besides Himself – to live with them and in them *(v. 17)*, to come alongside them and to assist them on their journey of faith and obedience, to be with them always and to teach them, and to bring to their memories all of Jesus' words *(v. 26)*; and second, that He would never desert them but even after His death would return to them.

Of course, He kept His promises. He did come back from the dead to be with them *(Lk. 24:36)*, and He did give them the Holy Spirit to guide and help them *(Jn.20:22)*. And the good news is that what Jesus promised to His disciples, He also assures to all those who trust in Him *(Mt. 28:19-20)*.

WHAT HIS FOLLOWERS ARE TO DO:

Jesus was aware of the needs of His disciples, so He took specific measures to assure that they would be provided for. We should do the same with those for whom we are responsible, such as our own family members or fellow believers that we are mentoring. When we see hardship or learn of potential difficulties that those close to us face, we must do what we can to alleviate the problems or to make provisions in advance to mitigate any negative effects.

Jesus gave help and guidance through the Holy Spirit and also through His own presence with the disciples, and we can do similarly for the ones God has brought into our lives and has placed in our care. We must be diligent in providing for their spiritual instruction, teaching and leading them in the ways of godliness and righteousness. Of course, this means that we ourselves must be prepared by studying the Scripture and by developing our own relationship with the Lord so we can share God's truth with them and assist in their spiritual growth.

Additionally, we need to remain present, both physically and emotionally, for those who depend on us. We must never abandon them! We should dedicate ourselves to staying involved as active participants in their lives, to be there for them whenever we are needed. Beyond our relatives or those we mentor, we can engage in a "ministry of presence" with friends, neighbors, colleagues, other church members, acquaintances, and even strangers in need. Sometimes, simply by being with people and spending time with them, especially those who feel lonely, neglected, or deserted, can provide encouragement and the strength to carry on.

And just as Jesus did, let's keep our promises. When we say we are going to do something, we must commit ourselves to making sure that it happens. Others will be counting on us, and we must not let them down.

JESUS PRAYS FOR HIS FOLLOWERS

When Jesus had spoken these words, he lifted up his eyes to heaven, and said, "Father, the hour has come ..." (Jn. 17:1a)

WHAT JESUS DID:

Jesus constantly prayed, communicating with His Father in Heaven. Now nearing the end of His life, Jesus offered up a prayer, recorded only in *John's* gospel, which included expressions of His desire for the sanctity and unity of His followers.

Jesus would soon be taken away from the ones He had chosen as His apostles, so He prayed for their protection from satanic influence and for their holiness by following God's word as they continued to live in a world filled with evil *(vv. 15-17)*. Jesus also prayed for the unity of all believers to come – the kind of unity Jesus shared with the Father – and for the great impact of such oneness: that the rest of the world would know that Jesus had truly been sent by God *(vv. 20-21)*.

WHAT HIS FOLLOWERS ARE TO DO:

We are encouraged by Jesus' example to continually pray for those close to us in the fellowship of Christian believers. Certainly, there are many things to pray for, and we should lift those to the Father as situations occur and needs arise. But let's follow the Lord and be sure to pray for the sanctity and unity of the Church.

"Sanctity" refers to the holy separation of believers from that which is antithetical to the righteousness of God. Note that Jesus did not pray that His followers be removed from the world. We are called to be a positive influence on others (*"salt"* and *"light"* – *Mt. 5:13, 16*) without appropriating any evil or worldly ways. Jesus gave a precise means of attaining that kind of holiness, namely, through the application of God's word of truth (i.e., the Scripture) to our lives. As we incorporate the words and ideas of the Bible into who we are, how we think, what we say, and what we do, we will become more like the Father, who by nature is holy. We are set apart for the special purpose of representing Christ to the world, so we need to always pray that God helps and guides us all toward His holiness through adherence to the divine word.

"Unity" expresses the oneness that is found in Jesus and the Father. Among other things, it is a unity of thought and purpose: Jesus and the Father shared the same mind and acted toward the same goal of redeeming the fallen world. We ought to pray that the unity of God and Christ can be realized in both the universal and the local Church. Instead of the seemingly endless divisions that we see in the body of Christ today, let us pray for oneness of direction and spirit. It is that unity which Jesus said would result in the world believing that we truly have supernatural roots and power. However, we assuredly will not reach that sort of unity without the Lord's leading and assistance, so let us continually lift this request in prayer before Him.

Even as His death was approaching, Jesus prayed for the holiness and oneness of all His followers. Let us who call Jesus Lord persistently do the same.

JESUS SINGS A HYMN

And when [Jesus and the disciples] had sung a hymn, they went out to the Mount of Olives. (Mt. 26:30)

At the end of their meal, before leaving the upper room, Jesus and His disciples joined together and sang a "hymn," perhaps one of the praise and thanksgiving songs from *Psalms 113-118* traditionally sung at Passover. Even with His impending trial, suffering, and death facing Him, Jesus lifted His voice in praise to the LORD God.

WHAT HIS FOLLOWERS ARE TO DO:

We should use our voices, as Jesus did, to acknowledge, thank, and worship our Heavenly Father, even during the toughest of circumstances. In feast or in famine, when everything is going smoothly or when troubles abound, let's exalt the name of God, whether with words or in song. As the psalmist says, *"Make a joyful noise to the LORD, all the earth."* (Ps. 100:1)

JESUS' TORMENT AND PEACE IN GETHSEMANE

Then Jesus went with them to a place called Gethsemane, and he said to his disciples, "Sit here, while I go over there and pray." (Mt. 26:36)

WHAT JESUS DID:

Jesus, we are told in *Jn. 18:2*, often went to an olive grove outside of Jerusalem called Gethsemane, a Greek word derived from the Aramaic meaning "oil press." Knowing the ordeal that lay ahead of Him in the coming hours, He was in tremendous distress and needed time in prayer with the Father. So, He removed Himself from the larger group of disciples and took His three closest apostles, Peter, James, and John, to be near Him for support and consolation in this time of great hardship, openly sharing with them the anguish He was experiencing deep in His soul *(Mt. 26:37-38)*.

WHAT HIS FOLLOWERS ARE TO DO:

We Christians also need to develop close relationships and friendships with a few other believers so that we can draw them near to us for help when we face difficulties. Yes, we are to rely on the Lord to care for us and guide us during good times and bad, but we should have trustworthy and reliable friends and family members as well who will come to our aid when called on, especially during hard times.

And when we are challenged by problems and overwhelming situations, we have to be open and honest with those who are closest to us about what we are feeling and how we are being affected. Let's not put on a false face of joy and happiness when in reality we are anything but joyful and happy. Instead, let's drop the façade and be transparent about our troubles so that others can come alongside us to share the weight of our burdens and help us to get through the roughest parts of our lives. Jesus called on those closest to Him to help Him through the torment He was facing, and we as His followers ought to as well.

*And going a little farther [Jesus] fell on his face and prayed,
saying, "My Father, if it be possible, let this cup pass from me;
nevertheless, not as I will, but as you will." (Mt. 26:39)*

WHAT JESUS DID:

The account continues: Jesus went away from the three apostles, and alone and in agony to the point where He sweated blood *(Lk. 22:44)*, He fell on His face before His *Abba* (Father) and three times prayed earnestly that He be spared the torturous death that loomed ahead, but ultimately yielding Himself not to what He wanted, but to His Father's will *(Mt. 26:36-44)*. In response to His prayer, an angel came to give Jesus strength *(Lk. 22:43)*.

Jesus' prayer is instructive to His followers in several ways:

- ▷ He prostrated Himself before God, both physically and spiritually. I'm not saying we should always be face down before God when we pray, but there is something compelling about the act of prostration before Him that can remind us of our submission to Him and His will.
- ▷ He openly bared His soul before God. We should also express to the LORD what we honestly feel. Don't hold back; let it all out! He already knows it anyway.
- ▷ He repeated the same prayer. Certainly, God hears every prayer, whether it's the first time or the hundredth time we have said it, but when we feel something so deeply that we need to say it over and over, our Heavenly Father does not reproach us. (See *Lk. 18:1-8*: Jesus taught us to keep praying and not to be discouraged.)
- ▷ God heard Jesus' prayer, but the answer was not what Jesus had asked for; He would still have to go to the cross. God responds to our prayers, too, by sometimes granting our petitions but at other times moving in a different direction.
- ▷ Jesus stopped praying His prayer after a time; He didn't go back and pray a fourth or fifth or sixth time. He had come to a place of acceptance of God's will and the strength to carry it out. As we pray, though we should not expect the appearance of an angel, we will reach a point of similar peaceful acceptance and divine strength to yield and commit ourselves to God's plan.

JESUS IS BETRAYED AND ARRESTED

While [Jesus] was still speaking, Judas came, one of the twelve, and with him a great crowd with swords and clubs, from the chief priests and the elders of the people. (Mt. 26:47)

WHAT JESUS DID:

Jesus' betrayal and arrest is described in all four gospels, each providing some details not found in the others. For instance, John says that the crowd that came to Gethsemane included soldiers and officers *(Jn. 18:3)*. In various translations, this armed group is described as having been *procured, obtained, brought*, or *guided* by Judas, and consisted of *a band, detachment,* or even *a cohort* (600 men!) of *soldiers*, along with some *officials, police, guards,* or *officers* from the *chief* or *high priests* and *Pharisees* or *elders.*

In the Synoptic accounts, Judas had given those with him a sign identifying Jesus, namely, they were to seize the one he kissed *(e.g., Mt: 26:48).* In Matthew's Gospel, Judas greeted Jesus as *"Rabbi" (v. 49)* and kissed Him, and Jesus directed him to get it over with quickly, addressing His betrayer as *"Friend" (v. 50),* just as He had taught His followers to love their enemies. John's Gospel describes Jesus, always concerned for the wellbeing of others, as telling the arresting crowd that they had come for Him but to let the disciples go *(Jn. 18:8).*

In a feeble and misguided attempt to defend Jesus, Simon Peter cut off the ear of one Malchus, (both named in *Jn. 18:10*), a servant of the high priest, but Jesus told his disciples to sheathe their swords, instructing them that those who use swords will be killed by swords *(Mt. 26:52).* Then, ever compassionate even while being arrested, Jesus touched the servant's ear and healed him *(Lk. 22:51).* Finally, in great fear for their own safety and lives, all the disciples left Jesus and ran off *(Mk.14:50; Mt. 26:56).*

WHAT HIS FOLLOWERS ARE TO DO:

There are several valuable take-aways from the arrest of Jesus that we who seek to emulate Him can apply to our own lives. For instance, we should take to heart the command to love our enemies and, as Jesus did, to view them as friends. While I don't think this is meant as a governmental principle or as national polity, it is absolutely a precept that we should all embrace and follow on an individual and personal level. There will be times when we are contested, misused, belittled, scorned, and betrayed. It is at those times that we can truly demonstrate the supernatural love of God. This is not a call for a meek and milquetoast reaction to opposition; it is, rather, a call for the courage and determination to live up to Christian convictions that are contrary to the ways of the world.

Also, let us seek the good of others above concern for benefitting ourselves. Though Jesus was being delivered into the hands of evil men, He advocated for the welfare of His disciples, and we should likewise care for other people even when we face troubles and hardship. We should deny the natural tendency of "Me first!" and give priority to the needs of those around us.

We ought to take a strong stance in denouncing wanton bloodshed, as well. Jesus teaches us that violence begets more violence. Let's raise our voices to decry brutal acts and urge that weapons be lowered so that calm and peace can prevail. Is the judicious use of force ever required? Yes. However, let's never resort to violence when other possible responses are available and efficacious.

A goal should be, as spoken of in *Isaiah 2:4*, that we turn our instruments of war and destruction (and the massive resources we devote to them) into implements of agriculture for the betterment of life.

Lastly, let's work to bring about restoration to the victims of violence, just as Jesus did when He thoughtfully healed the servant's severed ear. Whether the trauma is physical, emotional, or psychological, those who suffer from it should be given the attention and care they need to move toward recovery and renewal of life. We Christians should actively endeavor to engage in such kindness and help to administer and provide for appropriate treatment.

Jesus exhibited love, compassion, and a desire for peace even as anger and aggression surrounded Him, and we ought to show the same attitude and outward focus that lead to real acts of lovingkindness.

JESUS FACES ANNAS

So the band of soldiers and their captain and the officers of the Jews arrested Jesus and bound him. First they led him to Annas, for he was the father-in-law of Caiaphas, who was high priest that year. (Jn. 18:12-13)

WHAT JESUS DID:

Annas had served as High Priest for about 10 years (6 CE-15 CE), and his sons and now his son-in-law had succeeded him. He was the first official that Jesus faced, and Annas questioned Jesus about who followed Him and what He had been teaching *(v. 19)*.

Jesus answered directly and succinctly that He always taught openly and Annas could ask those who had heard Him about what He had said. Deeming this an impertinent answer to someone of such an exalted position, an officer hit Jesus in rebuke. But Jesus at that time did not just meekly let Himself be struck; instead, He bravely confronted the officer's action, demanding that the officer prove what He had said was false, but if it was true, he had no right to deliver a blow. *(vv. 20-23)*

WHAT HIS FOLLOWERS ARE TO DO:

One application of this incident in the life of Jesus is that we are never to allow a lie or wrongdoing to go unchallenged. Falsehood and injustice need a response, and as ones who believe in truth and righteousness, we who follow Jesus must be courageous, like our Lord, in opposing untruths and unrighteous actions.

Also, I wonder also if we would have the same confidence as Jesus in telling someone to ask others about the words we have spoken. Would we ever be ashamed if that which we said in the past and perhaps in private were repeated? Would we ever be caught in a lie? Would our words, if they were retold by someone else, reveal us to be foul-mouthed, a gossip, a braggard, a fool, or a hypocrite? As followers of Jesus, let's strive to always speak with honesty, sincerity, respect, civility, graciousness, self-control, humility, wisdom, and integrity, such that we are certain that our words, if reiterated by someone else, would reflect good, Christlike character and genuine godliness.

JESUS LOOKS AT PETER

Then they seized [Jesus] and led him away, bringing him into the high priest's [Caiaphas'] house, and Peter was following at a distance. And when they had kindled a fire in the middle of the courtyard and sat down together, Peter sat down among them. (Lk. 22:54-55)

WHAT JESUS DID:

The familiar story follows of Peter's threefold denial of Jesus when questioned by others in Caiaphas' courtyard: *I don't know Him; I'm not one of them; I don't know what you're talking about (vv. 56-60)*. At that moment, as the rooster crowed, Jesus, who was presumably waiting to be seen by Caiaphas, turned and looked right at Peter *(v. 61)*. It was then that Peter recalled the Lord's words foretelling his denials, and Peter with great anguish, left the courtyard and began to cry uncontrollably *(v. 62)*.

WHAT HIS FOLLOWERS ARE TO DO:

How might we imagine the look that Jesus gave Peter as he spoke angrily to those seated with him around the fire in Caiaphas' courtyard? Was it a look of disappointment, blame, and shame? I don't believe so because that was not in keeping with the character of Jesus. Peter was one of His closest disciples, the *"rock"* on whom Jesus had said He would build His Church and to whom the keys of the Kingdom of Heaven would be given *(Mt. 16:18-19)*, and Jesus always acted lovingly and compassionately, so I think His look to Peter would have reflected that love and compassion, and certainly the hope of redemption and restoration in the future.

We, too, who follow the Lord should not seek to fill others with shame even when they don't live up to their Christian convictions. Let's not express our displeasure with those who fall away or who fail to always affirm their faith in Christ. Also, we should avoid the "I told you so" attitude of superiority. We must remember that we are all sinners saved by God's mercy, forgiveness, and grace, and rather than cast blaming looks or point a shaming finger at fellow believers who do wrong, we need to pray for them and to embrace and encompass them in the love that Christ gave to Peter.

JESUS IS INTERROGATED BY CAIAPHAS

Then those who had seized Jesus led him to Caiaphas the high priest, where the scribes and the elders had gathered. (Mt. 26:57)

WHAT JESUS DID:

The religious leaders, presumably members of the Sanhedrin, had gathered in the home of the High Priest Caiaphas for this extraordinary (and perhaps illegal according to Jewish law) nighttime procedure with the intention of finding something that would justify killing Jesus. To this end, they made three attempts, only the last of which was successful for their purposes *(vv. 59-66)*.

Initially, they trotted out many false witnesses but found nothing worthy of capital punishment *(vv. 59-60a)*. Jesus was above reproach in His morality and conduct. Next, two people testified that Jesus had said He would destroy the Temple and rebuild it in three days *(v. 61)*. Jesus had indeed said that, though He was referring to His own body as the Temple of God; He had even previously told Annas to ask others what He had said *(Jn. 18:21)*. Perhaps if the religious leaders were really interested in His words, they would have asked what Jesus meant, but they were seeking His death, not further clarification, so He remained silent after their testimony *(Mt. 26:63)*, choosing not to explain His true meaning. *(More on Jesus' silence in the next segment.)*

Finally, the apparently frustrated Caiaphas asked Jesus directly if He was the Christ, the Son of God. Jesus' answer, **"You have said so"** *(v. 64a)*, was an affirmative response, as is more evident in *Mark 14:62a* in which Jesus replies, **"I am."** (Compare also *Mt. 26:25*, Jesus' reply to Judas earlier when Judas asked if he was the one who would betray Him, and Jesus said, **"You have said so."**) Speaking before Caiaphas and the other religionists, Jesus added that they would one day witness the coming of the Son of Man, an allusion to Jesus' own self-identification as this powerful heavenly figure (spoken of in *Daniel 7:13* and elsewhere). In reaction, the High Priest proclaimed that Jesus had uttered blasphemy, and the others gathered there pronounced their judgment of death. *(Mt. 26:64b-66)*

WHAT HIS FOLLOWERS ARE TO DO:

Christ's actions before Caiaphas offer us some examples to follow. Let us first seek to lead lives that are, like Christ's, above reproach. We will have failings, to be sure, but let it be our goal and ideal to be righteous in our words and deeds. Others who oppose our ideas and our ways will look for areas in our lives that they can readily seize upon to condemn or characterize as hypocritical. As we follow God's wisdom and submit to the guidance of His Holy Spirit, our speech and our conduct will be honorable and not open to valid criticism.

Additionally, there are times when silence speaks louder than words or when not saying anything is more judicious than talking. If truth has been stated by someone else, we don't necessarily have to add anything to it; truth can stand alone on its own merits without our further comments. As it says in *Prov. 10:19b*, **"whoever restrains his lips is prudent."** *(See the next segment for more on remaining silent.)*

Having said that, sometimes we cannot remain silent but must speak. Jesus answered the question of Caiaphas with the full force of conviction. As is commonly heard today, He spoke truth to power, despite being aware of the inevitable result of His words. When a situation demands a response, let's pray for the strength and courage of God to say what is right and what needs to be heard.

Jesus, our Teacher, has given us these life-lessons that we need to learn and apply.

JESUS' SILENCE BEFORE PILATE AND HEROD

And [the religious leaders] bound Jesus and led him away and delivered him over to Pilate. (Mk. 15:1b)

WHAT JESUS DID:

As we saw earlier in Jesus' hearing before Caiaphas and the other religious leaders, Jesus chose at one point to remain silent. He continued in this way during His initial appearance before Pilate when they were in the presence of those same religionists and again when He was taken to Herod.

The first interrogation by Pilate took place outside the Roman governor's headquarters and included the participation of the religious leaders. Jesus responded to Pilate's question as to whether He was the King of the Jews, answering in the affirmative, but when the religionists began to hurl accusations against Him, Jesus gave no reply, even when encouraged by the surprised Pilate to do so *(vv. 2-5)*. The subsequent discussion between Jesus and Pilate about Jesus' kingdom and about truth, as recorded in John's gospel *(18:33-38)*, happened inside Pilate's headquarters away from the Jewish religionists who feared ritual defilement if they were to enter that pagan area.

Jesus, a Galilean, was then taken to Herod Antipas, who had been given rule over the regions of Galilee and of Perea (on the eastern side of the Jordan River) after the death of his father, Herod the Great. It was Herod Antipas who was responsible for the imprisonment and execution of John the Baptist *(Mt. 14:3-10)*. Herod had heard of the wonder-worker Jesus and wanted to see Him perform a miracle, so he questioned Jesus extensively. However, as before, Jesus remained silent and offered no response. *(Lk. 23:7-9)*

So, Jesus did not speak three separate times during His appearances before the authorities: first, during part of His interrogation by Caiaphas, once again as He stood before Pilate and was indicted by the religious leaders, and once more when brought to Herod.

We might ask why Jesus chose to remain silent during those times; why didn't He take the opportunity to answer and to preach His message before these influential people? I believe He was just adhering to His own teaching to not give sacred truth and holy wisdom to those who would not welcome and appreciate it but would instead disregard and denigrate it *(Mt. 7:6)*. Jesus must have understood that whatever He said would have been rejected outright by those who heard Him, so rather than speaking His holy and precious words of truth, He held his tongue.

WHAT HIS FOLLOWERS ARE TO DO:

Simply stated, there will be times when remaining silent is better than speaking. If we realize that what we say, regardless of its veracity or possible spiritual value, will not be received or will be denigrated straight away, it may be better not to say anything at all. There are those who openly oppose Christ and who would belittle, scorn, or vilify His message, and instead of giving them the opportunity to heap derision on the word of God, we should, like the Lord, choose not to speak. Let's pray for divine guidance and for the discernment of when to talk and when to shut our mouths.

JESUS IS MOCKED, SCOURGED, & SENTENCED

And [Pilate's soldiers] stripped [Jesus] and put a scarlet robe on him ... (Mt. 27:28)

<u>WHAT JESUS DID:</u>

Pilate turned Jesus over to the Roman soldiers under his command – the entire battalion of some 600 soldiers turning out for this punishment. Jesus was brutally scourged, ridiculed, and pummeled by these vicious men. The soldiers tore off Jesus' clothing and with mock symbols of royalty covered Him with a red cloak (purple, in *Mark 15:17*), fashioned a crown of sharp thorns that they placed on His head, and put a reed in His right hand as a regal scepter. They knelt in front of Him in mock homage, hailing Him as King, and then spit in His face and struck Him with their hands (per *John 19:3*) and with the reed. *(Mt. 27:26-30)*

But in a remarkable display of courage and inner strength, Jesus did not resist or lift His hand or even raise His voice against them, just as He had taught His disciples: when someone hit them on one cheek, they were to turn and offer him the other cheek as well *(Lk. 6:29)*.

The badly-beaten Jesus was then presented by Pilate to the religious leaders and the crowds in an attempt to release Him. ***"Behold the Man!"*** Pilate said *(Jn. 19:5)*, perhaps hoping for a sympathetic response to the pathetic sight, but they would not be swayed from their desire for his death, and so Jesus was sentenced and led away to be crucified. *(Mt. 27:31)*

As followers of Jesus, we too may face ridicule and scorn, though most probably not to the brutally severe extent that the Lord experienced. There are people who oppose Christ and who will laugh at us or joke about our beliefs and our way of life. They will disparage our values and criticize us for not conforming to the ideas and practices of the world. We may be labelled derisively for what we hold to be true and how we comport ourselves. However, when that does occur, let's follow the example of Jesus and not return evil for evil. Stand strong in our convictions, yes, but always take the high and noble road and not debase ourselves by engaging in mean-spirited speech or actions.

Ours is the way of lovingkindness not hatred, of promoting wellbeing not destruction, of encouraging not cursing. We are not called to spit venom at others, but to share life-giving water in the name of Christ. When humiliated by those who would seek to strip us of our dignity, even publicly, we need to clothe ourselves in the meekness and humility of Jesus. When mocked, like the Lord before us, let's not lash out in knee-jerk anger, but rather let's hear the approving and uplifting voice of the Heavenly Father who holds us always in His loving and almighty embrace and who tells us that we are His children in whom He delights.

JESUS IS LED TO GOLGOTHA

And as [the soldiers] led [Jesus] away, they seized one Simon of Cyrene, who was coming in from the country, and laid on him the cross, to carry it behind Jesus. And there followed him a great multitude of the people and of women who were mourning and lamenting for him. (Lk. 23:26-27)

WHAT JESUS DID:

Jesus was obviously weakened from the brutal flogging and beating He had received at the hands of the Roman soldiers. Now forced to carry the heavy cross, or perhaps the crossbeam, on which He would be nailed, He was unable to bear its weight, and so the soldiers commandeered the assistance of a bystander, one Simon of Cyrene, which is in present-day Libya. Jesus, though certainly He had no real say in the matter, did not refuse the help when He needed it most.

(Note: In tradition, Simon of Cyrene became a Christian and later even a bishop; he was eventually martyred. He is today considered a saint by the Catholic Church. Simon is mentioned in the New Testament as the father of Rufus and Alexander [Mk. 15:16], and a Rufus is mentioned in Rom. 16:13, perhaps referring to the same person.)

The soldiers were leading Jesus to the place of execution, a hill outside the walls of Jerusalem called *Golgotha*, Aramaic for "skull" – or from Latin, *Calvary* – due to its cranium-like appearance. Along the route, which is today called the *Via Dolorosa*, or Way of Suffering, Jesus was met by a group of women who were grieving and weeping openly for Him. But Jesus, ever concerned for the wellbeing of others, told them to cry instead for themselves and their families in expectation of the terrible times ahead, undoubtedly foretelling the coming (70 CE) siege and destruction of Jerusalem by Rome (Lk. 23:28).

WHAT HIS FOLLOWERS ARE TO DO:

Some of us might love being independent and not needing the help of others. Even from an early age, we may want to do things ourselves without any assistance. Self-sufficiency in many areas is indeed commendable; however, there are definitely times when we can't go it alone and when we are unable to carry on by ourselves, as it was for Jesus on the way to Golgotha, and we must then accept the help of others when offered. Our pride might put up a fight and resist being given a helping hand, or we may selfishly not want to share the limelight with anyone else, but we need to swallow that arrogance and allow others to give us support when we truly need it. We must also realize that, in terms of our Christian mission, when we accept the help of others, we are giving them opportunities to participate in the work of ministry.

One other principle we might learn from Jesus as He spoke to the mourning women: We who follow Christ can see in His compassion for others, even in the most dire of circumstances, a way to conduct our own lives. When facing problems or hardship, let's not completely submerge ourselves in self-concern or self-pity to the point that we cannot look beyond our own situations. Our focus must encompass those around us and their needs, as well. Jesus always thought of the welfare of other people despite His own travails, and we ought to do likewise.

JESUS REFUSES A DRINK OF WINE AND GALL

And when they came to a place called Golgotha (which means Place of a Skull), [the soldiers] offered [Jesus] wine to drink, mixed with gall, but when he tasted it, he would not drink it. (Mt. 27:33-34)

WHAT JESUS DID:

Before Jesus was nailed to the cross, the soldiers offered Him a drink of wine mixed with a bitter-tasting substance called *"gall"* in Matthew and *"myrrh"* in Mark *(15:23)*. It apparently had soporific (some say even toxic) properties and was given to certain criminals about to be crucified to blunt some of the pain of their torturous death. Having tasted it, though, Jesus refused to imbibe. Later, while hanging on the cross, Jesus would cry out, *"I thirst"* *(Jn. 19:28)*, and be given a sponge soaked in vinegary sour wine, but not mixed with any narcotic, so He drank it *(v. 30)*. Why did He refuse the wine and gall mixture, then?

This was the time of Jesus' greatest testing. He knew the horrendous suffering He was about to experience. He had even prayed earlier in Gethsemane that, if possible, the Father would let this agonizing *"cup"* pass from Him *(Mt. 26:39)*. But ultimately, He submitted Himself to God's will, even if it meant dying on the cross. Having accepted the cup given to Him by His Father, He refused the strength-sapping, perception-dulling drink offered by the soldiers because He needed His full courage and His full awareness to be able to undergo this terrible ordeal.

WHAT HIS FOLLOWERS ARE TO DO:

When we encounter troubles and trials in our own lives, though assuredly nothing like that which Jesus underwent, an easy way to deal with those problems is to anesthetize or sedate ourselves with alcohol or drugs. Not wanting to face the reality before us, we drink booze or we pop pills to make us forget the ache and to deaden our senses so we won't feel so bad.

But we who seek to follow Jesus must not succumb to this temptation. We experience pain for a reason, whether to warn us of danger or to teach us life-lessons. I'm not saying that all pain is good and beneficial or that we should never take painkillers, but we need to avoid drugging ourselves to the point where we are numb and unaware of what is happening to us or around us. Like Jesus, especially in dire circumstances, we need to have a clear mind and to be strong and fully conscious as we face the hardships and experience the pain that frequently accompany life.

JESUS FORGIVES THOSE WHO KILL HIM

[The soldiers] crucified [Jesus] ... And Jesus said, "Father, forgive them, for they know not what they do." (Lk. 23:33-34)

WHAT JESUS DID:

Jesus had preached a gospel of the forgiveness of God, and He had taught His disciples throughout His ministry the importance of forgiving others. And so, true to His words, Jesus prayed to the Heavenly Father for the forgiveness of those who were in the very process of killing Him.

I believe, however, that His prayer went far beyond the Roman soldiers in charge of His execution but extended as well to all of us whose sin of commission and omission brought about the death of this innocent One. Jesus stated the reason for His petition, too: We don't understand the gravity of our evil words and actions. By our unrighteous speech and behavior, we turn away from Christ and His message, and instead silence Him and snuff out His presence in our lives. All our wrongdoing, our lack of holiness, whether we realize it or not, has the effect of separating us from God and His perfect will. Jesus compassionately begged the Father on all our behalf for the merciful forgiveness that would restore our relationship with Him.

WHAT HIS FOLLOWERS ARE TO DO:

A hallmark of our Christian life is to be forgiving of others, as taught and shown to us by the words and life of Jesus:

> ▷ It is an integral part of the Lord's Prayer: *"forgive us our debts, as we also have forgiven our debtors"* (Mt. 6:12).
> ▷ We should always be willing to forgive those who wrong us, not just once or twice, but even *"seventy-seven times"* (Mt. 18:22), i.e., indefinitely.
> ▷ Jesus warned us that if we don't forgive, we are held in a kind of prison until there is a complete change of heart. (See *Mt. 18:23-35*, The Parable of the Unforgiving Servant.)

So, let's learn from this supreme act of lovingkindness by Jesus even as He was being nailed to the cross to forgive those who do us wrong or harm. We must never hold petty grudges or develop long-term hardness of spirit that refuses to absolve. That is not the way of Christ, and it not to be our way either. No, we, like Him, are to be merciful, kind, understanding, compassionate, ... and forgiving.

JESUS PROMISES PARADISE TO
THE PENITENT CRIMINAL

Two others, who were criminals, were led away to be
put to death with [Jesus]. (Lk. 23:32)

WHAT JESUS DID:

Jesus was not the only one sentenced to die that day. Two criminals, perhaps thieves, robbers, or even insurrectionists, were also crucified on either side of Him. At first, both criminals joined the crowd in hurling insults at Jesus *(Mt. 27:44)*. But then one of them, facing his impending death and fearing God's certain judgment, seems to have had a change of heart and repented. He rebuked the other criminal and acknowledged that they were getting what they deserved for their crimes but that Jesus was an innocent man, guilty of nothing *(Lk. 23:40-41)*. The repentant thief then asked Jesus to remember Him when He came as ruler of His kingdom, and Jesus, caring and compassionate despite the torturous ordeal He was experiencing, with His hands extended by the cross to which He was nailed, answered and gave him the wonderful guarantee that he would be with Him that very day in heavenly paradise. *(vv. 42-43)*

WHAT HIS FOLLOWERS ARE TO DO:

Just as Jesus did with the repentant criminal despite his past, we too can make the same promise of paradise to all those who:

▷ understand that death and judgment before a holy God will one day come;

▷ change their mind and turn away from wrongdoing and sin;

▷ acknowledge faith in Jesus, who promised that He would acknowledge us before the Father *(Mt. 10:32)*;

▷ confess before God their sinfulness, which leads only to death, and beseech God's undeserved mercy, which brings life;

▷ accept that Jesus was the sinless one sent by the Father and slain unjustly for all our sins;

▷ believe that Jesus is indeed a coming King;

▷ receive Jesus' offer of forgiveness and His assurance that we will be with Him in paradise;

▷ are confident that Jesus will never forget any of us and have faith that through Him heaven awaits us;

▷ commit themselves into His care in this life and in the next.

This is the heart of Jesus' message, and we need to share in both word and deed this amazing pledge with the world.

JESUS CARES FOR HIS MOTHER FROM THE CROSS

*Standing by the cross of Jesus were his mother and ...
the disciple whom he loved ... (Jn. 19:25-26)*

WHAT JESUS DID:

Jesus' relationship with His mother Mary is portrayed in various ways in Scripture. We are told that at an early age, Jesus lived in submissive obedience to her and to his earthly father *(Lk. 2:51)*. Jesus' first miracle, the changing of water to wine at the wedding in Cana, was performed at the request of His mother even though He had told her that His time had not yet come *(Jn. 2:2-4)*. Mark's gospel describes Jesus' family, in response to His growing popularity and the opposition of religious leaders, as trying to seize Him because they thought He was out of His mind *(Mk. 3:21)*. Then, when Mary and Jesus' brothers showed up at the house where He was staying, He did not go out to welcome them but instead described those who did God's will as His true family *(Mk. 3:31-35)*. Nonetheless, Mary followed Him at some point and was present at the crucifixion of her son *(Jn. 19:25)*. She is also mentioned as with the disciples in Jerusalem after Jesus' resurrection *(Acts 1)*.

In the heart-wrenching scene near the cross, Mary watched as her firstborn son was being torturously killed before her very eyes. But Jesus, despite His own suffering, was always concerned for the wellbeing of others. Mary needed care, so Jesus told her to consider one of His closest disciples (traditionally portrayed as John the apostle) as her own son and assigned the disciple to provide for her as if she were his own mother. The disciple obeyed and received Mary into his home and family. *(Jn. 19:26-27)*

(Note: Tradition says that Joseph, Mary's husband, had passed away by then, leaving Mary a widow. And though Jesus had at least four brothers and two sisters (Mk. 6:3), one of whom, James, became a leader of the early church (Acts 15:13ff), we are left to wonder why they weren't responsible for the care of their mother.)

WHAT HIS FOLLOWERS ARE TO DO:

Jesus here gave His followers a clear example to emulate: We must look beyond our own circumstances, even during the hardest of times, to the situations of others. Rather than wallowing in self-pity or focusing only on the difficulties we face, let's be aware and responsive to those around us and to the difficulties that they might be experiencing, and then let's take active steps toward resolving their problems and meeting their needs. And if we ourselves are not able to directly supply what is required, we should do our best to engage and involve other people who are willing and have the means to offer support and provision.

The compassionate and caring love we see in the life of Christ compels us to look outward and not to ignore others and their needs but to seek to provide for them in whatever way we can.

JESUS' ANGUISHED CRY OF DESPAIR

And when the sixth hour had come, there was darkness over the whole land until the ninth hour. And at the ninth hour Jesus cried with a loud voice, "Eloi, Eloi, lema sabachthani?" which means, "My God, my God, why have you forsaken me?" (Mk. 15:33-34)

WHAT JESUS DID:

There seem to be two prevailing views regarding Jesus' anguished and desperate cry from the cross, questioning aloud why He had been abandoned by His Heavenly Father at this time of greatest need. One modern opinion is that Jesus had expected the Kingdom of God would soon arrive with Him, the righteous Messianic King, reigning over a redeemed Israel freed from the unjust rule of the Gentile world, and His cry voiced His profound despondency and sense of desertion. The other more traditional and Evangelical interpretation is that Jesus took on the sin of all humanity and even became sin on our behalf; thus,

He experienced a separation from His most-holy Father in Heaven, and His cry expressed the intense grief He felt as for the first time His communion with God was broken.

Regardless of the opinions, Jesus' lament was certainly echoing *Psalm 22*, spoken in His own Aramaic language, in which a royal figure such as King David described the torments and persecution by his enemies. During Jesus' crucifixion, darkness covered the entire region for three hours, and at 3 p.m., Jesus uttered words filled with tremendous pathos, grief, and desolation.

WHAT HIS FOLLOWERS ARE TO DO:

We who follow Jesus are not exempt from feelings of discouragement and despair. Becoming a Christian does not mean that our lives will suddenly be joyous and wonderful and that we will live happily ever after. That is the stuff of fairy tales and does not accurately characterize our walk with the Lord.

Like Jesus, there will be sad times of disappointment, despondency, and maybe depression. Circumstances will besiege and oppress us to the point where we feel deserted and alone in the universe. Our sinfulness will isolate us from experiencing the caring presence of God in all His holiness. And yet, even during those darkest hours, we can cry out to our Father in Heaven and express what we are feeling without shame or fear. God wants us to be real with Him, and we can be confident that, as we bare our souls before Him, He hears us and will respond in lovingkindness, for that is His nature.

JESUS' ASSURED CRY OF DELIVERANCE

Then Jesus, calling out with a loud voice, said, "Father, into your hands I commit my spirit!" And having said this he breathed his last. (Lk. 23:46)

WHAT JESUS DID:

Jesus had completed His mission here on earth. He had undergone the gruesome ordeal of the cross and now knew that His physical life was at its end. Despite the horrific circumstance that He was experiencing, He lifted His voice to God in the trust and assurance that He would soon be delivered, and surrendered His very spirit into the loving care of His Heavenly Father.

WHAT HIS FOLLOWERS ARE TO DO:

Jesus' actions on the cross are a simple yet dramatic reminder to us who follow Him that we are always and forever in almighty God's love and care. Jesus trusted the Father both in life and in death, and we should learn to do the same.

For us Christians, we are to walk in faith during the best of times and the worst of times and everything in between. Each moment while we are on this earth, despite our circumstances, we can be confident that our gracious Heavenly Father is present and is intimately and actively involved in our lives.

And at the appointed hour of our death, when our bodies die but our imperishable spirits go on, we can be equally sure that God will be there to welcome and embrace us. Thus, facing our departure from this corporeal world, we can with joyful anticipation call out to God as Jesus did and entrust ourselves into the care of the One who rules over this life and the life that is to come.

JESUS' RESURRECTION

And very early on the first day of the week, when the sun had risen, [some women disciples] went to the tomb. (Mk. 16:2)

After Jesus had died, His body was taken down from the cross by Joseph of Arimathea, an esteemed member of the Sanhedrin *(Mk. 15:43)* and a secret follower of Jesus *(Jn. 19:38)*, and Nicodemus, also a religious leader who had met with Jesus at night *(Jn. 3)*. They hastily wrapped His body in burial linens and laid it in Joseph's private tomb as the Sabbath was approaching when they could not do the work needed to properly prepare the body for entombment. A large stone was rolled across the entrance of the tomb *(Mk. 15; Jn. 19)* to enclose the stench and to prevent grave robbers or wild animals from entering.

The first to come to the tomb on Sunday were women disciples who brought spices to anoint the body of Jesus. Arriving at the tomb, they saw the stone rolled away, and entering inside, they saw a young man in white (identified in *Matthew 28:2* as an angel) who gave them the wonderful news that He had risen from the dead and was no longer in the tomb *(Mk. 16:4-6)*.

WHAT HIS FOLLOWERS ARE TO DO:

While I am not suggesting that we should hope to rise postmortem from our physical graves and return bodily to our earthly existence, I do believe that we who follow Jesus can apply His resurrection to our daily lives. Thus, we can seek to rise from those things which bring spiritual death and separation from God, such as sinfulness and unrighteousness and be dedicated to the pursuit of holiness, and righteousness in all that we think, say, and do. We must rise from selfishness to altruism; rise from deception to honesty; rise from corruption to integrity; rise from injustice to fairness; rise from anger and violence to patience and grace; rise from indifference to compassion; rise from wrongdoing to acts of goodness and lovingkindness. If we are held by earthly passions and desires, we need to rise out of their grip and conquer them in the strength of God's Holy Spirit. Let's raise our focus from the earthy to the heavenly and prioritize the spiritual and eternal over and above the physical and the mundane.

One day, we will all rise from death as Christ did, but until that comes, let's devote ourselves to leading lives marked by the resurrection power that can lift us from sinful ways, worldly concerns, and constant yearnings and into the realm of godly pursuits, heavenly values, and everlasting peace.

JESUS APPEARS TO SOME
WOMEN DISCIPLES

*So [the women disciples] departed quickly from the tomb
with fear and great joy, and ran to tell his disciples.
And behold, Jesus met them ... (Mt. 28:8-9a)*

WHAT JESUS DID:

This incident is recorded only in Matthew's gospel. The women disciples who had come to properly prepare Jesus' body for its entombment or burial had been told by the angel at the tomb that Jesus had risen from the dead and were on their way to share the good news with His other followers. The women were understandably feeling a mixture of fear and joy: fear from their encounter with an angelic being and joy from the thrilling news that Jesus was alive.

But while on their way, Jesus appeared to them, speaking the very understated word, *"Greetings."* Their reaction was to fall before Him in worship and to touch His feet, perhaps making sure He was not a ghostly apparition. Jesus then told them not to be afraid and to convey a message to the others to meet Him in Galilee. *(vv. 9b-10)*

WHAT HIS FOLLOWERS ARE TO DO:

Jesus appeared to these faithful women disciples and confirmed their joy with His presence, spoke words to calm their fears, and gave them the task of delivering a message to others. We who are followers of Jesus can do the same with those around us.

Let's seek to be present – available, active, engaged – in the lives of fellow believers. When they rejoice, let's affirm their happiness, giving thanks and praise with them to the Lord. When they are worried or afraid, let's offer our company and care and speak comforting words to assuage those fears. When they act in faith and worshipfully serve the Lord, let's acknowledge their trust and devotion and work with them to build an even closer relationship with our Heavenly Father. And let's enjoin upon them (and upon ourselves as well) the mission of spreading Jesus' message of mercy, forgiveness, and love and the power of God to conquer death.

JESUS COMFORTS MARY MAGDALENE

But Mary [Magdalene] stood weeping outside the tomb ... (Jn. 20:11)

WHAT JESUS DID:

Mary Magdalene was from the town of Magdala on the western shore of the Sea of Galilee. Scripture tells us that Jesus had cast out seven demons from her and that she and some other women had traveled with Jesus and His apostles as He preached and ministered throughout the region *(Lk. 8:1-3)*. All four gospels mention her at the time of Jesus' death, entombment, and resurrection: She was present at Jesus' crucifixion *(Jn. 19:25)*; she saw the tomb where Jesus' corpse had been laid *(Mk. 15:47; Lk. 23:55)*; she was among the women who first went to the tomb to anoint Jesus' body early on Sunday morning *(Mk. 16:1; Mt. 28:1)*; and she ran to tell Peter and another unnamed disciple that the tomb was empty *(Jn. 20:2)*.

Mary was understandably distraught when the One who had rescued her from demonic oppression and whom she had followed as a disciple was executed, and having returned to the empty tomb, she began to weep. Stooping to look into the tomb, she saw two angels and spoke with them briefly. Then, she turned and saw Jesus but did not recognize Him, supposing that He was a gardener, that is, someone who possibly took care of the tombs. The risen Jesus saw the anguish that Mary was feeling and came to her and asked her (though He must certainly have known) why she was upset. After she explained the reason for her tears, that Jesus' body was no longer in the tomb, Jesus comforted her by saying a single word – her name – showing His closeness to her. *(vv. 12-16)*

Nowhere in canonical Scripture is this described as a romantic or sexual or marital relationship as has been portrayed in popular film and novels, but rather a deep spiritual intimacy. Jesus knew Mary well, and when He spoke her name, she immediately recognized Him, called him *"Teacher,"* and embraced Him. Jesus then instructed her to tell the other disciples that He would soon ascend to God, the Heavenly Father. She obeyed and conveyed what she had seen and heard to the apostles. *(vv. 17-18)*

WHAT HIS FOLLOWERS ARE TO DO:

Let's follow Jesus as He leads us to compassion for others who are experiencing grief or pain. When we become aware that people are in distress, we must not ignore them or passively hope that someone else will deal with them. We need to see those who are hurting and to draw close to them, offering physical presence to assure them they are not alone, a sympathetic ear to listen to their troubles, and consoling words to help alleviate their sorrow. (Beyond that, of course, we must also be ever ready to share material support if a situation requires it.) As Jesus did, we should take active steps to provide comfort for the mournful and relief and restoration to the suffering.

JESUS AND TWO DISCIPLES ON THE ROAD TO EMMAUS

That very day [Sunday] two of [Jesus' disciples] were going to a village named Emmaus, about seven miles from Jerusalem ... (Lk. 24:13)

WHAT JESUS DID:

This incident, recorded only in Luke's gospel, occurred on a road leading out of Jerusalem through the village of Emmaus. These two men were followers of Jesus, though they did not recognize Him as He joined them and walked and conversed with them. Answering Jesus' questions about what they were discussing, they expressed their belief that Jesus had been a powerful prophet of God and their now seemingly-dashed hopes that He had been the one who would restore Israel. They also voiced their bewilderment at the reports that Jesus' tomb was empty and that some of the women disciples had seen and spoken with angels. In response, Jesus chided their lack of faith and understanding and explained in detail from the Scripture how the Messiah had to suffer and then be glorified. *(vv. 14-27).*

The story proceeds that as they approached Emmaus, Jesus acted as if He were going to continue farther on the road, perhaps not wanting to impose on these men's hospitality or more probably because He intended to appear to His apostles gathered in Jerusalem, but they insisted that He stay the night with them, and He accepted their gracious invitation. At supper, Jesus gave thanks and broke bread with the men, and it was then that the two disciples finally recognized Jesus, at which point, He vanished from their sight. The two men immediately traveled back to Jerusalem to tell the other disciples what had happened. *(vv. 28-35)*

WHAT HIS FOLLOWERS ARE TO DO:

We who follow Jesus can emulate His actions with these two men as we encounter those believers who are confused, saddened, or troubled by the circumstances in their lives. There are times when disciples of Christ will not understand what is happening to them or to their loved ones or when they hope for a certain outcome, but it fails to materialize. On those occasions, uncertainty, sorrow, and despair can easily set in, and that is when we need to come close to them, to meet them where they are, and to walk with them on their life journey.

What are some practical ways that we can, like Jesus, offer comfort and support to Christians who are questioning God and are unsure of their faith in Him as they face unexpected situations? Here are some ideas:

- ▷ We can first of all be present with them, not removed from them which could lead to their sense of isolation and loneliness.
- ▷ Also, we can engage them in conversation. By asking questions of those struggling with God, we can give them the opportunity to explain what is going on in their lives and to express how they are feeling.
- ▷ We need as well to be ready to speak the truth of the Scripture and convey the many encouraging promises of God, assuring troubled believers of the constant care of our loving Heavenly Father and of His perfect plan despite circumstances. However, let's not be overeager to pounce on them with Bible verses as an easy fix for their difficulties. Instead, we should offer a listening ear and a shoulder to cry on, and also be prepared to explain God's word.
- ▷ Let's never impose on the kindness of others. But if offered hospitality or gifts by those appreciative of our help and support, let's accept them with gratitude.
- ▷ We must spend time with Christians who are working out their faith in their daily lives, and this often means sharing meals with one another and moments of sacramental worship and thanksgiving. This will bring us closer together so that we can truly see each other as we really are.
- ▷ Finally, there will come a time when we have to allow those believers to stand on their own and work things out between them and the Lord. Thus, our separation from them (though not a complete vanishing from their lives) is needed for spiritual growth and maturity.

As Jesus leads, we follow.

JESUS APPEARS TO THE DISCIPLES IN JERUSALEM

As [the disciples in Jerusalem] were talking ..., Jesus himself stood among them, and said to them, "Peace to you!" (Lk. 24:36)

WHAT JESUS DID:

The disciples of Jesus were gathered together, perhaps in the same upper room where they had shared their meal before His arrest, but this is speculation. Presumably, they were in hiding from the Romans and Jewish religious leaders, fearing for their lives.

Jesus appeared suddenly among them, and though they had heard reports from others of His resurrection, Jesus' presence was astonishing. Thinking they were seeing the ghost of Jesus, they are described as *startled, frightened, troubled, doubtful, disbelieving,* and *marveling.* To calm their fears, Jesus invited them to look at His body and to touch Him *(v. 39)*. He even ate a piece of fish *(v. 43)* to prove that it was indeed Him, risen bodily from the dead.

The account in Luke goes on to say that He guided them into an understanding of the Scriptures *(v. 45)*, expounding to them from the *Tenach* (the Jewish Bible) to show that the Messiah had to suffer, die, and rise again, and restating His message of the need for repentance which leads to the forgiveness of sins *(v. 47)* which was to be spread throughout the world. And finally, He told them to wait in Jerusalem until they were **clothed with power from on high"** *(v. 49)*, certainly a reference to the coming of the promised Holy Spirit which would be sent by the Heavenly Father.

WHAT HIS FOLLOWERS ARE TO DO:

We who follow Jesus are all subject to questioning our beliefs at some times. Difficult circumstances will challenge our faith. Hardship, suffering, and loss can cause us to turn away from our trust in God's providence and love. We can become apprehensive and fearful when unexpected troubles confront us, unsure that God is in control and accomplishing His plan in our lives. When that happens, we need to step up and seek to comfort our worried and doubting Christian brothers and sisters as Jesus did with His disciples.

Let's share with those oppressed believers evidence from our own lives that support our trust in God. How has God shown Himself to be present and loving to us? What can we see as God's hand moving in us and through us? When in our lives has God brought about blessing out of pain, good out of bad? Can we point to specific ways that the Holy Spirit of God has guided and empowered us through obstacles and problems? Has our relationship with Christ resulted in a changed life evidenced by how we think, what we say, what we do, and how we interact with others? Everything – our attitudes and actions, our lifestyles, our use of money and material goods – should be proof of the reality of the claims we make about God and Jesus. Let's encourage and comfort those who are uncertain and anxious about God's loving care and plan by pointing to the ways the Lord has worked in us.

Also, we need to be prepared to share Scripture so that we, like Jesus, can help open the hearts and minds of those who experience doubt or fear, showing them the wonderful promises of our faithful Father to always hold them in His secure grip *(Jn. 10:29b)*. As God's truth is revealed in the Scripture, our doubts and fears can be alleviated, peace in our lives can be restored, and we can resume the divine mission of spreading the good news of Jesus.

JESUS IMPARTS THE HOLY SPIRIT

[Jesus] breathed on [the disciples] and said to them,
"Receive the Holy Spirit." (Jn. 20:22)

WHAT JESUS DID:

The words *rúa<u>h</u>* (Hebrew) and *pneuma* (Greek) can both be translated as "breath" or "spirit." Just as the Father had sent Jesus, Jesus was sending His disciples out into the world to spread His good news message *(v. 21)*, and they needed truly supernatural power to accomplish this task. Therefore, Jesus *"breathed"* on His disciples, just as God did when He breathed life into the first human *(Gen. 2:7)*, and gave to them the Holy Spirit, providing them with new life and strength to fulfill their mission and authorizing them to pronounce the forgiveness of sins *(v. 23)*.

WHAT HIS FOLLOWERS ARE TO DO:

Let's remind one another of the work that Jesus has commissioned us to do: preaching the need for a change of heart and habits, and the promise of God's mercy and forgiveness. We can often be so preoccupied with the demands of our daily lives that we neglect our true calling to spread Jesus' good news. Also, let's bind ourselves one to another in the body of Christ so that we can continually urge each other to be filled with the divine energy needed to bring people to Jesus and to confidently declare them absolved of sin. We must remember that we can accomplish this only through the empowerment of God's Holy Spirit; it is not something that we can do on our own, either separately or corporately. We need to constantly yield ourselves to His leading and to rely on His strength as we share the message of Christ.

And lest we grow weak or tired in our spiritual work, we should persistently encourage and invigorate each other through the inspiring words of Scripture and exhortations to stay the course and keep at it. Our mutual care and support can lift discouraged spirits; our availability and presence can breathe new life into old bones; our concern and understanding can revitalize depleted souls.

Jesus breathed the life-giving power of the Holy Spirit on His disciples so they could fulfill His commission of spreading the gospel, and we who follow Him today should continue with confidence and boldness that good work.

JESUS AND "DOUBTING" THOMAS

Now Thomas, one of the twelve, called the Twin, was not with [the other disciples] when Jesus came. (Jn. 20:24)

WHAT JESUS DID:

The apostle Thomas had not been with the others when Jesus appeared to them, and when told of Jesus' appearing, Thomas demanded physical proof – seeing and touching Jesus' wounds – before he could truly believe that Jesus had risen from the dead *(v. 25)*. Eight days later, John's account goes on to tell us, Jesus appeared in the locked room where His disciples were once again all gathered, including Thomas, greeting them with His customary words of peace *(v. 26)*.

Jesus then invited the skeptical apostle to look at and even touch His scarred body – the nail wounds in His hands and the spear wound in His side. Jesus told him not to be disbelieving but to believe. The disciple finally realized the truth and confessed Jesus as His Lord and God. *(vv. 27-28)*

Jesus then made the wonderful promise to all His followers throughout the ages: The apostle believed because He had seen with his own eyes the resurrected Jesus, but *"Blessed are those who have not seen, and yet have believed"* *(v. 29)*.

WHAT HIS FOLLOWERS ARE TO DO:

Jesus did not express anger at Thomas' lack of belief; instead, He met Thomas where He was in his journey of faith and urged him to test and see if he would truly believe.

We who follow Jesus should also realize that everyone comes to Christ from a distinct place and is at a different stage of walking with Him. In our interactions with fellow believers, we ought to consider their individual backgrounds and their current needs as they seek to grow in Christlikeness. That process of maturity often includes questioning one's faith and one's relationship with God.

When those doubts do arise in others, let's not react with frustration or discouragement, with disparaging remarks or anger. As Jesus did, we should meet people where they are spiritually and encourage those who are facing challenges of disbelief to examine their life with God and see if their faith is genuine or not. We should be available to let them talk about their doubts and to help them work through the obstacles to greater trust in the Lord. We can also share what Christ has done for us and show the evidence of a changed life. Through our words of comfort, through an understanding and sympathetic attitude, through compassionate and nonjudgmental support, and through the reality of our own experiences with Jesus, we can help others get through their times of doubt and unbelief.

Jesus did not force Thomas to believe, but He did present proof that would confirm faith in Him. We need to do the same. And yet, ultimately, faith is a personal matter, an individual decision and choice, and we must pray that God would remove the barriers to belief from those in doubt and reveal Himself clearly and decisively to them.

JESUS KEEPS HIS PROMISE
TO MEET IN GALILEE

But after I am raised up, I will go before you to Galilee." (Mk. 14:28)

WHAT JESUS DID:

Before the resurrection, Jesus and His disciples had eaten their last meal all together and were heading toward the Mount of Olives and the Garden of Gethsemane. Quoting from the prophet Zechariah *(13:7)*, Jesus foretold what would happen to Him: He, the shepherd, would be struck down, and they, His flock of sheep, would be scattered. However, He also said that He would be raised from death and made a promise to meet them in Galilee. It was Galilee where many of them were from, including Jesus, and where He had called many of them. It was where Jesus had begun His public ministry and had spent a great deal of time preaching the Kingdom of God, teaching about righteous living, and healing the sick and disabled.

On the day of His resurrection the angelic messenger(s) at the empty tomb repeated His promise to the women who had come to anoint Jesus' body, instructing them to tell His disciples that He was going to Galilee and that they would see Him there just as He had said *(Mk. 16:7)*. And Jesus kept His promise to meet them: After He had appeared to the disciples in Jerusalem, Jesus again showed Himself to them by Lake Galilee *(Jn. 21:1)*. Matthew's account says that the eleven remaining apostles went to a mountain in Galilee as they had been directed by Jesus *(Mt. 28:16)*.

WHAT HIS FOLLOWERS ARE TO DO:

We who follow Jesus as Lord should, as He did, always keep our promises. We Christians are to be honest in speech and faithful to our words. If we say that we are going to do something, we are committing ourselves to it and must do all that we can to see it through.

A person's word used to be a reliable bond; what was spoken would be upheld and acted on as promised. Not so much these days. People make pledges that they have no intention of fulfilling. They speak words that are devoid of commitment and that have no depth of assurance or trustworthiness. But that is not to be the way of the follower of Jesus. Our words are to be truthful and spoken with an unswerving dedication to fulfillment.

And if we have any inkling that we cannot keep our promise, let's not make it in the first place, remembering that once the words come out of our mouths and are heard by the ears of others, we are bound to them. Thus, let's think before we speak: Will what I am about to say be truthful and completely honest? If not, I should keep my mouth shut. Additionally, let's think before we promise: Is my promise something that I am able and intend to fulfill? If not, let me not speak it.

It is a great witness to the Lord we serve when others can say about us that we are people of our word. That shows that they trust us, and it reflects well on our faithful God. We Christians are to be promise-keepers, just like Jesus.

JESUS PREPARES A MEAL ON THE SEASHORE

Jesus said to [the disciples], "Come and have breakfast." (Jn. 21:12)

WHAT JESUS DID:

While they were all in Jerusalem, the risen Jesus had promised to meet the disciples in Galilee, which is about 80 miles from the holy city. Jesus met the disciples at the Sea of Tiberias *(v. 1)*, another name for the Sea of Galilee. In this account recorded only in John's gospel, five apostles were present (Peter, Thomas, Nathanael, and the brothers James and John) along with two other unnamed disciples. They had been fishing but had caught nothing. *(vv. 2-3)*

Jesus, unrecognized from the shore, told them to throw their nets on the other side of the boat, and they did so and subsequently hauled in 153 large fish. At that moment they recognized it was Jesus, and Peter leapt straightaway into the water and swam to Him. When the others arrived at the shore, they found that Jesus had prepared a meal for them of bread and a fish cooking over a charcoal fire. Jesus told them to bring some of the fish they had caught to put on the fire as well, invited them to have breakfast, and shared the food with them. *(vv. 4-14)*

WHAT HIS FOLLOWERS ARE TO DO:

These men had spent hours fishing through the night and would have certainly been hungry come morning. Thus, we understand from this scene in Galilee that Jesus cared for not only the spiritual needs of His disciples but for their physical needs, too. Like a good shepherd, Jesus fed His flock, and we who are committed to Him should do the same.

Spirituality is vitally important, to be sure; it is even to be our priority in life. But physical demands must be met as well. It is hard to tell a person suffering from famine about the love of our Heavenly Father. Nourish bodies with food in the name of Christ and explain that we are compelled by His love to do so, and then share the good news of God's mercy, forgiveness, and grace.

Of course, physical need may come in many forms: nutrition, housing, clothing, hygiene and healthcare, security, jobs, relationships, help with the demands of 21st century life, education, and even enjoyment and happiness. Let's be ready to offer what we have – material goods, financial resources, assistance in particular situations, expertise and experience, time and energy – to those in whatever need, inviting them to join us and to share in that with which God has blessed us. We need to stay committed to engaging in acts of lovingkindness and compassion to meet both physical and spiritual needs. Jesus did this, and we are to follow His example.

JESUS REINSTATES PETER

When they had finished breakfast, Jesus said to Simon Peter, "Simon, son of John, do you love me more than these?" He said to him, "Yes, Lord; you know that I love you." He said to him, "Feed my lambs." (Jn. 21:15)

WHAT JESUS DID:

Jesus had foretold Peter's threefold denial of Him, and that had come to pass. He also knew that Peter had wept bitterly over his cowardly and faithless behavior. Satan had temporarily pounded Peter, like one beats grains of wheat to separate the kernel from the chaff, but Jesus had prayed for Peter's return to faith and, once that had occurred, had commissioned him to strengthen the other disciples *(Lk. 22:31-32)*.

Now was the time for Jesus to confirm Peter's restoration and reassignment. Jesus never mentioned Peter's denials; he had already repented of his actions and had been forgiven. But Jesus here asked three times if Peter loved Him, certainly bringing to Peter's mind his statements in the courtyard of the High Priest on the night of Jesus' arrest.

Much has been written about the Greek verbs used in Jesus' three questions (sequentially, *agape, agape,* and *phileo)* and in Peter's response (*phileo for all three). Agape* denotes the highest form of love and is characterized as perfect and divine, sacrificial and unconditional, preferring one over all others; *phileo* is a more friendship kind of love, enjoying another's company, and is sometimes translated as "having affection for" or "being fond of" someone. Knowing this distinction is of real importance in grasping the significance and meaning of the interchange between Jesus and Peter as intended by the writer of John's gospel (though undoubtedly, the conversation between Jesus and Peter was in their native Aramaic).

Jesus asked His questions and allowed Peter to honestly appraise the measure of his love for the one he called Lord. Peter sadly realized that his relationship for Christ was not one of *agape* love but remained at the level of *phileo* affection and answered accordingly. Nonetheless, Jesus accepted Peter's response without criticism; and though by using *phileo* in His final question, Jesus seemed to have understood and acknowledged Peter's degree of devotion, He still graciously repeated three times His command to take care of His sheep and lambs. Thus, Jesus reinstated Peter by giving him the job of feeding and tending the flock of the Good Shepherd.

WHAT HIS FOLLOWERS ARE TO DO:

We can learn much from this weighty conversation between the Lord Jesus and Peter. First, Jesus did not directly forgive Peter, but His recommissioning of Peter to the task of caring for His other disciples showed that Peter's sinful denials had been pardoned and that Jesus wanted him to reengage in His mission. So, when others offend us or betray our trust or turn against us, if they express heartfelt contrition for their actions, let's reach out and draw them close and help them to become involved in ministering to the needs of other people.

In that same vein, we should not focus on failures but always keep looking for the best in our brothers and sisters in Christ. One does not need to be perfect to participate in the care and provision of others but just to have a genuine desire to be obedient to the Lord's commands, despite past failings or a realization of spiritual weakness or immaturity.

Also, we ought not be afraid to ask fellow believers about their relationship and commitment to Christ. And when they answer, let's accept their sincere responses without criticism or condemnation but with love and understanding. And if their level of devotion is not what we might hope for, instead of belittling them, we can offer words of encouragement and look for ways to help them find a place of service for the Lord.

Jesus knew Peter's past and heard his current responses and still wanted him to take a lead role in caring and providing for other disciples. We need to follow Jesus and reach out to embrace and inspire those who have turned from Him or are perhaps haunted by past spiritual failures and to bring them back into the body of Christ so they can take part in the Lord's work. This acceptance and reinstatement into ministry can heal past wounds and restore a sense of worth and usefulness in the Kingdom of God.

JESUS, PETER, AND THE BELOVED APOSTLE

*When Peter saw [the disciple whom Jesus loved following them],
he said to Jesus, "Lord, what about this man?" (Jn. 21:21)*

WHAT JESUS DID:

Jesus had just made the cryptic remark to Peter that when Peter was old, he would stretch out his hands and that another person would carry him where he did not want to go *(v. 18)*. The writer of John's gospel explains that Jesus was referring to the kind of death Peter would suffer *(v. 19)*.

(Tradition and later religious writings tell us that Peter was crucified in Rome in 65 CE under the persecution of Emperor Nero; tradition also claims that Peter requested to be crucified upside down because he did not deem himself worthy to die in the same manner as Jesus.)

Peter responded to Jesus' statement with a question to Him about another disciple, described as the *"disciple whom Jesus loved."* John's account explains that the beloved disciple was the apostle (in tradition believed to be John) who had leaned against Jesus during their last supper and asked Him about the identity of the betrayer *(v. 20b)*. Jesus' reply to Peter's question was that Peter was not to be concerned about the ultimate fate of the other apostle, even if Jesus wanted the disciple to live until His return, but rather Pete was just to follow Him *(v. 22)*.

WHAT HIS FOLLOWERS ARE TO DO:

When fellow believers talk about other members in the body of Christ, let's remind them that everyone's relationship with God is personal. Our focus is to not be on how others choose to follow Jesus but on our own walk with Him.

Additionally, just because something happens to us, whether in the spiritual or physical realm, it doesn't mean that it will happen to others. We must always be aware that our lives and our experiences are in the infinitely loving and capable hands of our Heavenly Father. God may decide to deal with us in a certain way while dealing with others differently. We must never think this unfair of God or wallow in self-pity. Even when faced with hardship, pain, or loss, let's do our best not to compare our own circumstances with those of other Christians. We need to make sure that we never question God's plan for each of us individually and never bemoan our fate or bitterly complain to God, "Well, what about him/her/them?!"

Jesus' words to Peter should be the words we speak to others and to ourselves every day: *"You follow me!"*

JESUS COMMISSIONS HIS DISCIPLES

[Jesus said]: Go therefore and make disciples of all nations ... (Mt. 28:19a)

WHAT JESUS DID:

Thus ends Matthew's gospel on a mountain in Galilee: Though some of His chosen eleven apostles still had doubts, Jesus commissioned them under His authority to go out and make disciples in every country, to baptize them, and to share with them all His teachings. Jesus finished this fourfold command by promising to be with them always and forever every step of the way *(vv.16-20)*.

WHAT HIS FOLLOWERS ARE TO DO:

We Christians need to remind other believers (and ourselves) of our Lord's command to make disciples from every country. Wherever we are – whether in our own nation or abroad, at home or traveling to other places, at work, school, or recreation, in our neighborhoods or during encounters with strangers, the Lord has told us to enjoin people in every place to follow Him. Let's not allow ourselves or other Christians to be lax or remiss in our faithful obedience to this order from our Lord. He came to spread His good news of the presence of the Kingdom of God, a realm where our gracious Heavenly Father reigns, and He has sent us out into our world to share that message. Let's repeat His command frequently to each other and remember that He has given us His authority to carry it out.

Jesus also taught us about compassion, mercy, kindness, and forgiveness, as well as about justice, righteousness, integrity, and holiness. He showed us the love of the Father and told us to be perfect in our love. We Christians should continually urge one another to take very seriously Jesus' words and exhort our fellow believers to be dedicated to leading lives in accordance with His precepts and to fulfilling His directive to share His teachings with others.

Additionally, we need to pledge ourselves to being present in the lives of those we mentor for Christ. We must remain available and involved with others who are walking in the way of Jesus. Emulating Him, let's stay committed to being there – accessible and actively engaged physically, emotionally, materially, spiritually – for our brothers and sisters in Christ.

Jesus sent His eleven disciples out to make more disciples, to baptize, and to teach observance of His commands. We should do the same by reminding and exhorting those in the body of Christ to trust and obey Him. And let's keep connected with each other and encourage one another with His promise to be with us always to guide and strengthen us as we seek to follow Him.

JESUS' ASCENSION

And [Jesus] led [the disciples] out as far as Bethany, and lifting up his hands he blessed them. While he blessed them, he parted from them and was carried up into heaven. (Lk. 24:20-21)

WHAT JESUS DID:

Jesus' ascension into heaven is described in the longer ending of Mark's gospel (*Mk. 16:19*, where Jesus is depicted as sitting at the right hand of God) and in Luke's writings at the very end of his Gospel and in the first chapter of The Acts of the Apostles. It occurred forty days after His resurrection (*Acts 1:3*) and in Luke's account took place outside of Jerusalem.

Before Jesus ascended, the disciples had asked Him about when the kingdom would arrive, but He responded that it was not for them to know and that it would happen in the Father's time. Their mission was to spread Jesus' good news in the power of the Holy Spirit which they would receive. (*Acts 1:6-8*)

Jesus blessed the disciples, that is, He prayed for God's help, goodness, abundance, and favor to be on them and was then taken from the physical world into the heavenly realm of the spirit

WHAT HIS FOLLOWERS ARE TO DO:

The first thing we can learn from Jesus' final words to His disciples while on earth is that we should encourage fellow believers not to focus excessively on the end times but rather to devote our energy here and now to spreading the good news of God's gracious mercy and forgiveness of sins in Christ. Jesus did speak on several occasions about the end of the world, so we should be aware of what He said and seek to understand it. However, we are primarily called to be His witnesses, to testify to His truth and life-giving message. We need to be mindful, too, that we can fulfill that calling only as we submit to the leading and empowerment of God's Holy Spirit.

And just as Jesus ascended from the earth, we can emulate Him by seeking to transcend the unrighteous material sphere and give primacy to that which is righteous, spiritual and holy. We should strive to rise above selfish desires to reach for a more elevated way of living filled with altruism and lovingkindness. We ought to break free from the sinful attitudes of hate, prejudice, greed, and revenge that bind us to a base, worldly existence and instead pursue the things of God, like love, fairness, justice, generosity, and forgiveness.

When we die, our spirits will rise to be with our Father in Heaven and with His Christ. Until that day, we need to follow the ascended life and teachings of Jesus, our Lord.

JOHN'S EPILOGUE

Now Jesus did many other signs in the presence of the disciples,
which are not written in this book ... (Jn. 20:30)

WHAT JESUS DID:

Jesus performed many more signs than what are recorded in Scripture, many more miraculous acts that gave authority to His words about God, about the Kingdom of Heaven, about leading lives of righteousness and compassion, and about Himself. After all, according to John's gospel, Jesus was actively engaged in His ministry of preaching, teaching, and healing for some three years. But the purpose of that which was written down is to produce and bolster faith in Jesus as the anointed son of the Father and to receive the eternal life that is offered through Him *(v. 31)*.

WHAT HIS FOLLOWERS ARE TO DO:

Even though not every deed that Jesus did was written down in the gospel accounts, we who follow Him have more than enough to learn and to emulate … actually, a lifetime's worth. May we simply trust and diligently obey!

PART THREE

Final Thoughts

FINAL THOUGHTS

Peter said [to the lame man], "I have no silver and gold, but what I do have I give to you. In the name of Jesus Christ of Nazareth, rise up and walk!" (Acts 3:6)

Having looked at the life of Jesus and what He did during His time of earthly ministry as portrayed in the four canonical gospels, we see actions repeated over and over by the Lord: He preached the Kingdom of God; He healed the sick and impaired; He freed people oppressed by demons; He provided for those in need, both spiritually and physically; He made disciples and taught them how to lead godly lives; He challenged hardhearted religious authorities and their rigid traditions; He spent time in prayer; He quoted Scripture; He raised the dead; He forgave sinners and their sinful past; He socialized with those outcast by their communities; He performed physical miracles that proved His spiritual authority.

Also, there are themes that are continually reiterated in the telling of His life story: the Fatherhood of God; the Kingdom of Heaven, its nature and growth; adherence to the moral law of the *Torah*; the need for grace, mercy, forgiveness, compassion, kindness and love; His identity as the Chosen One of God, the Messiah; the cost of discipleship; the reality of the demonic; the priority of the eternal over the temporal, of the spiritual over the material; the righteous use of money; the power of faith; warnings against false teaching and hypocrisy; the spread of the gospel; the end of the age; the vital importance of our relationship with God; humility and service of others; belief and trust in Him.

But rather than being a tedious or monotonous redundancy, there is real value in hearing Jesus' words and seeing His actions repeated time and again, for we can then learn exactly what He considered to be of greatest importance by knowing what He focused on while on earth. Jesus was well aware that His years here were limited, and so there was a precise kind of economy to His life: No wasted time, staying on mission, concentrating on the truly significant and essential.

Rarely do we learn something the first time we hear or see it; we often need to have it repeated several times before we actually get it. Thus, for instance, Jesus preached compassion, was moved with compassion, and acted compassionately, and when we hear it taught and see it modeled again and again, we are more likely to embrace and incorporate compassion into our lives. That was certainly true for the earliest apostles: The Lord had given them a constant example during His lifetime of showing lovingkindness, empathy, and mercy, and though they initially did not exhibit such behavior, after the Day of Pentecost (as recorded in the book of *Acts*) the disciples faithfully carried on Jesus' work of ministering to those in need. So, repetition is both good and necessary, a benefit for us all.

Finally, this book is meant to be one of exhortation and urging to believers in Jesus, including myself, who seek to emulate Him in how we think, speak, and act. I have sought to emphasize what Jesus did in His life and to encourage fellow Christians to follow His lead. That is why, in the sections on <u>What His followers are to do</u>, I have constantly used terms like "let's" and "we should" or "ought to" and "we need to" or "must." My humble and fervent prayer is that we Christians can see in the life and teaching of Jesus a way to obediently conduct our own lives, in truth and righteousness, for the glory of God.

Printed in the United States
by Baker & Taylor Publisher Services